LANGUAGE,]

General Editor.

Selected Titles

Questions of Conduct: Sexual Harassment, Citizenship, Government

Jeffrey Minson
Senior Lecturer in the Faculty of Humanities,
Griffith University, Queensland

150th YEAR
M
MACMILLAN

First published 1993 by
THE MACMILLAN PRESS LTD
Houndmills, Basingstoke, Hampshire RG21 2XS
and London
Companies and representatives
throughout the world

ISBN 0–333–46597–0 hardcover
ISBN 0–333–46598–9 paperback

A catalogue record for this book is available
from the British Library

Copy-edited and typeset by Grahame & Grahame Editorial, Brighton

Printed in Hong Kong

Contents

Preface and Acknowledgements

This book has been a long time in the making. Initially envisaged as a collection of essays written during the late 1970s and early 1980s, the new ground eventually covered by the book – notably the work on sexual harassment – grew out of a commission from the editorial group of the now defunct British feminist journal *m/f* to comment on Michel Foucault's histories of sexual ethics (Minson, 1986).

I am especially grateful to Parveen Adams for kickstarting the project and for stimulating my thinking on feminist matters generally. The essays on sexual harassment are an attempt to carry on the *m/f* tradition; I do not know how to thank it enough. Nor in this connection can I sufficiently thank Sharmila Mercer, who, having done her best to discourage me from straying onto this minefield, proved an endless source of technical information, comment and criticism. Beverly Brown helped me to clarify my views on Catharine MacKinnon's work. For advice and comment on some of the legal aspects of the sexual harassment essays I am indebted to Bill Lane; and for reminding me of the range of feminist argument which I would need to take into account I would like to thank Chilla Bulbeck and Gillian Swanson.

In turn, the expansion of the issues of progressive politics and liberal government raised by the question of sexual harassment into the entire block of essays that comprise Part II is due in no small part to extensive exchanges over the years with Mark Cousins, Paul Hirst, Barry Hindess, Ian Hunter, Nikolas Rose, Colin Mercer, Wayne Hudson and David Saunders. Hindess and Hunter have been particularly generous in the matter of written comment and criticism whilst the application of Saunders' formidable editing skills to one essay in particular has improved it no end.

Thanks of a no less heartfelt order are also due to Karen Yarrow and Lorraine Coutts for transforming the unsightly results of my archaic method of composition into readable copy; to Louise Goebel for her assistance in compiling the index; to Janice O'Brien's help with proof-reading; and to the Division of Humanities, Griffith University for all their financial support.

Several of these essays have been published elsewhere in modified versions: 'Kant, Rhetoric and Civility' in *Economy and Society* (1989, XVIII, 2), under the title 'Men and manners: Kantian humanism, rhetoric and the history of ethics'; 'Social Theory and Legal Argument' appeared in *International Journal of the Sociology of Law* (1991b, XVII, 3); 'Second Principles of Social Justice', in *Law in Context* (1992, forthcoming); 'Managing without a Politics of Subjectivity' under the title *Bureaucratic Culture and the Management of Sexual Harassment* (1991a), in the Occasional Papers series of the *Institute for Cultural Policy Studies*, Griffith University; and, 'The Participatory Imperative' in *Philosophy and Social Criticism* (1992, forthcoming).

I am grateful to all of the above for permission to republish these works.

Finally, I take this opportunity to express love and thanks for everything to Emily Cox.

J. P. M.

Part I
Introducing Ethical Culture

1 'The White Elephant's Nightmare'

Late in life, an ailing Henri Matisse, unable to use brush or pen, resorted to 'drawing with scissors'. Cutting out shapes from sheets of paper painted by an assistant, who then glued them onto paper under his direction, Matisse composed a vivid series of images from the world of popular entertainment, especially the circus. Together with some handwritten testamentary statements on the painter's craft, these images – one of which is entitled 'The White Elephant's Nightmare' – were published in the form of a *livre de peintre*, entitled *Jazz* (Matisse, 1947).[1] Over and above the political, legal and social concerns registered in its title, this is a book of ethics. To be more precise, it is about the conceptualisation and improvement of ethical conduct. I would like if I may to invoke the improvisatory skills and the serene confidence displayed in *Jazz* as a model for the way of doing ethics which has evolved in the course of following up the book's more specialised concerns.

Problems

What has sexual harassment got to do with citizenship? On the face of it, two discrete sets of questions are posed. The first concerns the implications of establishing sexual harassment as a distinct social problem in the field of social policy. In particular, I examine some of the implications of representing its ethical dimensions one way rather than another, in social theory, law, personnel management policies, and personal confrontations. The second set of questions have their origins in political theory. Here the focus is on the place of the citizen status, liberal values and institutions, participatory democracy and notions of community in attempts to rethink the ethical and political bases of the socialist and advanced liberal-democratic traditions. Let us say that one purpose of this book of essays is to suggest that sexual harassment and citizenship have less to do with one another and more to do with 'government' than is sometimes thought. To speak only a little less enigmatically, its aim is to draw out the consequences of conceiving sexual harassment and citizenship, both separately and together, as involving questions of ethical conduct.

What is the more general problem which draws these topics in social policy and political theory together and which calls for a measure of ethical improvisation? It is the widespread propensity in these fields, as elsewhere, to equate the ethical content of politics and government with idealisations of political community derived from the (overlapping) traditions of post-Enlightenment political and moral philosophy, emancipatory social theory and what I shall call political romanticism. In this equation, an inappropriately puritanical constraint is placed on what people are prepared to *count* as ethical constituents of politics, law and social policy. Whenever we evaluate a social policy solely according to how well it conforms to political principles, we shut our eyes to the policy's dependence upon norms and values which have evolved, in part autochthonously, out of the practices of 'government' (in a very general sense) through which the policy was formulated and put into effect. In which case, perceived disjunctions between government and political ethics (as articulated in political theories, ideologies, election promises, etc.) can only issue in denunciations of government or resigned acquiescence to its shortcomings. But do such disjunctions never reflect adversely on the composition of the ethical-political standards through which the disjunction is registered?

Equating the ethical content of politics, practical government, law, and social policy with political idealisations signals above all an intellectualist indifference to the means by which both political principles and governmental practice and policy are factored into personal life regulation. 'Relating oneself' to a principle may involve both more and less than conscious understanding of the reasons behind it, rational assent and commitment to its realisation, and conscientious expression of the principle in 'good behaviour'. For example, some people may agree with the principle of equality between the sexes but feel ill-at-ease with a particular normative workplace environment established in order to realise it. Is this response merely indicative of a hypocritical assent or might the problem occasionally lie elsewhere? Others may sincerely believe in the principle of open discussion as a means of making decisions but not know *how* to conduct themselves in discussion. They may lack the abilities and even be positively unsympathetic to the norms required either to keep discussions open or to bring them to a conclusion. Are these abilities and sympathies of no ethical moment? How could the meaning and value of discussion remain unaffected by such considerations?

These examples of the problems of translating political values into norms of daily existence hint at the sort of gap in predominant ways of evaluating the ethical element in politics, government, and organisational life which the approach to ethics developed across these essays attempts to plug. Its motto might be: no evaluation of the conduct of government without reference to the government of conduct and especially to the ways in which we govern ourselves. For some this motto may sound like a truism. Yet enquiries into citizenship from the perspective of the ethical conduct presupposed by it are surprisingly uncommon; whilst depicting sexual harassment as a question of conduct is nothing if not controversial.

Sources

To some extent, the air of improvisation surrounding this approach to the ethical stems from the errant relationships which the essays bear to the genres in which discussion of their subject is usually most at home. Too absorbed in historical, sociological and legal complexities, and insufficiently concerned with debates about matters of principle to pass easily for a work of moral and political philosophy, it also shies away from the vaunting ambition of most social theory (including the forms of analysis and critique associated with the 'personal politics' rubric). The seam of ethical affairs at which these essays seek to work – the relations between the conduct of government and the government of conduct – would be closed off were it the case that the price of shifting the centre of gravity of the ethical away from the standard *topoi* of moral and political philosophy was to be necessarily committed to explaining it (away) as the ideological effect of a global social structure.

In an interdisciplinary and non-professional sense of the word, this approach to the ethical might be characterised as *anthropological.* An historical anthropology of ourselves, it treats ethical attributes, categories, distinctions, and institutions, including those characterised by claims to social transcendence, as artefacts and instruments of definite cultural milieus. Various 'names' in the social science pantheon could be cited as particularly influential sources: notably, Foucault, Bourdieu, Mauss, Elias, Weber, Hirst and Hindess. More interestingly, perhaps, the most significant generic social-scientific source is what I take to be a paradigm-shift in the *history* of ethics. Surely one of the most unheralded intellectual 'events' in the recent history of the Humanities, this shift is partly the intellectual achievement of particular individuals and methodologies (some of Foucault's influence, for example, might be subsumed under this heading), partly a quieter and more diffuse effect of the professionalisation of historical argument about ethics (as exemplified in the admirable Cambridge University Press 'Ideas in Context' series).[2]

Traditionally, the history of ethics has been treated anachronistically, either as comprising a repository of potential contributions to timeless philosophical debates; as background and critical fodder for philosophy students; or as a vehicle for giving moral theory the dialectical form of a philosophy of history. Only in the last case does the history of ethics become an intellectually serious enterprise. In the first two cases, it is essentially a job for the servants. One result of making the history of ethics the business of professional historians has been a renewal of intellectual interest in ways of evaluating and acting upon conduct which have for some time now been widely considered (especially by philosophers) as falling below the threshold of ethical significance.[3]

At the top of this list of insufficiently considered ethical habits of mind stands the *rhetorical* tradition of ethical reasoning and practice. Inseparable from this rhetorical-ethical style are techniques of conscience-formation; régimes of good manners; moral pressure operating through honour and shame; casuistical literature and practice; diplomacy; negotiation; and characterological knowledge. To the extent that these unhallowed forms of ethical reflection live on in legal, managerial and administrative thinking, these 'practitioners' knowledges' can be added to the inventory of 'non-philosophical' influences on my approach to the ethical sphere.

To experiment with ways of analysing ethical matters which owe relatively little to modern moral philosophy is no doubt to sacrifice some of the precision which comes with philosophical training and with the conventional organisation of moral philosophical debate. It may not then be altogether idiosyncratic to invoke Matisse's method of *découpage* and the images of *Jazz* as an emblem of what is entailed in this rhetorically inflected way of engaging ethically with organisational life, law, politics and public affairs: the development of improvisatory skills to compensate for a disability; the construction of pattern and texture out of disparate materials and the capacity to 'divert' an audience. Or to compare the modern artist's challenge to the conventional priority of line over colour in regard to the meaning of a visual representation to the relegation of philosophy to a position of parity with academic disciplines and more mundane forms of organised reasoning in determining the meaning of ethical conduct.

Polemics

To make such comparisons is not to invite a general disparagement of moral and political philosophy. If in places I try to drive a wedge between their respective objects and those of 'governmental reasoning', this is not effected without the aid of some political philosophers' attention to the governmental realm and some moral philosophers' attention to 'impure' ethical forms. In any case, only the modern republican flank of political philosophy comes under sustained fire and this only insofar as it occupies the same ground as two more prominent 'enemies of promise': namely, a type of social theory which I call *sociological-structural critique* (sometimes just 'critique') and the ethos by which it is almost invariably driven: *political romanticism*. In both cases, the casualty of these approaches is a serious appreciation of the ethical norms and values informing governmental practice.

In the case of the sociological-structural critique, this incapacity or unwillingness to acknowledge the ethical weight of government stems from a self-imposed obligation to go to the causal roots of oppressive social conditions, track the full extent of their pervasive presence in the social and individual body and thereby register the need for radical social change. From this perspective, the down-to-earth ethical dispositions formed, for example, through the education system, the exercise of family or occupational responsibilities, and involvement in running political campaigns or organised pastimes are only interesting as objects of *suspicion*. It is 'society' in general and 'social subjects' (human individuals conceptualised in terms of their subjectivity) which form the main, dialectically-related, objects and horizons of analysis. The supposition that social relations form comprehensive ensembles generates the requirement to explain what enables them to continually function as wholes. Some underlying structure must be posited (the capitalist system, patriarchy, etc.) which to some extent transcends both given organisational-governmental forms and the consciousnesses of the social subjects in which its shaping effects are manifest. Yet structural determination is never complete. The core of indeterminacy built into the definition of human subjectivity is typically made the basis for 'resistance' and for a self-reflexive conception of the *work* of explanation as a 'critique' of the ideologies which help to sustain the structure. Critique restores to consciousness what makes its current forms (and limits) of awareness possible whilst hitherto evading it. Critique aggregates those 'fragments' of subjectivity and society which buck the system into the idea of an alternative form of social relations. Residing in 'prefigurative' forms within the present structure, this alternative to the governmental *status quo* forms the theoretical and imaginative basis on which an emancipatory society might be built (Hirst and Jones, 1987, pp. 21–22; Rose 1987, pp. 66–67).

Complications of this basic sociological-structural approach abound.[4] One reason for its resilience could be the insufficient attention paid by critics of critique to the question of how to analyse, to evaluate and to appropriate the *ethical* matters traditionally subsumed under the rubric of ideology. Many people see no acceptable alternative to the ethical-political stance required by sociological-structural critiques. One of the constructive aims of these essays is to assemble a repertoire of ethical dispositions with which friends of 'progressive' politics need not be ashamed of being associated.

The main ethical-political force behind sociological-structural critique is political romanticism. If we are to appreciate the extent of its purchase on progressive ethical and political culture, we would do well to follow Ian Hunter (1988) and Carl Schmitt (1924, 1986) in declining to define it by reference to the usual, frequently inconsistent historical inventory of rebellious artistic circles, preoccupations, themes, forms of action, privileged mental faculties, ideals or political allegiances. Not everything that 'stimulates Romantic productivity' can be identified with it (Schmitt, 1986, p. 74). Political romanticism is not only a name for dreamy (left- or right-wing) political ideals or a preference for community action-groups over trade-union committee work. Rather, romanticism refers to a *kind of ethical personality*, together with the techniques through which individuals acquire it and elaborate it in the course of relating themselves to the public domain (and vice-versa). In this perspective, the form of self-cultivation and personal-political involvements or detachments peculiar to political romanticism depends upon a way of reconceptualising the social universe which, as Hunter (*op. cit.*, pp. 184–85 *et passim*) has emphasised, was perfectly captured in Friedrich Schiller's *On the Aesthetic Education of Man*:

> It was civilisation itself which inflicted this wound upon modern man . . . Once the increasingly complex machinery of state necessitated a more rigorous separation of ranks and occupations, then the inner unity of human nature was severed . . . This disorganisation . . . was made complete by the spirit of government . . . Everlastingly chained to a single little fragment of the whole, man . . . becomes nothing more than the imprint of his occupation . . . When the community makes his office the measure of the man, when in one of his citizens it prizes nothing but memory, in another a mere tabularising intelligence . . . can we wonder that the remaining aptitudes of the psyche are neglected in order to give undivided attention to the one which will bring honour and profit? (Schiller, 1791, 1967, pp. 33, 35, 37)

By means of a series of metaphors and binary oppositions which have hardly dated at all, politics and 'civilised' society are in this passage hypostatised to form a unified object of conscientious objection. Crucial to the formation of the romantic personality, then, is a highly generalised, ethical knowledge of the way of the world, of what it was, where it is going and above all how it is governed, which is simultaneously an assertion of dis-identification with it. Government, in Schmitt's (*op. cit.*, p. 17) words, is identified with 'everything which gives order and consistency to what takes place – regardless of whether it is the mechanical calculability of the causal or a normative nexus' (Schmitt, 1986, p. 17).

The yardstick against which the general inadequacy of governmental norms and procedures is registered is the *telos* of the Romantic personality: perfect all-round development. The specialisations of function attendant upon governmental organisation are subject to a metaphorical interpretation. Institutional specialisations introduced a violent split in our subjective and social being; a mythopoeic 'wound'. The essentially mechanical 'spirit of government' disrupts the possibility of organic, harmonious forms of integration of the self and social relations. In this anticipation of the English cultural commonplace, 'the dissociation of sensibility', lie the seeds of contemporary critiques of bureaucracy on the grounds of its fostering only the rational or instrumental faculties ('a merely tabularising intelligence'), to the exclusion of one's emotional or sexual dispositions.

To be sure, my personal sense of self and its infinite possibilities of cultural development may well be constituted by my identification with some collective cause. It is not the individualism of romantic approaches to politics and government that is so damaging; but rather their reduction of organised social life to a purely (inter)subjective form of significance and the 'expressivist' practical stance to which this gives rise. The condition for self-fulfilling involvement in the government of social life is the suspension of belief in all institutional specialisations, every operative distinction, institutional norm or procedure, time-frame, and binding decision (Schmitt, *op. cit.*, p. 17). All of these objective exigencies can only be experienced by a romantically formed conscience as a limit to be transcended. The implications of that suspension of normative governmental realities and binding decisions is that the political field has to be reconceptualised as purely the *occasio*,[5] as Schmitt calls it – the vehicle or opportunity – for an ethical work of self-transformation whereby things which society keeps apart must be held together in creative tension or ultimately synthesised in some higher 'third term'.

One point of convergence between political romanticism and sociological-structural critique is their conception of the individual as an historical and structural concentrate of an indefinite community. 'The romantics transform every instant . . . into an historical moment, . . . and . . . every moment . . . into a point in a structure' (Schmitt, *ibid.*, p. 74). Another point of convergence lies in their characterisation of organised reason as ideological. Binding normative exigencies are seen as simultaneously concealing and manifesting the underlying global realities which make them possible and which they seek to repress. 'The "backstage" that conceals the movement of reality is everywhere being constructed', says Schmitt (*ibid.*, p. 14). A sense of power and the itch to subvert is induced by this (all-)knowing attitude to the wiles of the system. Belief that the source of oppression cannot be touched by specific governmental reforms does not mean that the scope of meaningful political action can only be global and revolutionary: revolutionary organisations may be found as alienating as any others. Nor does suspension of belief in organisational norms and procedures (committees, for instance) preclude using them as occasions for staging political-romantic self-involvements. Alternatively, the value of one's engagement in government may be anxiously disavowed.

Political-romantic commitment to permanent openness should not be confused with the more pragmatic forms of openness associated with a committment to working for organisational reform:

> . . . that kind of openness is nothing more (or less) than a resolution to be differently closed, to rearrange the categories and distinctions within which some actions seem to be desirable and others less so; whereas the openness (apparently) desired [in the romantic ethos] . . . is . . . a *general* faculty, a distinct muscle of the spirit whose exercise leads not to an alternative plan of directed action but to a plan . . . to be directionless, to refuse direction, to resist the drawing of lines, to perform multiplicity and provisionality. (Fish, 1989, pp. 310–11)

These remarks call to mind all those post-structuralist variants of political romanticism, in which the stake of personal-political struggle is no longer the whole person that we once were, or could become, were we to transcend the compartmentalising limits of the governmental. Far from being its victim, the integrated self becomes, on the contrary, an (always incomplete) imposition and an instrument *of* government. And yet (as will be seen in Chapter 2), what could be more in the spirit of Schiller and his romanticisation of Kant? Here, too, we find the same permanent injunction 'to perform multiplicity and provisionality', the same supporting assumption of a freedom to occupy and to dialectically 'play' across a plurality of social and personal roles as desired; and the same moral qualification. These desires shall not utterly negate (though once again they may subsist in tension with) limits to desires. The key to the harmonisation of personal desires and regulatory mechanisms is always dialogue, communal self-government, democratic choice. Any regulatory mechanism which has not been willingly chosen or created is experienced as an arbitrary limit, to be 'disintegrated', as Schmitt puts it, and ultimately transcended. Whether one believes in revolutionary action, or in subverting organisations by opening them up to critique and unending dialogue, the basis for involvement in public affairs is essentially a *magical* faith in the releasing effects of dialectical processes:

> Freude, schöner Götterfuncken . . .
> Deine Zauber binder wieder,
> Was die Mode streng getheilt.
> Alle Menschen werden Brüder
> Wo dein sanfte Flügel weilt.[6]

Ending my outline of the romantic ethic on this note serves as a reminder not only of how simultaneously corny and moving political-romantic sentiments can sometimes be, but also of the fact that what is at issue in my use of 'political romanticism' as a term of criticism is much *narrower* than everything for which romanticism as an historical movement has historically stood. To expose its baleful influence on 'progressive' approaches to politics, government and organisational life is not to slight values and aims on which it has succeeded in acquiring a virtual monopoly, such as community (see Chapter 9) or innovation and openness to the future. Quite the reverse, by comparison with its influence, for instance, upon music or painting, romanticism as applied to politics and government persistently fails even in its own terms to deliver on its promises. Yet to end on 'Ode to Joy' would also be inappropriate if it threatened to undermine the insistence that the writ of political romanticism runs much *further* than a tendency to aestheticism and outright utopian radicalism in politics.

Summing up, the characteristic of political romanticism targeted in these essays is not simply the aesthete's or the political radical's rejection of government. It is a much more widely shared 'trained incapacity' to seriously engage with the conduct of government and its diverse relations of dependency upon the government of conduct.

Phantasies

All thought is at least touched by phantasy. What are the greatest hopes and worst fears invested in affirming the value of an 'anthropological' mode of description and a 'rhetorical' style of ethical thinking about political questions over that of political romanticism? The hopeful phantasy could be expressed as the desire to establish once and for all that political-romantic imperatives commit their adherents to an endless rut of oppositionalist enclave-thinking. On the positive side, the hope would be to contribute to the development of an alternative horizon of ethical and political expectations. Without impugning the importance of the task of reassessing socialist ideals, I am more concerned with the mundane ethical dispositions one needs to cultivate in order to live out (or with) one's commitments to socialism's more ethically demanding political aims. What sort of ethical *habitus*, as Bourdieu (1977) would say, which habits of mind and supportive local environments does one need in order to make oneself capable of being smart and daring and inventive in pursuit of socialist aims? Or in order to know when and how to compromise, as changing circumstances and the exigencies of responsible government dictate? Or how to relate oneself to political disappointments? Socialist ethics and the ethics of a socialist are not quite the same thing. By comparison with political romanticism's ennervating propensity to permanent self-questioning and its incitement to paranoia about the workings of government,[7] the confident aura of Matisse's *Jazz* images could be taken as a symbol of the affective note which my 'rhetorical' approach to the ethical would like to strike. Is there not a form of *practical* ethical confidence which is 'a social phenomenon' – whereby a certain attitude of trust in one's own and others' capacities for ethical reflection is predicated upon the existence of 'social confirmation and support' (Williams, 1985, pp. 170–71)? The value of the rhetorical tradition rests on its being just such a repository of resources for intelligent ethical-political reflection.

Chance would be a fine thing. Political romanticism may have its competitors, but it also possesses an unshakeable grip on contemporary ethical and political culture. Still, the phantasy of criticism and reconstruction at least captures the direction of the arguments, even if supplementation and damage-control rather than displacement is the order of the day. And could there be a more appropriate mnemonic for that phantasy of dislodging the deadening effects of political romanticism than Matisse's image of 'The White Elephant's Nightmare'? All the more so if in addition it goes proxy for a certain fear regarding one of the main potential *objections* to this whole enterprise.

With their Renaissance-humanist pedigree, the extent to which the rhetorically shaded ethical forms pitted against the political-romantic ethos can be disentangled from their aristocratic, archaic and otherwise unappealing origins is at least an open question. Should that prove impossible, then the boot would be on the other foot. It is not political romanticism but the case against that it would be more appropriate to characterise as a 'white elephant'. This is the 'nightmare' prospect hanging over *my* argument: a nightmare peopled by supercilious masters of the courtly art of fine crawling; Marlovian imperialists, all male-ego and oozing cynicism; and most damning of all, the 16th century painter Arcimboldo's lugubrious librarian, his head and body composed entirely of rare books!

Improvisations

It remains to plot the essays' course, together with some of their interdependencies, especially those bearing on the question of the relationship between 'sexual harassment' and 'citizenship' and the implications of viewing them as involving questions of ethical conduct.

Chapter 2, 'Kant, Rhetoric, and Civility', puts the case for reconnecting ethical reflection to the realm of rhetorical skills and 'self-fashioning' and for a related reassessment of social manners. In so doing, it attempts to allay feminist concerns that these accomplishments of 'civilised' ethical culture represent a poisoned chalice. It is in this connection that the question of sexual harassment first emerges: in the event of women having to confront it personally, could not 'civility' and rhetoric work for rather than against them?

The example raises bigger questions about the implications of different ways of ethically representing this problem for the possibility of effectively regulating it, garnering public support for its regulation, and for how the various *limits* to regulation will be construed. The ensuing essays on the sexual harassment issue (Chapters 3 to 6) are all built around a contrast between the answers to those questions yielded by my 'ethical cultural' approach and the political-romantic ethos enshrined in sociological-structural critiques. In Chapter 3, the general outlines and problems of this critique are sketched, along with an alternative way of seeing the issue; in Chapters 4 and 5, this approach is further extended in the course of examining aspects of the sexual harassment issue as it arises in the US and Australian anti-discrimination law; Chapter 6 looks at some historical and contemporary ethical-cultural dimensions of personnel-management policies. The polemic running through these essays pitches the unproductive consequences of the political-romantic form of conscientious objection fostered by sociological-structural critique against the advantages of also building in, rather than denigrating, the no doubt 'apolitical' norms and values of civility upon which the legal and infra-legal government of sexual harassment trades. If to do so involves questioning the received wisdom that sexual harassment is 'not a moral issue' but a question of 'personal politics', then so be it.

The *anti-positivist* epistemological attitudes towards administrative and legal reasoning inculcated by the critique also come in for questioning.[8] The inverse of this romantic scepticism in respect to governmental expertise is an inflated view of the significance of social theory in the work of social reform. In Chapter 4, Catharine MacKinnon's theory of sexual harassment is taken as an example of this tendency. In contrast, the ethical-cultural approach seeks to rescue the 'positive' technical knowledges of the issue built up by legal, trade union, managerial and administrative practitioners from the enormous condescension of romantic social theorists.

This confidence in the judgements of practitioners is not based on the assumption that their knowledge is 'value-free'. The policies in question and their attendant knowledges make no sense independently of some mixture of both governmental and pro-feminist political-ethical investments. The prime example is the legal and managerial construction of sexual harassment, in effect, as an issue of 'inequitable manners'. Nor, despite their deliberately localised focus, are these legal and managerial approaches necessarily closed off to broader perspectives. As I try to show in Chapter 6, the *modus operandi* of sexual harassment management policies may indeed be linked to a more diffuse history of organisational culture. But the linkages established through the ethical cultural approach are more varied than the critique supposes.

Finally, legal and managerial approaches to sexual harassment do not pretend to be *all-* knowing about it and arguably ought not to be criticised for failing to examine it from every possible angle. The price of informativeness and political efficacy is the acceptance of blindspots. A sub-theme of Chapter 5 is the justifiability of excluding psychological dimensions of sexual harassment from the calculations of a personnel management policy; at least for most purposes.

The relationship between the psychical and the social thus takes its place in a series of broader issues raised by this work on the construction of sexual harassment as a social problem. Two issues in particular stand out. The first arises from the intermittent evidence of a disjunction between 'politics' and 'government'. The second concerns the less-than-ideal constituents of ethical culture in the work of government. The key to the further elaboration of these issues in Part III is the dependence of definitions and policies pertaining to the problem of sexual harassment upon *liberal* forms of reasoning. For instance, the norms of 'equitable manners' embedded in regulatory apparatuses immediately solicit reference to *citizenship statuses*. Analysis of limits to regulation and the associated disadvantages of representing the ethical issues at stake solely in terms of political principles introduces considerations of *pluralism*. In conjunction with the history of bureaucratic culture, this in turn raises questions about attitudes to *inequalities and hierarchies* in a democratic culture which is also by necessity heavily 'governmentalised'. The constraints upon informal contestations of sexual harassment raises questions about the *limits and alternatives to participative politics.* Is the 'liberal citizenship' which is invoked in representing and governing sexual harassment the same animal as the liberal political philosophy which undergoes ritual death at the hands of the sociological-structural critique? The reconsideration of liberal citizenship and its limits which is suggested by this distinction can only be taken so far in the context of a case-study. It is in the broader context of the problem taken up in Part III – the place of liberal and libertarian categories in socialist thinking – that some of the implications of viewing liberalism as not only a political philosophy but also a form of governmental reasoning are worked out in more detail. The status of both liberal and radical-participatory versions of citizenship, the value of free discussion, and the 'associationalist' concept of a democratic society are considered. Once again, political-romanticism comes in for criticism. In the light of the ethical-cultural significance of rhetoric, for instance, empathising, truth-oriented dialogue is not necessarily preferable to discussion-by-negotiation. In the light of the person-forming aims of government, active citizenship may not always be more preferable to some of the more passive varieties.

Let us hope that this introductory chapter has at least succeeded in hinting at what is distinctive and contentious in the proposal to view sexual harassment and citizenship as questions of ethical conduct. Is it not also a little clearer how 'sexual harassment' and 'citizenship' both are and are *not* related to one another? Investigation of the arts of governing sexual harassment certainly involves asking what it means to be a citizen in a liberal polity. The former's ethical dimensions cannot, however, be adequately caught in the ideal of citizenship by itself. Still less can sexual harassment be regarded as a problem which can only be seriously addressed by pushing citizenship in a more socialist direction in such a way as to make it more hospitable to feminist aims. *Radicalising* citizenship will not help socialists solve their *own* problems, let alone anyone else's.

The trick is to find a way of appreciating citizenship which is not caught up in the political-romantic phantasy of a general dialectical 'process' of personal-and-political emancipation. The aim of these essays is to convey some of the objections and alternatives to that phantasy arising out of attention to the ethical purposes, responsibilities, techniques and limits of liberal government.

2 Kant, Rhetoric and Civility

A Supplement of Humanism

> *Cleomenes*: In the culture of gardens, whatever comes up in the paths is weeded out as offensive and flung upon the dunghill; but among the vegetables that are thus promiscuously thrown away for weeds, there may be many curious plants, on the use and beauty of which a botanist would read long lectures. The moralists have endeavoured to rout vice, and clear the heart of all hurtful appetites and inclinations. We are beholden to them . . . as we are to those who destroy vermin and clear the countries of all noxious species. But may not a naturalist dissect moles, try experiments upon them, and inquire into the nature of their handicraft without offence to the molecatchers, whose whole business is only to kill them as fast as they can?
> *Horatio*: What fault is it you find with the moralists?
>
> Bernard Mandeville (1732, 1971)

It is commonly assumed that the ethical content of progressive politics is an exclusive amalgam of Enlightenment-humanism and romanticism. It is also assumed that the ethical is an essentially unworldly realm of principles, values and ideals. The ethical contents of participatory democracy, social transparency, equality, self-realisation, the socially harmonious and ecologically sustainable society, etc., designate ideal, that is *perfect* states of affairs. Only on this transcendent condition can they provide a measure of the world's shortcomings and a lodestar for its reformation. It is on the strength of these twin assumptions that debates on the limits of post-Enlightenment humanism typically tend to stall. 'It is impossible to defend human rights out of one side of one's mouth', it is said, 'whilst deconstructing the idea of humanity out of the other'. The choice is either to espouse modern humanism, as the ultimate ethical point of progressive politics, irrespective of its explanatory and practical drawbacks; or to leave the ethical virtually out of account, treating it as an ideological epiphenomenon, as an object for political calculation, or as a matter for 'personal' asides and unreflective practice. This essay works to question the assumptions that (post-)Enlightenment humanism and progressive ethics are synonymous and that the ethical in general is identifiable with the realm of ideal perfection. Its aim is to evade that Hobson's Choice.

To this end, it is not enough to weed out its foundationalist and perfectionist ingredients – to treat 'human rights' as discursively and institutionally (rather than transcendentally) grounded statuses (Hirst and Woolley, 1982, p. 131f); or to replace perfection by visions of 'practopian' betterment (Toffler, 1981, p. 368). Hirst and Woolley's (*op. cit.*, p. 138) assertion that 'motivating people to behave in altruistic . . . and conscientious ways without transcendent goals . . . is not a matter of "ideals" or "morals" but of a daily mechanism of conduct, keyed into practices and institutions' illustrates how readily anti-foundationalist arguments on modern humanism founder on the two assumptions in question. The pressure of the commonsense identification of 'morals' with 'the ideal' leads to 'conscientiousness', etc. paradoxically losing their moral quality on becoming institutionally embodied in conduct. Take away the ideals and what is left in humanism, ethically speaking, that is, in Lévi-Strauss's phrase, good to think with? What is at issue, then, is not the general validity of modern humanism but its claim to a monopoly of values and ideals, unrestricted applicability, and self-sufficiency in the matter of ethical practices.

But where are the ethical supplements of modern humanist ethics to be sought? Taking a cue from Bernard Mandeville's *Enquiry into the Origins of Honour*, this enquiry retraces certain 'paths' laid down by post-Enlightenment humanist ethics in the course of historically establishing itself, and reconsiders some of the ethical flora and fauna which lay in its path and which it sought to eliminate in a series of ideological combats. The task is to discriminate between the weeds and vermin of pre-humanist ethics which may deserve to be cast on the dungheap, such as the ideal patriarchalist household, and components of pre-humanist ethics which arguably deserve better.

For the marginal status of many pre-humanist ethical modalities in modern ethical culture is not only due to their unwholesome political past but also to that movement of *purification* alluded to by Mandeville and entailed in the assumption that the ethical can be exclusively identified with its ideal forms. What is thereby excluded is *inter alia* the worldly means whereby individuals are interpellated by an ethical standpoint and instructed in ways of relating themselves to it and practising it; and the means and conditions of its enunciation and defence. Question these exclusions and a Pandora's box of demoted terms opens up for potential 'reoccupation' (Blumenberg, 1983). To the 'universalist' Enlightenment humanist ideals of equality, the value of altruism, and the universalist form of the moral obligation can be opposed the view that ethical practices may be conditional upon considerations of *status* and the acquisition of particular *abilities* or may be self-regarding instruments of *mastery*. To the romantic ideal of dialectical self-realisation through the harmonisation of oppositions within self and society can be opposed a *cultivation of manners* aiming at the *betterment* and *extension* of the self. To the moral condition or emotion of guilt can be opposed those of shame. But of all the exclusions entailed by identifying the ethical with its perfectionist forms, none is more momentous in its consequences than the dissociation of ethics from *rhetoric*.

The 'supplement' to the then established Christian and 'civic humanist' ethical repertoire proposed by Mandeville himself was of course 'self-liking', the propensity to think (overly) highly of oneself and its supposed concomitants, the love of honour and fear of shame. Only by the most procrustean argument could the elements of pre-humanist ethical culture foreshadowed here be reduced to the cynically egoistic terms of Mandeville's own polemics. However, even if honour and shame are irreducible to masks of self-interest, they remain, ethically speaking, hybrid terms at best (Lamb, 1983). To sharpen the focus of Mandeville's colourful depiction of moralists as indiscriminate destroyers of valuable ethical life-forms it is necessary to historicise it and to exemplify it in contemporary ethical culture.

One of the strengths of contemporary feminism, certainly in Australia and North America, has been its capacity to make areas of sexism – workplace sexual harassment is a conspicuous example – subject to legal regulation and managerial responsibility to an extent that might not have been thought possible. A condition of these 'femocratic' successes arguably lies in the fact that a key outcome of this work has been the emergence of a social imperative to institute workable régimes of manners, partly, through legal and managerial initiatives. An ulterior concern of this essay is to clarify what is at issue in current feminist debate about the utilisation of such measures for the reform of manners, by asking whether this mode of (self-)government is hopelessly in debt to its discredited cultural past.

Kant and the 'Progress' of Modern Humanism

Three themes of post-Enlightenment humanist ethics will be singled out for examination from the standpoint of what they (attempt to) exclude: the universalisation of the constituency of ethical 'statements' (including actions), the dissociation of ethics and rhetoric, and the marginalisation of manners. (The related exclusions of honour-and-shame will be touched on in passing.) To grasp these contours of modern humanist ethics one cannot do better than to begin with Kant.

Kant's centrality to modern humanism might be disputed. Does not the specification 'post-Enlightenment' imply a progression from 'one-sided' Enlightenment rationalism to the various diversifications of the ethical associated with the romanticisation of culture? And what could be.more representative of the Enlightenment 'past' than the Kantian concept of duty and its rational grounding?

However, this assumption of a progressive reaction against, or enrichment of, Enlightenment philosophy only makes sense from within the perspective of modern humanism which it is the task of this essay to interrogate.[1] Major constituents of romantic ethical culture such as perspectivism, the play-principle and the valorisation of 'the man of feeling', for example, pre-date the romantic movement. Kant's moral philosophy may itself be read as a reaction against 'sentimentalist' revisions of the sterner varieties of Protestant thought.[2]

Moreover, only with extreme circumspection did the man whom in Chapter 1 we treated as the paradigm case of a Romantic philosopher, Friedrich Schiller, seek to 'go beyond' Kant. The 'infinite liberation' afforded by the moral law is not in doubt. However, it can only be realised when 'Duty, stern voice of necessity' moderates the censorious tone of its precepts[3] and its initially external and hence pervertible aspect. Only then can Reason's ostensible opposite, Nature (meaning all that is aesthetically 'agreeable' to the *sensuous* side of man) enter the picture as Reason's partner in the dialectical enterprise of man's self-rule (Schiller, 1801, 1982, pp. 179–81). Modifications to Kant's 'philosophical system' are thus only necessitated by the fact that its 'technical' form veils the sacred truth embodied in the moral law from our feeling. Duty and inclination must be harmonised (Schiller, *ibid.*, pp. 5, 17, 179–81). Similarly, contemporary embarrassment with 'Duty' cannot hide the persistence of a large grain of universalistic normativity even in the most emancipatory modern ethical culture.

Kant: Universalisation, Altruism and Guilt

In case modern readers have forgotten, then, the 'moral law' is imposed on all rational beings in the form of a universal, lawlike obligation (Kant, 1785, 1948). The necessary universalisability of moral imperatives is linked to the assumption that they can only be justified by virtue of their rational form. Their justification cannot be contingent on being vouchsafed either by authority (e.g. divine command) or on what Kant called 'anthropological' considerations (such as the empirical presence of virtuous inclinations).

Moral imperatives are not indifferent to a set of ultimate humanistic moral goals (Kant, 1964, pp. 51–53). However, such imperatives must be based on impersonal 'reasons for action' which any rational being (human or otherwise) possessed of a capacity for independent (self-) reflection and a good will would judge for themselves to be valid. On that basis alone should agents submit themselves to moral imperatives.

Kantian moral obligation is 'universalist' in at least four respects. *All* humans, irrespective of social status, are potentially subject to moral obligations and equally objects of moral respect and concern. Moral imperatives are *obligatory* on whomsoever is 'subject' to them; *opting* to subject oneself to moral constraints savours of a spectatorial-aesthetic attitude. Moral action is differentiated as such by dint of the extent to which it is *altruistically* motivated, as opposed to its accruing to the benefit of the moral agent (one 'ought' to help anyone in danger, not only a loved one). Finally, disobeying the moral law elicits condemnation before the court of conscience: i.e. a state of guilt. A purely altruistic ethic has no place for *shaming* ethical subjects.[4] There is no necessary connection between shame and moral responsibility (Richard, 1971, pp. 252–53). The condition of shame represents a negative personal benefit: damage to self-esteem.

The practical (as opposed to 'technical') sides of Kantian ethics, Schiller (*op. cit.*, p. 5) tells us, 'stand revealed as the immemorial pronouncements of common reason'. Yet, for all their contemporary 'obviousness' these assumptions about morality all have a history . . . and a pre-history. It has become an historical commonplace that prior to the Enlightenment – Christianity only partly excepted – the practice of virtue was widely regarded as as expedient means whereby a privileged elite might, if it so desired, ennoble itself. Pre-Enlightenment ethics presents us with the spectacle of ascetic moralities in which our three rules of ethical universality – universality of constituency, obligatory applicability and their related ideal of altruism are conspicuous by their absence and in which the ethical credentials of shame are not in doubt.[5]

As Foucault (1984) remarked, to make oneself the subject of prescriptive statements in Western antiquity is a mark of illustriousness and a kind of beauty. Cultivating mastery over one's impulses and passions is commended to (rather than required of) those in authority as a token of fitness to rule over social inferiors. Self-restraint – to be able to say no to one's impulses when circumstances make it expedient – is in this perspective the very mark of freedom. The 'free' man surpasses the 'condition' of slavery in the sense of not being subject to his passions.

Let us not exaggerate the 'alterity' of pre-humanist ethics. Just as the 'master moralities' of Antiquity attribute only limited ethical attributes to slaves and a special kind of moderation to women,[6] so (post-)

Enlightenment ethics also admits exceptions to ethical status, for example, the diminished responsibility, or incapacity to enter contracts, of minors and the insane. Kant himself would even exclude women from the possibility of acceding to the status of 'active' citizen (Mendus, 1987). Obviously, then, Enlightenment ethics is not uniformly hostile to hierarchy. Lyons (1973) has shown how Bentham's work can be read as, in part, a programmatic professional ethics of subordination addressed to managers or other sorts of 'superior'. However, these differences between pre-Enlightenment and modern ethics are not annulled on some neutral middle ground of exclusions. In classical Greek philosophy, the soul was commonly compared to a polity, a complex of rulers and ruled, each part of which is allotted its natural share of virtue in accordance with its 'natural' condition. For example, women need only acquire the modicum of practical wisdom required to manage the household and to check their supposed propensity to garrulousness and gossip. Those in positions of authority are encouraged to cultivate a fuller complement of the virtues. Your superiors are in that sense your moral betters.

In general then, by contrast with modern humanist ethics which *makes exceptions* to a general rule, pre-humanist ethics *makes inclusions* for limited purposes into a privileged moral hierarchy. Qualifying the difference between a humanist ethos and its pre-humanist forebears in this way allows us both to recognise and to set limits to their incommensurability. Notably, it enables us to make the point that the ethical categories of equality and hierarchy are not mutually exclusive cultural principles of legitimacy which can be neatly assigned to 'modern' and pre-modern societies. For instance, the ancient virtue of *sophrosyne* or moderation and associated 'practices of the self' were neither restricted only to women nor seen only as a means of men's personal ennoblement. J-P. Vernant (1982, pp. 60–68) recalls two 'egalitarian' deployments: (i) in the new codes of martial virtue associated with the development of the phalanx, stressing the subordination of the 'hoplite' (footsoldier) to a common discipline; and (ii) in the civic ethos associated with the democratic institutions of the polis. Similarly, the agonistic 'logic' of shaming – which seems to display through all its variations a remarkable cross-cultural constancy – presupposes the equality-in-honour of the offended challenger and the offender (Bourdieu, 1965, pp. 197f).

Given these limits to the discontinuities between Enlightened and pre-Enlightenment ethics, is there any reason why pre-Enlightenment conceptions of ethics as a means of self-empowerment and of exercising responsible power over others cannot be detached from a notion of natural hierarchies? But what if the forms of pre-humanist ethics described here were subject to criticism even in their own day, and on grounds which correspond to the perspectives of a modern humanist? Too much historical continuity in criteria of moral evaluation would upset my argument by suggesting that pre-humanist ethics was inherently flawed.

With its assumption of a 'democracy of souls', Christian ethics has doubtless over the centuries provided the means to criticise benighted forms of pre-Enlightenment ethics such the tradition of mysogyny (de Pisan, 1405, 1983, pp. 28–29). To what extent Christian asceticism and charity can be identified with modern understandings of altruism is more doubtful, if this implies the existence of a perennial moral opposition to the idea of ethics as an instrument of privileged self-enhancement.

An indication to the contrary is provided by Peter Brown's (1967) wonderful biography of St Augustine. Christian ascetic brotherhoods and communities took over the self-ennobling ascetic rationales and practices of their pagan forebears, many of whom, such as Plotinus for the young St Augustine himself, functioned as exemplars. The 'mature' Augustine's attack on the Pelagian doctrine of the will is based on his controversial conviction that the Christian ascetic life is not a 'triumph of the will' but rather a consequence of divine grace. (Whence his doctrine of predestination and insistence that the Church admit persistent sinners, as opposed to constituting itself as a pure sect.)

St Augustine's writings are notable for their heightened sense of the price and paradox of self-denying altruism unsupplemented by divine grace. Undoubtedly, what is in question here is not simply the possibility of putting others' welfare before one's own, i.e. altruism as a *maxim of principled conduct* (e.g. don't just think of yourself). The question with which Augustine was concerned was rather the absolute necessity (for the sake of salvation) and the absolute impossibility (without God's help) of attaining a highly paradoxical *state of desire*. The believer is asked to cultivate the purification of the moral motive to the point of eliminating all (narcissistic) personal pride in performing a moral deed. Altruism as a maxim of good conduct may be perfectly indifferent to the contingent mixtures of motives informing particular individuals' moral actions. It is only when altruism incorporates an ideal state of desire – the perfect *will* – that the presence of such an admixture comes to signify an 'egoistic' detraction from the moral quality of an action. Altruism is paradoxical and controversial enough within Christianity. What should be said about attempts within modern humanist frameworks to cultivate desire for a total overhaul of motives independently of the religious condition of possibility for altruism; that is, independently of 'grace'?

Rhetoric

The divorce of ethics from rhetoric is a further and less often noticed characteristic of modern humanism. It can be related to the historical epistemological realignment of the ethical domain associated with the rise of foundationalist projects for moral and political sciences, and the accompanying separation of fact and value. Philosophically rationalised in 'emotivist' theories of ethics, this separation issues in the moral-relativist view that moral judgements or actions are not objectively grounded but express personal values, orientations to the world, or existential choices. As termini of moral reasoning, they are not subject to rational debate or justification.

Emotivism is more than a detached academic philosophical view on the meaning of moral language: it has become embodied in contemporary ethical culture (MacIntyre, 1981, p. 21). To a surprising extent, this 'expressive' view of ethics is as much heir to eighteenth- and nineteenth-century moral science projects as it is in conflict with them. Denying that moral values can be scientifically grounded leaves a crucial epistemological condition of possibility for moral science projects untouched: namely, the attempt to divorce ethics from the institution of *rhetorical* skills and erudition.

Rhetoric as an institution was organised around the written formalisation of the ancient art of persuasive oratory, combining instruction and entertainment, wisdom and style.[7] Established as a school subject, it evolved during its Renaissance heyday into an art of written (mainly verse) composition. Even then, it continued to retain and renew connections with scholarship, law, religion, political speech, court society, diplomacy, letter-writing and other areas of life (Ong, 1971). Originally arising to pre-eminence with the advent of the democratic institutions associated with the ancient Greek polis, the art of rhetoric signified a shift in the forms of power invested in human speech, from the incantatory power of ritual formulae or the 'last word' of a monarch to the persuasive force of an address to a democratic assembly or to the jury in a legal tribunal (Vernant, 1982, pp. 49–60). However, rhetoric has not been confined to the domain of 'the management of language' for political or pecuniary ends (Vernant, *ibid.*, p. 50). Firstly, at times rhetoric assumes within its compass elements of discourse which – on certain formal philosophical criteria – ought to fall within the domain of 'reason' as opposed to 'persuasion'. Notably, it embraces invention (*inventio*), the part of rhetorical theory and technique concerned with 'finding' good arguments by running through the 'places' (the topic headings) appropriate to a given subject matter;

and arrangement (*dispositio*), whereby the constituents of a discourse are assembled in relation to one another and to its overall aims as well as its intended effects (Vickers, 1988, pp. 62–64 *et passim*). Secondly, the parts of rhetoric known as *elocutio* (style) and *actio* (delivery) have served as a support for various aristocratic 'body techniques' aimed at the refinement of conduct and relationships, physiological functions and demeanour. The 'art' of rhetoric informed not only written composition but also personal composure.

Rhetoric might be seen as one of four (frequently overlapping or competing) ways of articulating ethics as a form of knowledge prior to the Enlightenment era; the others being dialectic, prophecy and allegory. In spite of all their differences from one another (and their own highly developed rhetorical dimensions), the figures of the philosopher, religious prophet and allegorist are united in their appeal to a truth transcending mundane understanding. This transcendence, the foundation, authorising guarantee and inspiration of their discourse, forms the basis of their respective forms of exclusivity. No matter how this precious truth is obtained (disciplined philosophical reflection, divine visitation, esoteric hermetic studies, it is a truth which owes nothing to conventional wisdom. It will inevitably be misinterpreted, cheapened or found unbearable and rejected by all but the pure-of-heart or the initiate (Murrin, 1969, pp. 21–53).

By contrast, ethical thought subsumed within the classical art of rhetoric will by definition be attuned to the received opinion – the stock of commonplace wisdom – of the audience to whom it is addressed and whom it attempts to persuade (Murrin, *ibid.*, pp. 3–9). Compare the stark choice presented to the people of Jerusalem by the Old Testament prophet Jeremiah – repent or perish! – a demand which its author expects to fail (*ibid.*, pp. 23–27). Schematically, moral oratory is based on principles of canonical *authorisation, decorum and emotive appeal*. To be effective, wisdom must be well expressed, authoritative and calculated to 'please'. It was of course precisely these worldly and calculative elements which formed the basis of ancient philosophical and Christian patristic attempts to morally discredit rhetoric.[8]

These reproaches include a powerful *ad hominem* ingredient – they place the probity and sincerity of the orator's character under a cloud. However, the force of these reproaches did not only rest on notorious abuses of the rhetorical art (such as the unscrupulous commercial practices and self-aggrandising tactics of the ancient Sophists (Kennedy, 1963)). Rather the entire tradition was vulnerable to the extent that rhetorical education entailed the cultivation of what has been called a 'mobile sensibility' (Greenblatt, 1980, pp. 224–25). A student of rhetorical composition and delivery would be taught not merely how to present alternative (including morally bad or improbable) points of view, but also how to recreate in themselves the 'emotional' concomitants of that viewpoint and its typical human representatives. Antique 'historical' writings afford many examples of these devices for capturing the interest and sympathies of an audience (Auerbach, 1953, pp. 34–40). Cultivation of mobile sensibility could also embrace more permanent personal characteristics and mannerisms. In the Renaissance heyday of such rhetorically inflected 'self-fashioning' (Greenblatt, *ibid.*, pp. 1–3) an aspiring courtier might well follow Baldesar Castiglione's advice: 'Just as in the summer fields the bees wing their way . . . from one flower to the next, so the courtier must acquire grace from those who appear to possess it and take from each the quality that seems most commendable' (Castiglione, 1528, 1967, pp. 66–67).

The person in this perspective is a heterogeneous accretion of winning ways. Yet both in practice and theory, rhetorically inflected self-fashioning is not exhausted by this 'other-directed' theatricality. The extent to which the honour of a lady or gentleman was an 'indwelling quality' not contingent on external sanction was a matter of debate, certainly among Italian court intellectuals (Bryson, 1935).

Vulnerable to attack though it may have been, wholesale repudiation of rhetoric was unheard of. Plato is not the exception he was once thought to be. As Vickers (1988, p. 133), Welch (1988) and many others have pointed out, Plato's assumption of an alternative, philosophical rhetoric, informed by dialectic, as the Platonic dialogue form reminds us, is not indifferent to the art of persuasion. Besides, rhetoricians were quite capable of defending the ethical credentials of their practice (Vickers, *op. cit.*, pp. 149–196). Hannah Gray (1968) documents Renaissance-humanist arguments against 'merely intellectual' medieval discourse on virtue which allegedly neglected to induce its audience to go down the path of virtue.

However, once again following Mandeville's advice, there may also be reason not to spurn some of the less edifying aspects of oratorical composition. The 'epideictic' branch of rhetoric, initially arising out of ancient Greek public ceremonies and rituals and given over to panegyric in praise of gods and men, soon came to embrace speeches in censure and denunciation (Dixon, 1971, p. 23). Whilst in theory simply the correlative of the art of praise, this denunciatory oratical mode came to be elevated into a quite distinct art of malicious invective rivalling its opposite number. This *ars vituperandi* came to acquire its own history, rationale techniques, exemplary exponents and in the archaic figure of Momus, even its own 'presiding deity' (Pippin Burnett, 1983, p. 55). The master of classical invective was the seventh-century poet Archilochus, who, claims Anne

Pippin Burnett (*ibid.*, pp. 16–17), was as much honoured by antiquity as Homer himself.[9] Alongside epideictic poetry, the art of abuse was 'one of the two poetic practices essential to social life', serving as a vehicle of moral pressure and as a kind of knowledge useful for dealing with enemies (*ibid.*, pp. 55 n. 2, 57).

Truly, in the art of blame we have a mole after Mandeville's own heart. In much Renaissance writing and drama, as in 'real life', the interlacing of ethics and rhetoric invested the former with an *agonistic* dimension (Ong, 1971, p. 66). The idea of ethical discourse as a way of fighting might well be the subject of some modern 'experiments'.[10]

Kantian Ethics: Reason *v* Persuasion

Sapere aude! Have the courage to use your *own* understanding! What light does Kant's (1784, 1970) 'motto of Enlightenment' cast on rhetorical ethics? What light does this rhetorical-ethical tradition throw back onto Kantian representations of the ethical?

The obverse of this call for the emancipation of individual reason is the 'self-incurred' inability to reason 'without the guidance of another' (Kant, 1970, p. 54). The explicit target of the motto in the essay 'What is Enlightenment?', is the hegemonisation of the individual's rational powers by religious and political authorities (chiefly the former). In this regard, though in different ways, both moral-philosophical and historical-political commentary have concurred with Kant. Characterising the ethical in terms of its rational form has, since Weber (1968), been widely (and plausibly) interpreted as a work of 'disenchantment' which played a role in reconstituting the ethical as an autonomous zone of individual ethical self-determination. When all sensible criticisms of the implications of viewing ethics as 'a private matter' have been accepted, this construction of a general-purpose capacity for independent thought and personal responsibility is almost certainly a cultural achievement to be defended. Only partly mythical, such a capacity can be spelled out independently of philosophical versions of 'the motto of Enlightenment' which work (like Kant's) by relocating a supposedly ultimate capacity for transcendence, which was hitherto vested in religious and/or political authority in the rational 'good will' of human beings.

However, both essentialist-philosophical and historical-political commentaries on the 'Enlightenment' aspect of Kantian ethics tend to construe its intended targets too narrowly. *Rhetoric* may attempt to ground ethical judgement on (worldly, personal) authority, but that fact hardly exhausts its ethical import. Kant's 'disenchantment' of ethics may be linked not only to his laying the ground for its detachment from compulsory religion, but equally to its attempt to dissociate ethical judgement from its rhetorical conditions of enunciation and impact. May we not ask whether this emancipation of ethical reason from 'external' authority was not won at too high a price?

Ex hypothesi, if the validity of ethical judgements is made independent of external authority in general, then no ethical respect can be paid to the authority of the one who enunciates the judgements, even where this is based not on superior social status but on their personal characteristics and, not unrelatedly, on their rhetorical competence, on how well the judgements are expressed. From where Kant stands, none of this is of any *ethical* importance. 'Virtue', Kant (1797, 1964, p. 41) tells us, 'cannot be defined as a mere aptitude'. The one aptitude required for moral judgement on Kant's view, applying universal principles to particular cases, is construed as the untheorisable and unteachable *gift* of 'mother-wit' (Kant, 1781, 1933, p. 177).

In clear contra-distinction to Renaissance humanists, Kant is emphatic that there is no place in moral education for *inducements* to virtue. Ethico-rhetorical education looked to historical narratives as a perennial source of inspiring deeds and personages: *historia magistra vitae* (Kosselleck, 1985, pp. 21–38). For Kant (1803, 1971, pp. 179–80), 'everything is lost' when moral education is based upon 'examples'. Pupils must behave well from their *own*'maxims'; not on the basis of the commonplace aphorisms or *sententiae* to which the term 'maxim' traditionally referred (Curtius, 1953, pp. 57–61). Kant's 'moral' maxim is a subjective imperative which has been derived from general principle by moral agents' use of their own understanding. What is the use, asks Kant, of an education system's producing 'packmules of Parnassus', laden with 'copious' ethical erudition, but incapable of understanding general principles and applying them to particular cases (*ibid.*, pp. 170–71)? These derogations of rhetorical ethics (and information) drawn from Kant's (1803) treatise on education coincide exactly with the *Groundwork's* attitude towards adulterations of the categorical imperative: 'Unmixed with the alien element of added empirical inducements, the pure thought of duty has by way of reason alone an influence on the human heart so much more powerful than all further impulses [to be moral]' (Kant, 1785, 1948, p. 75).

The rhetorical element in these 'impulsions' (or benevolent 'inclinations') to ethical conduct is made explicit when Kant repeatedly deploys an analogy between moral teachers' offering 'inducements to be moral' in the form of 'charms and pleasures' and 'the highest welfare of life' in addition to the 'sublime' incentive of duty, and doctors who 'spoil their medicine . . . by their very attempt to make it really powerful'. It is beneath the dignity of the will to be ethically motivated after the manner of an Epicurean philosopher (Kant, 1788, 1956, pp. 91–92; 1785, 1948, p. 75n).

Kant's Enlightenment-humanist attempt to ground moral judgement not on religious or other personal authority but on impersonal rational criteria is thus dependent to a quite considerable extent on loosening the traditional ties between ethics and rhetoric. The cost of 'emancipating' ethical thought from its impure accretions is the effacement of the very notion of ethical competence. The loss entailed by this effacement of the rhetorical dimensions of the ethical will be illustrated shortly in relation to the question of whether the supposed benefits of rhetoricised ethics can be recouped in the present.

Kantian Virtue and the Demise of the Social Virtues

A further consequence of Kant's attempted reduction of the ethical to its purely rational form consists in the exclusion from morality 'proper' of a series of 'social virtues' which are inseparable from rhetorical self-fashioning: namely the moulding of character and conduct with a view to 'pleasing' others. In his *Lectures on Ethics*, Kant (1775–80, 1963, pp. 236–37) writes that:

> accessibility, affability, politeness, refinement, propriety, courtesy and ingratiating and captivating behaviour . . . call for *no large measure of moral determination and cannot, therefore, be reckoned as virtues.* They demand no self-control and sacrifice . . . They relate to the pleasure and charm of social intercourse and to nothing else. (my emphasis)

Kant concedes that these so-called social virtues may serve as 'a means of developing virtue'. In *Über Pedagogik*, 'manners, politeness and a certain judiciousness' figure amongst the necessities of moral cultivation above 'discipline' ('the taming of wildness') but again falling well short of moral-cultural enlightenment (Kant, 1803, 1971, pp. 122–3). The antithesis between virtue proper and the social virtues is sharpened wherever it is used to support what became the commonplace Romantic distinction between (ethical) culture proper and 'mere' civilisation:

> We are *civilised* to the point of excess in all kinds of social courtesies and proprieties. But we are still a long way from the point at which

we would consider ourselves *morally* mature . . . an application of this idea [of morality] which only extends to the semblances of morality, as in love of honour and outward propriety, amounts merely to civilisation. (Kant, 1784, 1970, p. 49)

Kant's disparaging remarks remind us of how manners have, like rhetoric, come to be associated with all the supposed artificiality, superficiality, insincerity and duplicity of an aristocratic culture committed by tradition to the value of *otium*, or freedom from 'base' occupations. A combination of developments, from capitalist commercialisation and industry to social democratic and artistic currents have progressively made this aristocratic grandeur itself appear 'otiose'. Apart from its disgraced aristocratic ancestry, the realm of good manners is also tarnished by its related associations with 'patriarchal' cultural forms.

Here, for instance, is David Hume's epitome of gallantry, precisely reflecting the association which is still so current between manners, aristocracy, 'civilisation', and female subordination:

A man is lord in his own family . . . hence he is always the lowest person in the company attentive to the wants of everyone . . . Gallantry is nothing but an instance of the same generous attention. As nature has given man the superiority above women, by endowing him with greater strength both of mind and body, it is his part to alleviate that superiority, by . . . a studied deference . . . for all her inclinations . . . Barbarous nations display this superiority by reducing their females to the most abject slavery, by confining them, by beating them, by selling them, by killing them. But the male sex among a polite people *discover their authority in a more generous though not less evident manner*, by civility, by respect, by complaisance. (Hume, 1741, 1963, p. 133, my emphasis)

As feminist jurists have long pointed out, this sense of propriety towards women and the associated moral standards respecting their 'honour' were also historically bound up with a legal regard for women as their husband's or father's property (cf. Chapters 4 and 5 below).

Less obviously, the ethical standing of manners is further demeaned by its association with *disciplinary* habit-formation. Historically, the inculcation of manners has not been limited to aristocratic men and women. Pocock (1985) has drawn attention to the emergence of a new concern with manners inside the civic humanist tradition, as a means of equipping the bourgeois citizenry of an increasingly commercialised world with a new sort of civic virtue. In place of anachronistic views of civic virtue in which man is essentially destined to display his virtue in the public forum, attempts are made to reconstitute the individual as a bearer of the apolitical rights and capacities for restraining the passions required by a commercial society.[11] Certainly, the 'manners' which, to an eighteenth century observer such as Adam Ferguson epitomised the difference between 'rude' and polished nations, were neither restricted to, nor invariably attempted to ape, those of the aristocracy:

> Every profession has its point of honour and its system of manners; the merchant his punctuality and fair dealing; the statesman his capacity and address; the man of society his good breeding and wit. Every station has a carriage, a dress, a ceremonial. (Ferguson, 1767, 1966, p. 189)

It is not difficult to spot a referential coincidence between the 'manners' discussed in these philosophical-historical discourses and the 'disciplinary' habits formed through the knowledges, agencies and institution-building, the programmatic ambitions and population-management techniques associated with the historical development of 'police' (Minson, 1985, pp. 19–29, 102–13).

This coincidence between manners and 'common' discipline points to a third reason for the ethical demotion of manners: the rise of new programmes and techniques as well as values aiming at the 'government' of the self. These programmes and techniques work by fostering autonomy, where the disciplines sought only what Foucault (1977) called a 'docility' appropriate to individuals' being harnessed to productive work and other institutional aims and activities over which they have little 'say'. Post-disciplinary technologies of the self do not renounce discipline but work by fostering passions which some of the earlier disciplines sought to keep in check. These techniques seek to transform institutional spaces hitherto traversed by a fine normative mesh into an environment more conducive to discretionary decision-making and displays of initiative (Rose, 1989). 'Post-fordist' developments in personnel-management and production engineering would be an example. It is the establishment of these programmed *régimes of informality* throughout the social body which, alongside an associated 'cult of intimacy'[12] (Coleman, 1982, pp. 52f) contributes as much to the diminished status of manners as its associations with aristocratic artificiality and patriarchalist domination. Civility in the modern world has not lapsed merely by default, through parental irresponsibility, etc., as 'letters to the editor' are wont to complain. It has also been deliberately cast aside in favour of other ways of making people responsible. It will be the task of the next section to question this depreciation of civil manners.

The Origins and Impact of 'Civility': Norbert Elias

The persistence of the reputation of manners for superficiality is apparent even in analyses which treat it seriously. Bourdieu (1977, pp. 94–95) alerts his readers to the importance accorded to 'seemingly insignificant details of dress, bearing, physical and verbal manners' in all societies which try to transform the cultural attributes of their members. The necessity for this attention to the 'unnecessary' is traced to these societies' propensity to use the body as a *practical mnemonic* for 'the fundamental principles of the arbitrary content of the culture'. The effectivity of this 'trick of pedagogic reason' lies in the fact that by 'embodying' these principles in the form of seemingly insignificant social requirements of demeanour, a series of petty conducts etc. then fall below the threshold of consciousness and hence are quarantined off from the possibility of voluntary deliberate transformation. Accordingly, 'the concessions of politeness always contain political concessions'.

In this argument, manners breach the rule that nothing whatsoever should be done without first subjecting it to rational evaluation. In effect they fail to pass a Kantian-rationalist test of social transparency. Manners are the dubious embodiment of the dominant ideology. Paradoxically, they are not superficial to the extent that their superficial appearance is itself a trick of the ideological apparatus. Yet they retain their superficiality to the extent that their meaning derives from some other, more fundamental place. To pursue a history of manners along Bourdieu's lines is not likely to shed light on a pluralistic contemporary ethical culture characterised by its singular *lack* of a uniform ideology. By contrast, it is Norbert Elias's eschewal of the assumption that the duty of the student of manners is to recover their unconscious in the name of critical enlightenment which makes his approach so illuminating.

In three remarkable books, Elias (1978, 1982, 1983) sets out both to establish and to explain the historical dimensions of certain sorts of sensibility and ways of dealing with others associated with 'civilised' societies, in

(i) the shaping of the feelings of shame, delicacy, and embarrassment and – the evolution of bodily proprieties, e.g. regarding spitting, urinating, defecating, nose-blowing, farting and eating habits;
(ii) the cultivation of an art of detached (self-) observation, description,

and circumspection in dealings with others;

(iii) a lesser yet recurrent theme – the transformation in socially approved relations between the sexes – an elevation in the cultural status of (noble) women and the imposition on men of courtesy towards women.

These forms of sensibility, reasoning and self-controlled conduct, argues Elias, do not originate, as had often been argued, either in the (Counter-) Reformation conscience or in capitalist accounting. The roots of civility run back to the 'courtly' forms of social organisation associated with the Absolutist-monarchical phase in the passage from feudal organisation to the modern 'professional-bourgeois-urban-industrial' age:

> At a certain stage in the development of European societies individuals are bound together in the form of courts and thereby given a specific stamp . . .   As a central figuration of that stage of development . . . this aristocratic court society developed a civilising and cultural physiognomy which was taken over by professional-bourgeois society *partly as a heritage and partly as an antithesis* and, preserved in this way, was further developed. (Elias, 1983, pp. 39–40; my emphasis)

Forming as they do 'models and style-setting centres' (Elias, 1982, p. 5), the European Absolutist courts are the key to the more pervasive cultural institution of affective and bodily restraints in the West. Elias's macro-sociological argument, which is both a case study in sociological theory (the 'figuration' of court society is intended to mediate agency and social structure) and a history of 'modernity', will not be examined as such. A more selective reading of Elias is proposed, in which his work provides a critical commentary on the (post-)Enlightenment attempt to exclude civilised manners from the realm of ethics properly so-called.

According to Kant, the superficiality of manners hinged on the lack of inward self-determination and control involved in their exercise. It is this assumption which Elias' (1978) study puts in question. Drawing upon late medieval and Renaissance etiquette manuals, he demonstrates a dramatic change in thresholds of embarrassment and delicacy. A token of this transformation is the casual, unembarrassed tone of the influential manual of civil conduct compiled by Erasmus in 1530 (Elias, *ibid.*, pp. 53f). *Civilitas morum* may well have been classified by Erasmus as 'the grossest branch of philosophy' (*ibid.*, p. 76) but the leading sixteenth-century intellectual did not regard it as beneath his attention. Formally addressed to the offspring of princes (though many equivalent texts were addressed to adults), *De Civilitate Morum Puerilium* ('On civility in children') nonchalantly and drolly recommends his readers to refrain, in the interests of 'outward bodily propriety' from a range of unsalubrious practices which well-brought-up 'moderns' would scarcely dream of, let alone be seriously tempted to publicly engage in, such as playing with excrement. Examples from the area of behaviour at table include blowing one's nose onto the tablecloth and searching around in the stewpot with one's hand for the largest hunks of meat (the latter manifesting 'want of forebearance').

The detail and tone of the treatise suggest that its recommendations are motivated by neither native disgust nor hygiene. Rather Renaissance rules of bodily propriety place adherents at an appropriate distance from social inferiors and superiors.[13] Only as a result of a protracted 'civilising process', in which the spectrum of prohibited bodily acts is gradually both broadened and deepened, do 'spontaneous' feelings of embarrassment and disgust regarding bodily functions become motivating forces for restraint. It is no doubt at this point, but only then, that the 'social virtues' of propriety can appear, as they did to Kant, as infra-moral capacities which did not draw on any significant degree of self-government. This attitude towards the field of civilised manners not only underestimates the accumulated strata of (un)conscious repression tied to social training – in Kant's words, the 'moral determination' underlying civilised manners. Such an attitude almost certainly also overestimates the proportion of people in 'civilised society' who have been inducted at all, let alone 'to excess', into civilised proprieties.

To see whether Kant's representation of the arts of self-observation and circumspection in personal relations as intrinsically superficial fares any better in the light of Elias's history, the latter's broader argument on the 'sociogenesis' and organisation of the Absolutist courts must first be sketched in.

For Elias, the relative triumph of European monarchies over the centrifugal tendencies of feudal political organisation was partly contingent on the 'courtisation' of the warrior nobility. Divested of their erstwhile military functions and financially dependent upon royal favour for the maintenance of their estates, the French princely aristocracy discussed by Elias (1982) were compelled (until the death of Louis XIV) to near-permanent attendance at Versailles. In turn the monarch was bound to his aristocracy by origin and culture: as the premier *gentilhomme*, he needed the company, service and respect of the traditional nobility, 'the outward splendour and prestige of his reign' (Elias, 1983, p. 196).

He also needed them as a counterweight to the powers of the *noblesse de robe*. This non-princely 'bourgeois-aristocratic' and professional bureau-cratic caste was in turn made dependent on royal patronage, contesting particular princely privileges but 'never . . . the institution of privilege itself' (Elias, 1982, p. 178). The absolute sway of royal rule flows from the fact that each of the competing 'courtised' groups 'needs him in their conflicts and because he can play one off against the other' and thereby stave off their claims on *his* powers and prerogatives (Elias, 1983, p. 168).

In this finely-tuned conflictual context of extreme dependence on the opinion and favours of superiors, neither professional status, competence, wealth, property, nor even a noble pedigree counted independently of royal recognition. It was in this context that French court society became such a notorious forcing-house for the cultivation of manners. A royal decision, for example, as to who would hold the King's right sleeve during the morning dressing ritual served as 'a literal documentation of social existence' (Elias, *ibid.*, p. 94). Palpably absurd though they frequently seemed even to participants, the meticulous daily round of royal rituals and entertainments were as essential as they were inescapable. For it was by these means that the shifting distributions of power, rank, favours and prestige were symbolised and so determined.

'Court rationality,' writes Elias, 'derived its specific character . . . from the calculated planning of strategy in the face of the possible gain or loss of status' (Elias, 1983, p. 93). In this incessant competition for status, where reputations rise and fall by the minute, to successfully enact one's prestige, to create and maintain the appropriate social distance between oneself and every other courtier required powers of circumspection and observation: the cultivation of a keen sensitivity to one's own and others appearance; the nuances of posture, speech and gesture; 'the moulding of facial muscles and . . . facial expression' (Elias, 1982, p. 276). The cultivation of self-knowledge (one must know one's motives if one is to mask them) was also an asset. So was the capacity to 'read' the motives of others. These arts of existence were disseminated in books of memoirs, letters, maxims, poetry, novels, pen-portraits and etiquette manuals.

The 'court rationality', argues Elias, belies the assumption that courtiers' preoccupation with appearances and good form betokens an intrinsic superficiality. This assessment of court life itself springs from a subse-quent 'structure of social existence'. It forgets the aristocracy's systematic exclusion from pursuits which might have made them independent of courtly ritual. Simply put, only when capital and professional opportunities ('relatively mobile foundations of existence') were freed from the yoke of the court society, i.e. from confinement to a single locus of recognition, accreditation, etc., can non-admission into 'polite society' weigh less heavily. So even in this 'worst case', preoccupation with manners need not be thought irrational, superficial and lacking in inward moral determination in every respect.

From a contemporary point of view, the charge of superficiality is a way of expressing doubt about whether instituting changes at the level of manners could ever contribute to significant cultural and political changes. Elias's broader arguments on the role of manners in shaping 'modernity' suggest that it can and has. The 'police' of courtly manners, he argues, provided as important a prototype for the conversion of 'external into internal compulsion' (1983, p. 221) as capitalism and protestantism. The civilising and cultural physiognomy developed in court society was not totally rejected but taken over by bourgeois-professional society *partly as a heritage*, for example through the agency of 'the disciplines', in professional ethics, 'middle-class respectability', etc. The purchase of this heritage even extends, Elias shows, into romantic love itself (Elias, 1983, ch. 8).

The 'courtisation' of the European warrior aristocracy, argues Elias, brought about an improvement in women's social standing and in men's behaviour towards them. 'It was not men but women who were first liberated for intellectual development, for reading . . . ' (Elias, 1982, p. 81). In the twelfth century reorganisation of French medieval courts, women's very exclusion from martial activity gave them a head start. From these slight beginnings, aristocratic women's educational standing steadily improves, culminating in the unprecedented intellectual equality associated with the seventeenth-century French salon culture which sprang up in noble *hotels de ville* after Louis XIV's death.

Elias's general argument has been criticised on account of its evolutionist tendencies (Lasch, 1985). Historical investigations of learned women would tend to suggest that women's 'head-start' was soon clawed back (La Baume, ed., 1980). A more promising parallel development traced by Elias (1983, pp. 242–43) concerns rules of 'social distancing'. The inaccessability of women to any men apart from their husbands was not predicated solely on ideologies of delicacy, modesty, chastity, courtly love, etc. Gentlemanly conduct also embraces daily rules of bodily restraint through which women of a certain status are constructed as a locus of bodily integrity. 'If a lady asks you to sit beside her, runs a medieval 'motto for men', do not sit on her dress, or too near her . . . . ' By the time of Louis XIV (Elias, 1982, p. 90) these constraints become more demanding. In Chapter 3, I will offer further arguments on why these constraints are not merely an embodied 'mnemonic' of patriarchal ideology.

In addition, there is a connection between these constraints on relations between the sexes and the possibility of the postponed satisfactions and painful joys associated with the 'discipline' of romantic love (Elias, 1983, ch. 8). Romantic thought and practices of the self have undeniably provided models for hybridising conventionally distinguished male/female attributes (Vogel, 1987). Alongside the cultivation of respect for women's 'physical' space, the link between romantic love and courtly self-restraint drives a further wedge between restructuring conduct through the vehicle of manners and patriarchal assumptions of women's secondary to men.

Rhetorical Ethos and Reform of Manners

> Almost all worthwhile human life lies between the extremes morality puts before us . . . between force and reason, persuasion and rational conviction, shame and guilt, dislike and disapproval, mere rejection and blame. The purity of morality . . . conceals not only the means with which it deals with deviant members of its community but also the virtues of those means. (Williams, 1985, pp. 94–95)

This essay has sought to bring out the 'virtues' of associating ethics and rhetoric, the cultivation of manners and seeing ethics as a vehicle of (self-) empowerment. The aim was to suggest that these components of pre-Enlightenment Western ethical cultures sustain a sufficient measure of logical and historical independence of their unedifying historical origins to justify their incorporation within the *ethos* of social democrats, feminists or other reform-minded categories of citizen. They could be seen as aids to living out or living with their 'progressive' commitments. Though having little to say on rhetoric or manners, Bernard Williams's attack on the modern 'morality system', distinguished from older ethical outlooks by the privileged place it gives to 'pure' moral obligation, provides a model for demonstrating the extent to which these outlooks are actually embodied in a subterranean and largely unappreciated fashion in contemporary ethical cultures.[14] But to go any further down that road would be to exceed the scope of this essay. Let us conclude with a warning about 'in-principle' problems of reincorporating rhetoric, followed by a provisional attempt to spell out some of the formal attributes of a rhetorically inflected ethics and its implications for a reform of manners.

To call for the redemption of the rhetorical *tout court* would be absurd. The boundaries demarcating rhetoric from adjacent arts and sciences are too historically variable to justify any simple act of reclamation.[15] A cautionary note is all the more necessary if, as here, the purpose of reoccupying the rhetorical terrain is a supplementation of modern humanism. Do we wish to accede to Welch's (1988) depiction of Plato's synthesis of dialectic and philosophical rhetoric as engaging whole human beings? Or to Lanham's (1976) construction of *homo rhetoricus* as a perennial embodiment of the play-principle? Further examples (extending to post-structuralist relatives of these avowedly humanistic recuperations) could be multiplied. It is no exaggeration to say that the bulk of twentieth-century arguments for a return to rhetoric represent not a negation but continuation of Romantic humanism.[16]

The problem with modern humanistic thought is its perfectionism. Staten's (1984) formalisation of Wittgenstein's and Derrida's assault on philosophical propensities to identify entities with their ideal 'thinkable form' neatly encapsulates the problem posed by the exclusions of rhetoric, the social virtues, honour-and-shame, etc. entailed in the establishment of post-Enlightenment ethics. How can the material or practical concomitants of a virtue, for example its metaphorical properties or the way it is taught, be extraneous to what makes it a moral virtue, if these are necessary not only to its practice but to its very enunciation? It is with a view to meeting this formal problem that in this essay the ethical is conceived 'ethnographically' as a realm of 'material culture', in which the more uncomprising, ideal, self-denying components are not privileged in the order of analysis over its 'lowlier' practical ingredients.[17] Amalgamating the series of hints punctuating the historical argument, let us now see what corresponding refiguration of the ethical emerges when those marginalised elements are foregrounded.

One such material ingredient is the *performantial* side of ethical judgement or action. Bringing the rhetorical back into ethics formally amounts to requiring moral agents to adjust the material expression of a moral judgement to the conditions and impacts of its enunciation. In consequence, truth and justification become a necessary but not a sufficient condition for the 'adequacy' of ethical judgements.

Foreshadowing the concerns of Part II of this book, we might try to illustrate the implications of this statement by reference to the contrasting ethical stances open to a woman who finds herself relying on her own resources when faced with sexual harassment. A rhetorically informed ethical stance requires one to take responsibility for the fact that ethical judgements or actions are performances that may or may not come off. In the case of sexual harassment this could mean questioning the wisdom of 'uncontrolled' responses – displays of hatred, moral indignation or outrage (even if the unrestraint may be part of the performance of indignation). Losing one's temper is one thing, honouring emotional outbursts with an ethical-political licence is something else. One consequence of an emotivist ethical stance of this kind is an abdication of personal responsibility which manifests itself in studied or naive indifference to both the power and the fragility of the ethical.

On the one hand, ethics-as-personal-political expression is indifferent to the *power*-effects invested in the material instrumentalities of ethical actions and judgements. There is nothing to be ashamed of in the exercise of power *per se*, but neither should one pretend indifference to the power of some kinds of riposte to sexual harassment to wound, to get someone the sack, to put them in an impossible position, or to give someone a means of backing down without losing face. Ethical emotivism ignores the possibility that such objectionable conduct may be stopped more effectively if objections are put in one tone or style rather than another, by one person rather than another, on one occasion of its occurrence rather than another.

The licensed spontaneity associated with an emotivist-humanist stance also renders it indifferent to the endemic susceptibility of the ethical to being undone by moralism. For example, a collapse into moralism – the self-righteous parade of virtue – threatens in personal confrontations over sexual harassment, whenever what is at stake is resistance on the part of the perpetrator which takes the form of refusals to be ethically interpellated by feminist values or even by the very word 'sexism'. In such circumstances, simply to assume the moral high ground, that is, to refuse to calculate on which *style* of ethical action or judgement is most appropriate in the circumstances, is to risk being placed, however unjustly, in the ineffectual or brittle posture of the moraliser, and to allow the offender to present himself (especially to others) as more sinned against than sinning.

Calculation in this context need not be exclusive of emotion. Lowering one's moral tone need not entail lowering one's voice. The ancient *ars vituperandi* might be recalled in this connection. By contrast with the expressivist outbursts of rage or indignation here we have a calculated art-form fuelled by the intensities of *malice*. No one could recommend it unreservedly (its borderline ethical status is what makes it interesting). Yet it might be wondered whether a 'rightful' malice, with its calculative commitments, is not finally a more responsible or even congenial moving force than indignation.

These speculations about the likely effects of different ethical styles in combatting sexual harassment call to mind a second component of a rhetorical ethos. To be a moral agent presupposes more than merely being human, possessing 'reason', 'will', and integrity. A person's ethical standing in a rhetorical perspective (which in this regard recalls Aristotelian ethics, Williams, 1985, p. 36) is predicated on the acquisition of *capacities*, such as the capacity to make a telling moral point, to effectively carry out or follow through a virtuous action, or to judge character (Brown, 1986). Kosman (1980) develops a parallel perspective on the space within Aristotelian ethics for the education of the passions, how to bring within our power (which may not be the same as bringing under conscious control) what we undergo rather than do, that is, our dispositions to be affected in certain ways.

'Ethical authority' need not be solely attached to the occupation of positions of power or social privilege. It can also flow from a combination of competences and personal characteristics. To those who tend to identify a 'progressive' moral-political stance with a commitment to eliminate social inequalities, it may appear scandalous to qualify some people as less ethically competent than others, for example on account of their irascibility or lack of assertiveness. Yet the implications of this rhetorical concept of ethical competence will be neither unattractive nor unfamiliar to such persons. For it suggests the possibility of reconnecting the ethical sphere to the requirements of enhancing personal powers, not as a way of lording it over (supposedly natural) inferiors, or cultivating a generalised competitiveness, but rather as a way of handling oneself in personal conflicts, especially where one's opponent enjoys certain institutionalised power-advantages.

Honour and shame would inevitably loom large in a rhetorical ethics. To an extent this entails spurning the spiritual ideal of altruism. Admitting a rhetorical outlook into ethics, it will be said, turns it into a form of self-service, of which honour and shame, as in Mandeville, would be the egoistic accompaniments. The point of questioning the usefulness of altruism (or rather the altruism/egoism dichotomy) is not to deny the importance of unselfish conduct. It is rather to question whether the practical ways in which we *teach* people to put others' welfare before their own must, as Kant thinks, be anchored in an altruistic *state-of-soul* if they are to be effective.

Kant's hostility to moral education through 'examples' is echoed in contemporary critiques of the use of 'role-models' as a means of addressing problems of sexual harassment in the workplace. The superficial manners taught in this way do nothing, it is said, to address the real problem. Yet concern for appropriateness of demeanour is not restricted to the (alleged) superficies of behaviour but goes to questions of mental disposition. How could the modifications of posture, gesture, speech, and facial expression discussed in Elias's history of manners be reduced to behaviour? To take a modern example, non-sexist household manners might be thought to require not only an equitable performance of chores but also the cultivation of an 'eye' for when they need doing. Similarly, to make workplace sexual harassment the target of a policing of manners may not be the recipe for superficiality it first appears to be. Certainly, when one thinks of the dramatic psychic and social changes historically brought about through the régimes of manners identified by Elias, they appear out of all proportion to the seeming insignificance of the localised surfaces on which they operate.

Postscript (16 December 1991)

A limitation of this essay consists in the fact that the historical dislocation of ethics and rhetoric discussed in it makes almost no mention of the impact of the Reformation and Counter-Reformation on Western ethical culture. Undoubtedly many of the techniques of spiritual direction, religious education and ecclesiastical policing deployed in the course of attempting to Christianise European populations between the fifteenth and eighteenth centuries drew to a greater or lesser extent upon the humanist rhetorical tradition. What was Jesuit education without rhetoric? Yet it is equally apparent that every clearcut example of (Counter-) Reformation uses of rhetorical techniques (e.g. in casuistical reasoning) can be readily matched by examples of spiritual techniques which are in crucial regards non-rhetorical. A notable example is the aleatory techniques of Bible-reading aimed at making God's word strike the 'hearts' of men and women.

To exaggerate the scope of rhetoric is inevitably to romanticise it. The fact that the essay itself draws attention to romantic appropriations of rhetorical traditions does not prevent it from intermittently collapsing all the dimensions of ethical training into their rhetorical dimensions. That way lies post-structuralism. If 'discourse' is not governed by transcendent(al) epistemological yardsticks, *then* 'everything is interpretation all the way down' and the discursive realm is correspondingly 'rhetorical' from top to bottom. No such scepticism animates these essays, in which a rhetorical approach to ethics is accompanied by a cheerful, neo-positivist endorsement of *localised knowledges of social conditions*. The fact that some of their terms of reference are irreducibly normative and culturally relative does not detract from their capacity to be informative, to put certain social myths to rest, etc.

Part II
To Govern Sexual Harassment

An Introduction to Part II: 'What Would He Know About Sexual Harassment?'

Mark Twain's advice to politicians was: *never apologise, never explain.* Partly in acknowledgement of the powerful expectations about the ethical ('ideological') credentials of those who write about sensitive feminist issues, partly in defiance of those expectations, but mostly because I lack the makings of a politician, I decided to preface these essays on sexual harassment with a brief explanatory comment.

Even friends are apt to look askance at the idea of a man's writing on sexual harassment. Not only has the author not personally been on the receiving end of it; he also has no first-hand acquaintance with, or specialised training in, the legal and managerial machineries which have been established to combat it. If these ethical and technical disqualifications were not enough, the original seeds of my work on this topic lay less in political interest than in a search for a brief example through which to illustrate the contemporary pertinence of Foucault's study of ancient sexual ethics. If thought is shaped by its origins, here is a case of 'male theory' if ever there was one.

Be that as it may. But even without these unworthy origins it is doubtful if the arguments themselves can get by on the strength of their author's personal commitment to fighting sexual harassment. They do not dwell on details. Rarely is the misery and extent of the problem evoked. In truth, the arguments make for neither heartwarming nor horrendous reading. The only question is whether they draw attention to insufficiently appreciated problems, limits and tactical possibilities which cannot be conjured away by pointing to their author's gender.

But no arguments can be assessed on their merits if even well-disposed readers feel put-off or puzzled about their purpose. Some readers may be put off by the polemical and occasionally prescriptive tenor of the argument. Successive revisions have failed to curb either of these tendencies as much as I would have liked. It may, however, be possible to forestall puzzlement about the rhetorical angle.

To enquire into the 'point-of-view' behind these arguments is to enter a confusing realm of phantasy comprising several, not always consistent, perspectives. The first of these ideal 'inscribed readers', glimpsed, so to speak, through a rear-view mirror in the course of writing, re-reading and rewriting, is the Equal Employment Opportunity Official or Practitioner. She or he may on different occasions wear the face (and dress) of a lawyer, a manager or management consultant, or a trade unionist. Sometimes the 'family resemblance' between these figures is quite remote. Yet all have in common a preparedness to engage in painstaking, technical and sometimes 'compromising' work of establishing or operating *procedural* mechanisms for handling sexual harassment complaints and policies for preempting them. She or he will have both definite commitments to feminist objectives and values whilst also being more or less attuned to the constraints on their realisation imposed by their professional standing. One rhetorical aim of these essays is to praise as well as to analyse the work of 'EEO' Officials.

The second figure appearing in my mental rear-view mirror is what in Australian legal parlance is called the Complainant. The figure is always a woman and not always a feminist. She is frequently a young worker in a vulnerable sexual/economic position *vis-à-vis* her superiors. But on other occasions she appears more self-assured and in a more secure and powerful occupational position. Faced with unbearable pressure from sexual harassment she is given to asking bluntly: what can your general theories or procedures do for me? Or my co-workers?

A third figure in the mirror is an Active Feminist who may also be a Practitioner herself, but in any case has no problem seeing such work as capable of furthering at least some feminist aims. Where she differs from EEO practitioners most starkly is in the deliberately crude nature of her investment in feminism, which consists in kicking up a fuss wherever women are treated disparately or their distinctive wants or sufferings ignored; and demanding to know of any law or policy what there is in it for women. In this figment lies something of the 'pro-feminist' point-of-view from which these essays are written, overlapping with and sometimes contradicting my sympathetic view of the Equal Employment Opportunity Practitioner and others of that ilk.

A final, even more diffuse figure to which some of the arguments make appeal is an Unknown Citizen. Sometimes male, sometimes female, my Unknown Citizen has no consuming involvements in politics beyond an interest in the news. On occasions, this Citizen is also a man who finds someone he knows at work to be the subject of a sexual harassment complaint and who he feels is entitled to fair treatment. The point about this Unknown Citizen is that his or her support for measures against sexual harassment can neither be taken for granted nor written off as a lost cause. Where support is forthcoming it may not be for recognisably feminist reasons. For feminism my Unknown Citizen presents a problem analogous to the Christian conundrum regarding 'the virtuous pagan'.

These 'inscribed readers' are certainly a motley crew, each figure taking on a different physiognomy (the manager giving way to a legal practitioner, for example) according to the topic at hand. Equally apparent should be their ideological disparity, the imaginary authorial identification in some cases being intense and sustained, in others tactically motivated and temporary. At times their agreement and approval is sought, as I try to look at the issues from their standpoint. At other times I pointedly refuse to look over my shoulder. But there is also the authorial wish to enlighten and to assist. Where do these figures come from? Insofar as they are 'chosen' at all, the basis of the choice evidently lies in judgements about the merits of different ways of combatting sexual harassment and consequently about the diverse sorts of people whose views *count*. These judgements come out of a commitment to a liberal-pluralist way of governing premised on negotiated alliances and the evasion of insoluble and destructive ideological conflict. The price of political pluralism is that public policy cannot be exclusively premised on political principles.

'What would he know about sexual harassment?' The multiplicity in the points-of-view informing the argument confronts *ad hominem* criticism with the need to broaden its terms. What ought to be in question is not only what *I* know about sexual harassment, but also whether what my 'inscribed readers' know about it is worth knowing or not.

3 Ungovernable Conduct?

Introduction

'Feminism has brought America closer to the democracy it ought to be and has found words like sexual harassment for events that ten years ago were called life.' Gloria Steinem's observation (made in a 1983 interview for the *Guardian*) registers the fact that in the English-speaking democracies it was only in the 1970s and 1980s, through a combination of feminist campaigns, sociological surveys and widely publicised legal cases, that sexual harassment was baptised as a *bone fide* social problem in legislation and case-law, official complaints procedures, personnel-management policies, news stories, and so on.

The reference to 'democracy' implicitly draws attention to the official liberal warrant for recognising sexual harassment as a matter of public concern. A liberal-democratic polity ought to promote equality of condition between the sexes. At law, sexual harassment is construed as discrimination, denying women the opportunity to participate in the public world of work and education on an equal footing with men. In short, it amounts to *a denial of citizenship*. Taken together with her optimistic view of these developments as a stepping-stone to true democracy, Steinem's remark encapsulates what would usually be called a liberal-feminist perspective on the politics of sexual harassment.

To say the least, this optimism about the prospects of current social policy on sexual harassment and on related equal employment opportunity (EEO) issues has not been universally shared. The subject of this chapter is an influential theoretical critique of EEO policies which fastens on to the individualistic liberal ideology and the 'sex-role' paradigm of sociological theory on which they are thought to rest. The aim is to expose the political-romantic mould in which this 'sociological-structuralist' critique of liberal policies on sexual harassment is cast and in its place to suggest a more modest repertoire of concepts, objects and questions. The result is what I will call an *ethical-cultural* rationale for such policies, which prepares the ground for the more detailed arguments on management and legal policy regarding sexual harassment in Chapters 4 to 6.

The argument is not simply a rebuttal of one side of the liberal *v.* anti-liberal debate but rather an attempt to recast some of its terms. The plausibility of sociological-structural critiques does not entirely rest on the appeal of political romanticism (formidable though that is); it also thrives on weaknesses in prevailing understandings of what liberalism itself entails. Any statement of liberal philosophy which revolves too exclusively around an abstract moral-political ideal and legal status of 'equal citizenship' leaves itself open to attack. But the main feminist anti-liberal critique in turn stands or falls on its strategy of attacking EEO policies at the level of their political-philosophical, legal or ideological presuppositions. This critique can only be met by restating the liberal rationale for these policies in such a way as to demonstrate their irreducibility to the lexicon of political-philosophical ideals or politico-legal statuses. Only if the latter can be effectively connected up to relatively apolitical, *governmental* forms of calculation and their institutional accoutrements, I argue, can it be asserted with confidence that the liberal citizenship supposedly protected and extended through governmental interventions is more than an edifying idea or an ideological snare.

Identification and clarification of the *ethical* elements in these connections between law, political ideals and the government of conduct is the main task of these essays. Only in that light can the part played by liberalism in the normative passage of sexual harassment from 'inevitable fact of life' to 'governable social evil' alluded to by Gloria Steinem be seen, not as a subject for critique but as a minor achievement. However, there are grounds for refusing to go along with Steinem's way of evaluating the regulation of sexual harassment in terms of its approximation to a generalised democratic ideal.

Foundations of Male Dominance, or the Limits of Liberal Sociology

What is meant by sexual harassment? Let us begin with the sort of working definition used in the mainly Australian and North American legal, administrative, trade union and corporate-management, and sociological survey literatures which have provided the empirical bases for my work. There, unlawful sexual harassment is unwanted, unsolicited and unreciprocated conduct of a sexual nature which is primarily, though not exclusively, directed against women; which takes place mainly in the workplace and in educational institutions; and which has detrimental effects on the terms or conditions of her employment or education. This conduct may be physical (from rape to touching sexual parts of the body); verbal (jokes, propositioning, comments on appearance); or related to seeing and being seen (ogling, pin-ups).

This definition would not pass unchallenged in sociological-structuralist analyses. But before we approach this critical literature, we need a detailed example of the sort of liberal-feminist sociology in which such a definition is at home and which provides the critique's obligatory foil. Barbara Gutek's (1985) study of workplace sexual harassment nicely exemplifies both the 'sex-role' model and the liberal assumptions and tactics in question. The findings of a survey of 827 women and 405 men working in Los Angeles are linked to a theory of workplace sexual harassment and a remedial management policy.

Gutek analyses workplace organisations into sets of role relationships, that is, shared and sanctioned normative expectations concerning job-related tasks and demeanour. Sexual harassment is not a product of 'individual deficit' or male–female biology but rather a sociological phenomenon, resulting from 'a carryover into the workplace of gender-based roles' deemed inappropriate to work (Gutek, 1985, pp. 15–16). Initially, this 'sex-role spillover' is attributed to the culturally determined 'salience' of gender – the insistence that an individual's sex always makes a difference (*ibid.*, p. 17); and to men's persistent enactment of sex-role stereotyping as a condition of social acceptance.

But what in turn determines this 'sexualisation of the workplace' (*ibid.*, p. 122) and hence the inappropriate attention to women workers' gendered characteristics at the expense of their occupational abilities? Well, more women than men occupy jobs in which physical attractiveness and personality matter. Where there are gender minorities in a workplace they are more likely to be women than men (*ibid.*, pp. 146–7), few men being motivated to do traditional women's work. 'The woman in a man's job' becomes in effect a 'role deviate' in a work environment which, being numerically dominated by men is in any case more sexualised by dint of the central place of swearing, sex-talk, dirty jokes and pictures, bravado, etc. in the male sex-role. Whence the salience of gender and the opportunity to act out sex roles.

The fact that sexual harassment incidents typically have more to do with power than attraction is acknowledged. So is the fact that where a gender difference obtains in supervisor–supervisee relations, women's structurally disadvantaged place in the sexual division of labour ensures that the supervisee role is far more likely to be a woman. However, critics will observe, little *systematic* attention is paid to the implications of gendered hierarchies and power-relations (e.g. only five out of eighty-four questions in the survey make reference to them). The main burden of structural explanation is borne by 'sex segregation' – men's *numerical* domination in mixed work environments and their ensuring sexualisation.

Having framed the problem in this manner, Gutek draws out the policy implications. Affirmative action policies are needed in order to redress the sex-ratio problem. A concerted personnel policy is sketched, comprising not only individual remedies for sexual harassment *via* grievance procedures but also measures informed by a broader 'goal of preventative medicine' respecting workplace 'motivations' (*ibid.*, p. 177). 'Preventative' measures include staff education, the conscription of managers as role-models, attention to 'styles of address', and incorporating a record of sexual harassment conduct as a factor in organisations' work performance appraisals and reward and promotion structure (*ibid.*, pp. 173–77). The overriding aim of the recommendations is to establish ' a professional work-environment where employees are treated in a professional manner' (*ibid.*, p. 173). The study ends as it began, on an astonishing note of optimism concerning the willingness and capacity of management to eliminate this 'not particularly resistant' problem, on her estimation, by the mid-1990s (Gutek, *ibid.*, pp. 19, 178)!

Within the United States, Gutek is nothing if not an authority on the subject. Sociological studies of this kind may not be state-of-the-art in some academic circles, but they retain a real social and political currency. As well they might. In the following chapter, I will be looking at the possibility of taking a critical distance from the explanatory claims of sex-role sociology, whilst defending the strategic value of both the empirical and normative knowledge yielded by it. At this point, Gutek's study will serve as a ready reference for the sort of problem-definition and policy options which the sociological-structural critique believes it has to surpass.

Foundations of Male Dominance or the 'Limits' of Liberal Sociology

In the eyes of this critique, it is questionable whether anything distinguishes sexual harassment from other forms of women's oppression in the way the powers-that-be suppose. Similarly, laws and policies on sexual harassment are frequently assumed to be driven by a liberal-patriarchal logic afflicting all EEO policies. For these reasons, despite the familiarity of the arguments, it will be useful to begin by anatomising the critique in its most general form before proceeding to outline its ramifications for the sexual harassment issue.

In conformity with our earlier sketch of sociological-structuralism, general theories of women's subordination insist that all sexist phenomena and experiences are systemically related effects of an institutionally reinforced, ubiquitous structure of asymmetrical power-relations operating across the male–female divide. This power-structure operates simultaneously at the level of institutions and at that of the ideological, identity-forming forces which shape (whilst partly eluding) experience in various sex-specific ways. Expressing itself through 'manifest' acts of sexist discrimination 'located at an empirical level', this structure underpins and to that extent exists independently of particular sexist phenomena (Grosz, 1988, pp. 93–94). There is no institution, social activity or amenity, bodily demeanour, body of knowledge or categorisation which is not saturated with male-supremicist assumptions; and nowhere more so than when they lay claim to the supposedly gender-neutral, rational virtues of impartiality, equity, impersonality, and universality. Premised on the feminine qualities they attempt to exclude, these rational categorisations and models of behaviour are the very work of patriarchy (Lloyd, 1984). This unnatural antinomy of the subjective and the objective finds institutional support in the crowning liberal-patriarchal, *ideological* dichotomy between (masculine) public and (feminine) private spheres which is at once at the heart of the sexual division of labour and the sexual division of the soul. Not only manifestly discriminatory conduct but 'normal' organisational behaviours, too, have to be seen as the socio-pathological acting-out of more or less unconsciously determined, embodied sexed identities (MacKinnon, 1979, 1987).

Yet for all its depth and ubiquity, patriarchy is characterised by a fatal insufficiency and contradictory character; patriarchal domination is persistently resisted.[1] The forms of sexed subjectivity on which it depends always need to be (re-)asserted and 'negotiated' in myriad struggles which may or may not end in women's favour. The system cannot therefore operate only by coercion or exclusion of the feminine and is open to destabilisation.

The more the insufficiency and contradictoriness of the structure is stressed, the more the presence of the structure of male dominance in the social and political field takes on a fugitive quality (retreating into dialectical alloys of structure-and-agency such as Connell's (1987) 'projects'). The very notion of an underlying patriarchal structure which could be the target of a global feminist strategy of social transformation is then likely to be found too abstract and deterministic. Structural determination arguments, it is said, underestimate women's capacities for resistance. They exaggerate the unity of women's and feminists' perspectives across class, ethnic, and national differences. And they sometimes overinvest in a '1960s' counter-hegemonic 'alternative society' scenario, involving the coalescence of euphoric, consciousness-raising direct actions and 'prefigurative' institution-building (e.g. Altman, 1980) at the expense of less 'ideologically sound' sites, forms and subjects of intervention, such as those associated with bureaucratic organisations and institutions of the state (Eisenstein, 1985, 1990). In some 'post-structuralist' perspectives, a general revolutionary strategy directed against the core institutions of male supremacy gives way to attention to apparently 'surface phenomena' of power, conflict, (mis)behaviour, and so on (Pringle and Watson, 1990, pp. 232, 242). In view of the characteristics which this kind of critique shares with political romanticism (the impossibility of pinning it down to determinate forms of political action; the supposition of an essentially hidden structure manifesting itself in surface institutions, conduct, etc.; the penchant for perpetual self-problematisation and displacement), it cannot be stated with confidence that the post-structuralist turn in feminist theory represents an unambiguous break with the political-romantic and sociological-structuralist 'past'.[2]

Fatally dependent upon sex-role sociology (as exemplified in Gutek), EEO policy on women, say adherents of the critique, takes an incorrigibly superficial view of what has to change and how. The sources of sex-discriminatory conduct are assumed to run no deeper than the ideological prejudices associated with sex-role socialisation. The solution to it is there-fore resocialisation into non-sexist role behaviour. Both the analysis and the strategy understate the structural-institutional power-relations involved and the depth and intensity of the grip of gender-identifications upon individuals. The affront to a man's self-esteem on being asked to do 'women's work', for example, is irreducible to the imposition of a fixed set of learned role stereotypes upon natural persons who are otherwise sexually differentiated only along biological lines (Connell, 1987, p. 50). These sexual identifications have been too deeply scored into the body and the psyche to be shaken off by exposure to a non-sexist role-model (Game and Pringle, 1983, p. 223).

The superficiality of the theory of sex-roles parallels that of the liberal-philosophical pillar of EEO policies. Women's oppression can only be registered as so many disparate transgressions of liberal principles of rational, fair and and equal treatment; or in other words, as 'a case of imperfect citizenship' (Franzway *et al.*, 1989, p. 14). To the extent that equal opportunity criteria of merit, efficiency, and normal professional conduct express 'masculinist' standards of public life and are blind to women's domestic responsibilities, distinctive talents, social disabilities, desires, affective dispositions, etc., they can only be expected to be of positive use to a few token women willing and able to play the game by the existing rules. Even where such policies seem to have discernible progressive effects, this can only reflect their capacity to chime in with (and lend legitimation to) capitalistic or technocratic-rational ideologies in which men also have a major investment (Connell *op. cit.*, pp. 263, 264).

On the strength of the intellectual foundations of EEO policies in liberal ideology and sex-role theory, Franzway *et al.* (*op. cit.*, pp. 15–17) can only conclude that these policies are 'theoretically rootless to a striking degree' and that liberal feminism has 'reached its conceptual limit and can go no further in its own terms'. We shall see.

The Critique of Sexual Harassment Policy

Structural-sociological critiques of liberal-feminist law and policy thus come down to concerns about the *arbitrary limitation* on the types of sexism targeted for official action; the *superficiality* of the elements of sexism singled out; and the bogus *objectivity* or disembodied abstractness of the element of women's personhood picked out for legal protection: namely, her status as an individual citizen. How do these charges of arbitrariness, superficiality and bogus objectivity and universality operate with respect to sexual harassment regulation?

It will be generally agreed that 'sexual harassment' in the legal sense is not a 'natural kind' of sexism. Behaviour which is unlawful in the workplace, for instance, would not necessarily be so in the street. Misogynistic insinuations about a woman's intellectual capacities would not count as sexual harassment. In some critics' eyes:

> The very act of producing a workplace definition effectively separated off these particularly located harassment behaviours . . . This separation . . . permits people to draw the conclusion that actual *solutions* to sexual harassment can be found within discrimination legislation, the operation of tribunals and . . . unions'. (Stanley and Wise, 1987, p. 61)

> Sexual harassment is merely the most blatant part of a more pervasive exercise of sexual power. In marking out the limits of what is acceptable the EEO-based apparatus actually validates the remaining field of power relations and in this sense it is integral to compulsory heterosexuality. (Game and Pringle, 1986, p. 290)

Here, the non-inclusive nature of legislative definitions and their workplace equivalents is taken as a sign of a wholly unjustifiable arbitrariness and bogus objectivity: a female experience of long standing has been renamed, and one bit of it, those forms of *workplace* harassment which are characterised by their explicitly *sexual* content, artificially fenced off from the bulk of the sexist harassment experienced by women in their homes, streets, shops, everywhere and everyday (Stanley and Wise, *op. cit.*, p. 80). No less than the tabloids' 'office romeo' version of events (Stanley and Wise (*ibid.*, pp. 39–40), the 'workplace definition' distorts and trivialises women's 'gut' experience. For example, its terminology suggests that it is a 'uni-sex' problem. In contrast, the 'bedrock feminist analyses' which first drew public attention to the issue in the USA (the authors cite Farley, 1978 and MacKinnon, 1979, in particular) portrayed workplace sexual harassment as but one locus of manifestation of 'the real problem . . . men-in-patriarchy'. Stanley and Wise's alternative definition of sexual harassment as 'every unwanted and unsought intrusion by men into women's feelings, thought, behaviours, space, time, energies and bodies' (*op. cit.*, p. 71) places it, cognitively and politically, well beyond the scope of any official investigation or definition, let alone administrative 'solutions'.[3]

To set official limits to what can count as sexual harassment is to convey the impression that the problem of the harassment of women is limited to a few supposedly deviant men who practice the more extreme and explicitly *sexualised* ways of 'doing male power'. This allows the equally 'culpable behaviour' (*ibid.*, p. 79) of the sexual harasser (on their definition) who turns off his wife's favourite TV programme or intrudes on women's private conversation in a pub to go unsanctioned (*ibid.*, pp. 4, 165–66). Official definitions do nothing to challenge the general 'cultural license' to treat women as 'sexual game', with all the 'unsolicited and non-reciprocal aggression' that entails (Farley, 1978, pp. 13, 53). Within the workplace itself, the selective definition casts a legitimating shadow over both non-sexual forms of harassment and ways of exercising sexual power which operate not coercively but through the register of (shared) pleasures, such as routines of 'heterosexist' sexual banter or the staging of phantasy relationships (Pringle, 1988, pp. 94–95).

In the eyes of the sociological-structural critique, the limitation on what counts as sexual harassment is not arbitrary at all but rather a work of the liberal public–private distinction. Official definitions and procedures are either indifferent to or simply incapable of handling 'sexual harassment' which takes place in either 'private' *spaces* (i.e. outside the public world of work), or 'private' *interpersonal relations* in the informal 'underlife' of the workplace itself. For some, action against it is only contemplated on account of its being regarded as an unseemly transgression of that distinction (Olsen 1983, p. 1551, cited in Graycar and Morgan, 1990, p. 369). How absurd, therefore, to suppose, with Gutek, that sexual harassment represents an adventitious 'spillage' from the personal ('private') sphere into the 'public' world of the economy which could be mopped up by legal or managerial action. Sexual harassment at work is not so much a deviation from the social order as a way of reinforcing it.

To the extent that the case against EEO policies on sexual harassments amounts to accusing it of treating symptoms rather than causes, the arbitrary limitation charge overlaps with that of *superficiality*. Sex-segregation, for instance, is not a cause of sexual harassment, as Gutek would have it, but to a large degree its effect (Farley, 1978, p. 53). Obeying an age-old 'historical imperative', workplace harassment provides 'the patriarchy' with the material basis needed for its reproduction by systematically locking women into a position of economic inferiority and reinforcing traditional notions of women's place as homemakers (Farley, *ibid.*, p. xvi). It tends to keep them down by contributing to their confinement to low-paid, sex-segregated job-categories. It thereby keeps them out of 'non-traditional' jobs (for women) with better prospects.

If this functional imperative of the patriarchy holds good, once again, what could be more futile than EEO reforms such as those proposed by Gutek? Liberal sociology seeks to establish norms of professional conduct through enlightened discourse on the irrationality and unfairness of the sex-role behaviour in question, alternative role models and complaints procedures and sanctions. For some, this is to adopt an individualistic approach to problems of personal politics, an approach which fails to insert women's oppression into the larger structural-and-political dialectic of socio-historical change (Connell, 1987, p. 53).[4] Worse, to propose a régime of conduct aimed at changing 'role behaviour' is to reduce the issue to a question of *manners and morals*. For many commentators the very mention of sexual harassment and these words in the same breath is a sign of one's understanding's having been derailed (MacKinnon, 1979, p. 173; Bularzik, 1978, p. 39; Graycar and Morgan, 1990, p. 369).

This suspicion is certainly understandable. During the furore over the recent allegations of sexual harassment levelled against US Supreme Court nominee Clarence Thomas, for example, media reports persistently associated the incidence of sexual harassment in American political life with the reputation of male senators and congressmen for 'womanising' and general immorality. This habit of likening sexual harassment to a sexual peccadillo confirms some feminists' suspicions about the law's being a 'male-protection racket'. Like the girls in the nursery rhyme, sexually harassed women shall enjoy 'protection' only at the hands of a male-dominated moral police: 'when the boys came out to play, Georgie Porgie ran away' (Stanley and Wise, *op cit.*, p. 6). And the precondition for official intervention on this view is that sexual harassment shall be construed as a transgression of a patriarchal code of sexual manners in the public domain.

For instance, insofar as EEO policies on sexual harassment require men's compliance with 'acceptable standards of conduct between the sexes' (Farley 1978, p. xv), they may be perceived as merely treading in the unliberated footsteps of nineteenth-century feminist philanthropists in the 'social purity' campaigns against the sexual exploitation of women in factories (Bularzik, 1978). There, sexual violence against women was ideologically construed as a problem of vice in the workplace ('shameful behaviour' which 'no lady should bear'). To characterise coercive sexual behaviours in the language of manners could only mean committing today's feminists to their nineteenth-century middle-class sisters' acceptance of the values of female modesty, chastity and its economic and social concomitants: women's subordination to a patriarchal property system. To speak of sexual harassment as a problem of manners is to restrict feminist demands to requests for the protection of their presumed superiors against only the most conspicuously malign consequences of that subordination.[5]

Finally, talk of manners in this connection is also likely to be seen as complicit with social expectations of women's passivity and quiescence, and hence with traditional assertions of men's superiority with respect to social inferiors through 'exercising familiarities which the subordinate is not allowed to reciprocate' (Farley 1978, pp. 15–16). These 'familiarities' range from bodily contact, assuming close physical proximity and an 'explicit', sexually aggressive posture, to teasing and using familiar terms of address. It is not therefore surprising, given women's generally subordinate and vulnerable economic position and the norms of female passivity, if they find themselves under a moral pressure not to 'make a fuss' about sexual harassment (e.g. to politely laugh along with sexual banter at their expense).

Surely, then, to think of sexual harassment as a breach of manners is to understate the evil and to mislocate the source of sexual harassment in the most offensive way. It is to blind oneself to the social-pathological construction of masculinity which generates this behaviour on a regular basis and to the rather more profound moral issue at stake, namely, the transgression of women's *personal integrity* and right to self-determination. However, it is not by treating it as a moral issue but only by linking sexual harassment to the power structures that produce it, and hence politicising it, that any real change can be brought about (MacKinnon, 1979, p. 173).

'Political' alternatives to liberal EEO procedural forms of action to which critiques make appeal include attempting to mobilise trade union action (Hadjifotiou, 1983); organising non-unionist women workers and guerilla warfare against purveyors of sexist humour (Farley, 1978; 13–14, 211); feminist counselling facilities for victims (Alliance Against Sexual

Coercion, 1981) and calls for informal action by women. Direct action draws upon the resources of 'women's culture' with its streetwise understanding of men's weaknesses and capacities for masquerade, pastiche, and ridicule (Stanley and Wise 1987, pp. 132f, 166, 183f; Pringle 1988, pp. 102–103, 265–66).

Few critiques recommend total opposition to procedural action. Official measures may be variously turned to women's advantage, either by using them as occasions for consciousness-raising about the underlying patriarchal realities (Game and Pringle, 1986, p. 290); or by a more protracted involvement aimed at remaking official measures themselves in the image of a specifically feminist vision of equality (MacKinnon, 1979). For Lin Farley (1978, pp. 44, 211) procedures and popular campaigns alike can only hope to make a serious impact on sexual harassment if they can be harnessed to a world-historical synthesis of the workers' and women's movements.[6]

What a contrast there is between this grand scenario and the information about women's experiences, the changing fortunes of legal actions, feminist campaigns, the range of available complaints, procedures, etc., which take up most of Farley's book. This is only the most extreme example of a discrepancy between theoretical-political frameworks and practicalities which is very common in the sexual harassment literature, including some workplace manuals (see Chapter 6). Whether sociological-structural perspectives can generate policies representing a serious advance on the sort of personnel management measures commended by Gutek remains to be seen.[7]

However, sociological-structural explanations do have considerable ethical-sensitising effects. All social science makes some ethical statement. Nobody can gainsay the 'consciousness raising' impacts of feminist sociological studies of sexual harassment on public opinion, the law, and so on – irrespective of differences in their respective explanatory frameworks. Sociological-structuralism however, offers to shape a specifically romantic form of conscience. An ethical-cognitive repertoire of concepts is provided which 'places' adherents at an alienated distance from 'official' powers-that-be and the organised forms of reasoning at their disposal. What might it mean to refuse this invitation to alienation from liberal doctrine and policy?

Never Mind the Cause: an Ethical Cultural Approach

If the point of the exercise is to feel our way towards a more policy-oriented liberal rationale for regulating sexual harassment in the workplace, then neither an alternative general theory of sexual harassment nor an abandonment of all theoretical argument in favour of exclusive concentration upon the details of particular policies will serve. Instead of asking what is sexual harassment and why does it exist, it might be more appropriate to examine *how* it exists. In this way a more circumscribed and descriptive enquiry is inaugurated. What, we must ask, has been and is likely to remain *the most effective way(s) of representing and attacking* sexual harassment as a social evil which is intolerable in a liberal democracy? Under what circumstances? For which purposes? In which terms? Through which agencies? With what likely effects? In short, never mind the underlying causes of sexual harassment, look at the forms of its 'problematisation' (Foucault, 1991).

Given the lack of social unanimity over whether workplace sexual harassment constitutes a distinct problem of sex-discrimination or even whether it is a problem at all, a defensible liberal rationale has to account for the *particularisation* of the issue to designated sites and conducts. And it must explain why the labour of signifying the ethical unacceptability of sexual harassment is not simply a matter of giving official recognition to a pre-given reality. In other words, it has to clarify why some ways of representing and attacking the problem are likely to be more persuasive and effective than others.

The question of representation might be framed as follows: How did sexual harassment become etched-in as a contour in the manifold of women's moral experience of the workplace, as something which was no longer to be tolerated? Under what circumstances was men's 'cultural license' to badger and bully women (or worse, of course) to some extent withdrawn and a license to speak up about it extended? Under which of its aspects was this behaviour picked out as a possible cause of action at law; as a subject of complaint to management, or indeed as something which could be credibly contested on an informal, face-to-face basis? Following Foucault's (1984a) terminology, all this can be termed the question of the *ethical substance* of sexual harassment. The next question is, which is the most appropriate *ethical stance* (polemical style, argumentative tack) to adopt, the better to attack the problem? That is, which approaches on the part of unions, individuals or EEO professionals are more likely to persuade managements to take the issue seriously? Or to induce individual men to think twice about certain habitual ways of conducting themselves and to manage their demeanour and behaviour differently? Finally, which ethical posture is best calculated to secure the widest possible *public* acceptance of the need to outlaw this conduct?

To venture a short answer to these questions of ethical stance and substance in the form of a hypothesis: *it is only in relation to the objectives, techniques of ethical culture, and limits of a liberal style of 'governmentality' in Foucault's sense that sexual harassment can be recognised as an ethically unacceptable and administrable social problem.* In order to elaborate this hypothesis, it will be helpful to remind ourselves of what is meant by an 'ethical culture' which is not the realisation of moral principles; and to sketch out the idea of a 'liberalism' that is irreducible to an ideology of individual liberty; a style of 'government' that is irreducible either to state apparatuses and policy or to the terms of political ideologies and programmes; and a 'citizenship' that neither can nor should be 'perfect'. We will then be in a position to restate a liberal rationale for seeing sexual harassment as a denial of liberal citizenship . . . but also as something else besides.

Ethical Culture, Government and the Conditions of Citizenship

First and foremost, the term 'ethical culture' signals a commitment to extending what counts as ethical beyond the realm of moral and political principles. It draws attention to the less-than-ideal material-cultural components, practices and competences of an anti-sexual harassment ethos which are built into the way in which the problem is defined for the purposes of governmental action and into the various ways in which the problem is dealt with. Nobody is moved to act by principles alone. Why? Both the presence of self-regarding impulses and the absence of ethical abilities guarantees that this is the case. All the principled 'reasons for action' in the world, then, will not on their own supply the *means* – the tasks of behaviour – by which the average man on the shop floor or in the manager's seat can be brought to perform the ethical work upon themselves required if they are to manage their occupational relations with women differently.

Notable amongst this array of practical ethical thinking and practice, I will argue, is the representation of sexual harassment as in effect a problem of *manners* which have to be *policed*. Is sexual harassment in no way comparable to gross forms of rudeness: i.e. to behaviour and bodily demeanour calculated to make the other feel embarrassed, for example, or self-conscious, ill-at-ease, humiliated or distracted from her work? (For other analogies see Chapter 5.) All analogies can only be taken so far. A régime of manners aimed at inducing men to manage their occupational relations with women differently means, for example, checking their propensity to stare at women in sex-specific ways. It means making them self-conscious about the frequently invasive ways in which men are culturally disposed to take up space. Nevertheless, the affective consequences of sexual harassment go beyond the consequences of men's behaviour towards women: nobody likes being stared at. This normatising ingredient in liberal regulation and policy can be married to the formal obligations, prerogatives and anti-subordinative imperatives of equal citizenship ('inequitable manners'). But it cannot be, either logically or historically, *derived* from the liberal political–philosophical ideal or legal statuses of citizenship (let alone from more radical concepts of social equality). The element of respect for a woman's bodily integrity – *or a man's* for that matter – is not a derivative of liberal political philosophy.

The same can be said in regard to a further, and also less-than-ideal ethical constituent of a liberal-governmental policy on sexual harassment: the advisability of the need to cultivate what can loosely be called a *rhetorical* style of response to it. It is necessary to endow principles of social justice with a persuasive form; or to give people other reasons, both ethical and not so ethical, to comply with their demands. A rhetorical style may serve as a means of empowering women in confronting sexual harassment informally (as foreshadowed in the previous essay); in legal argument, and at the conciliation stage of a legal complaint (see Chapter 5). More generally, and perhaps even more controversially, a rhetorical style is inseparable from the need to work into one's calculations the *pluralist* political milieu in which measures against sexual harassment have to operate. This means acknowledging the *ethically controversial status of the category of sexual harassment itself and hence according a limited tactical recognition to those who oppose its official regulation.*

It is not only a matter of recognising the diversity of cultural belief-systems (both ethnic and intra-ethnic). Beyond these 'multicultural' considerations, there is also the more basic fact that the objects on which the government of sexual harassment attempts to act are themselves *social actors*. Not only by virtue of Farley's 'cultural license' to treat women as 'fair game', but for other reasons too, the male population have been accustomed to expect a certain freedom of action even within highly regulated environments. (Women, too, expect to enjoy at least some of these freedoms.) Only within certain limits (or else at the cost of provoking serious resistance) can their actions be forcefully constrained by law, or management policy and informal responses.

Finally, if a policing of manners and a rhetorical commitment to pluralism are to be made central planks in the rationale, this carries implications for the way in which the *citizenship dimension* of the issue itself is conceived. As we shall see in Chapters 5 and 7, it too must be refashioned in such a way as to bring out its own less-than-ideal, ethical–governmental underpinnings as well as its pro-feminist implications.

For the price of constructing sexual harassment as a 'social' problem of liberal government is to set limits to the extent to which either its definition or its treatment can afford to express not only feminist but also overly controversial *liberal* principles. Part of the point of the 'ethical culture' denomination is to question the conventional wisdom that emphasis on its ethical dimension implies treating it as a private matter divorced from the underlying social realities of power; and hence to underline the drawbacks of overpoliticising the issue. It also signals a corresponding scepticism about according more than a subaltern role to 'social theory' in determining appropriate policies on sexual harassment or even what sort of a problem it is. It is not to the underlying structures which supposedly cause it that we need to look in order to specify the broader context which is relevant to assessing the prospects of sexual harassment policies; but rather to that broad yet less ineffable way of posing and acting upon social problems which Michel Foucault has called 'governmentality'.

Governmentality and Feminism

Foucault's concept of governmentality refers to a loose amalgam of objectives; techniques of social investigation; and policies, institutions and practices directed to the constant care and improvement of populations. It signifies a general form of organised reasoning, embracing practical ways of posing and addressing social and economic problems. As such, 'governmentality' both puns and conceptually cuts across the traditional division of labour between the history of institutional structures and the history of thought; for example, in the way it puts the history of western 'individualisation' in touch with the history of European nationhood, family reform, marketisation of social relations, etc.[8]

The phenomena of governmentality have to be linked to two further criss-crossing developments which are crucial both to its understanding and to its historical misunderstanding. If the population is to be 'improved' by governmental measures this is for the purposes of strengthening the absolutist monarchical state (or principality). Here, governmentality is linked to a *centralising bureau-based political strategy* aimed at partly disempowering both aristocratic and religious *loci* of power. Absolutist régimes strive to transform warrior-aristocrats into courtiers and/or state functionaries; and to displace contentious theological concerns from the objectives of government in favour of attempting to enhance, not the salvation but the chances of survival and the standard of living of populations. But at the same time, the forms, techniques and purposes of attempting to rule populations in this intense way seem to have been borrowed from *patriarchalist* models of how to govern a household 'economy' and (initially to a lesser extent) from *pastoral* models of spiritual direction (Foucault, 1979, 1981).

In liberal political philosophy, the liberal polity has been historically represented as the antithesis of the absolutist 'police state'. But how would matters stand were liberalism to be seen not simply as a political-philosophical doctrine based on setting limits *to* government, but also as both a philosophy and an 'art' (i.e. technique) *of* government (Burchell *et al.* 1991; Minson, 1985)? To some extent, liberal governance renders the lives of individuals and associations (families, firms, churches . . . But also revolutionary parties) out-of-bounds to state interventions except under limited conditions. It offers citizens the opportunity to pursue their own life-plans and interests (individually or in association with others) in some 'anti-social' as well as socially desirable ways. It equips them with the capacities and dispositions to do so. However, when one reckons with an historically expanding number of normative grounds for intervening in private spheres (including the economic and the familial) and the permeability of these spheres to 'outside' expert advice (as well as their *desire* for it), it becomes apparent that the burdens of government have to some extent been not so much cast off as shifted onto the shoulders of individuals and associations themselves.

Liberalism so construed is not necessarily antithetical to all aspects of absolutist governance. If anything, it represents a way of attempting to refocus and even to intensify the governmentalisation of individuals inaugurated in absolutist programmes of 'police' such as those of the German 'cameralists' (Small, 1909). The fact is that a good proportion of what we take to be paradigmatically liberal policies predates the age of representative democracy and the doctrines of liberty and anti-statism with which we now associate modern liberalism.[9]

This possibility of tracing liberal-governmental policies to an origin in illiberal political regimes confutes analysis of liberal policies – including those with feminist leanings – solely as an expression of, or a failure to express, liberal political principles or ideologies (e.g. Holcombe, 1983, p. 5). Liberal techniques of government have been deployed in the service of a variety of political-philosophical agendas. One and the same governmental policy may be presented so as to appeal to conflicting political agendas. Indeed, the attempt to steer a passage between socially divisive political viewpoints takes us to the very heart of liberal government, irrespective of its political shell. This is not to imply that it is ever independent of political agendas. Governmentalisation does not signify an inexorably depoliticising tendency towards the rationalisation of existence.

Rather, liberal policies always involve a set of *negotiated transactions* between the registers of the political and the governmental (Miller and Rose, 1990; Burchell, 1991).

In the light of these scattered remarks on liberalism and governmentality, let us consider one of the central props of the sociological-structural critique: the assertion that liberalism is premised upon the ideology of a mutually exclusive division between public and private – preeminently institutionalised through the discourse of *contract* (e.g. Siltanen and Stanworth, 1984; Pateman, 1988).

From the perspective of a history of what might be called *the governmentalisation of sexual difference*, it might be another story. Let us limit ourselves to a few summary counter-hypotheses. Firstly, if the idea of a mutually exclusive division between public and private is a liberal invention, it is one that belongs not to the modern age of capitalism, liberal-democracy and meritocracy, but rather to the early modern absolutist era. The primary axis of this would-be exclusive division between private and public is not work and home but the domains of political authority and civil society. And the purpose of absolutist attempts to exclude the diverse forces comprising civil society from participation in the work of political government was not the exclusion of women but rather the exclusion of fomentors of social division and internicene civil warfare. Partly under the pressure of a variety of political imperatives, for example the growth of demands for 'social' political rights, partly as a consequence of its own momentum, modern liberal government depends, as we have seen, upon a *multiplication* of public–private differentiations.[10] The (limited) negative liberties vouchsafed by contractual agreements are only part of the story of the liberalisation of social relations in the interests of improving living standards, morals, etc. In some instances, as we will see in Chapters 4 and 5, contract law is a condition for, rather than an obstacle to, subjecting parties to *social* norms and obligations through infra-legal interventions. Liberal governance today is not essentially an attempt to create and enforce the illusion of a singular division between 'the' public and 'the' private; and to consign women to the latter.

Furthermore, the pre-liberal-democratic origins of what we now see as liberal social policies might make us think twice about the derogatory use of the term 'paternalistic' in respect to 'protective' policies aimed at improving women's conditions. Early modern governmental and police literature is quite explicit in its paternalistic attitude towards the populace, which it seeks to reshape and energise for the benefit of the prince and his principality (Small, 1910). It is the populace in general, and not only or especially its female (or even its poorest) members, who are compared to children deemed as yet incapable of behaving themselves without close supervision. The language of paternalism might be regarded as something like a *placeholder*, merely a way of registering – *metaphorically* – a set of incapacities, disabilities, and vulnerabilities which it is the function of government to alleviate. They need not therefore be conceived as inherent in a given category of individual or social group. Whether or not the ensuing governmental policies are at odds with either governmental or political-ideological concerns with equality and autonomy can only be judged on a case-by-case basis. In other words, the *protective* objectives of sex discrimination legislation and policy are not amenable to a singular patriarchal-proprietal interpretation.

For this is to assume that the model of all 'good' government is a republic of autonomous self-governing citizens. However, even at the level of principle, liberal government cannot be conformed to the rules of what Foucault (1981) called the 'city-citizen game'. The specifically governmental model of the relations between rulers and ruled is according to Foucault much more akin to a pastoral, 'shepherd–flock game'. Friends and critics of liberalism alike have yet to fully reckon with the extent to which the liberal concept of citizenship itself is as much a product of government calculations as it is of political-philosophical idealisations of a community of rational self-governing individuals (see Chapter 7).[11] Liberal-governmental reasoning, according to this hypothesis, constructs citizens after its own fashion as both objects and agents of care and attention. If so, this casts doubt upon the appropriateness of characterising all liberal-governmental problematisations of sex-inequalities as ostensibly calling attention to women's 'imperfect citizenship' (in the modern political philosophical sense) whilst in reality serving as a vehicle for the institutionalisation of a liberal variation on patriarchal rule.

For the effect of this perspective is to obliterate the importance of *governmental* equalisations and autonomisations which may be more site- or task-specific; more contingently related to one another; and more pluralistic in their value-orientations than their political-philosophical equivalents. For instance, some problematisations of wives' subject-status historically arose in the context of governmental concerns about, say, the health and welfare of children, seen as a national resource (Hodges and Hussain, 1979, p. 96). In such a case (with its bearing on the social reconstruction of the mother-wife figure), governmental thinking on familialisation of the populations makes reference to value-laden objectives such as autonomy and equality. Thus there may be warnings against trying to oversee too much or in too much detail; or attempts to foster the capacities of particular family members to pursue their own private well-being; or to distribute social and economic competences (e.g. economically useful skills or concern for their own physical or psychological health) and benefits (such as access to education) more evenly amongst populations through the reshaping of family relationships and responsibilities. These objectives may diverge from political-philosophical ideals of a free and fair self-governing political community, including feminist ones. But can it be doubted that these governmental styles of reasoning and intervention did something to open up genuine fault-lines in traditional forms of patriarchal dominance and – for all its ideological impurity – constituted many of the power-bases and lines of advance for feminist movements (Minson, 1985, ch. 8)? Whether inadvertently or by design, these governmental developments not only make traditional patriarchal institutions appear 'backward'. They also establish the subordination of women in all manner of institutions, including formally liberal ones, as *a new type of (un)ethical fact* of which political governments and the community at large must take account.

This is not to issue a moral blank cheque to all governmental problematisations of patriarchy. Rather, the facts pertaining to the interdependencies of feminism and governmentality at which I have been hinting make it implausible to denounce EEO-based governmental interventions simple on the grounds of their failure to operate in accordance with feminist or even liberal moral-political principles of social justice and to treat other forms of justification (health reasons, etc.) as so many ideological ruses. To do so is to underestimate the polymorphous nature of the social conditions and the autochthonous governmental norms and values through which the array of conducts now called sexist came to be constituted as an interconnected series of social problems.

The need to break the critical habit of repeating rather than dislodging the private–public dichotomy has not of course been lost on a number of feminist writers. But, with few exceptions, the tendency is to resort to a distinction between ideology and real practice or else to a notion of dialectical interaction. In neither case is there much attempt at conceptual development of the space in which the juxtaposition and/or interdependencies of private and public dimensions is supposed to occur. Spanning as it does the realms of state administration, the 'social mission' of private organisations, and the domestic care of children, the concept of governmentality represents just such an attempt.

Governmentality, Civility and Sexual Harassment

Crude though it may be, this attempt to link the historical constitution of the 'field' of 'sexist' behaviours to the bandwagon of social governance has unsettling implications for the 'arbitrary limitation' and 'superficiality' arguments against EEO policies on sexual harassment.

How much critical mileage can be made out of the bare fact that the 'same' behaviour is not uniformly treated as unlawful?[12] Not every region in the social body lends itself equally to the same kind of policing or to being policed at all. To take a simple instance, Gutek's recommendation that a record of sexual harassment ought to weigh against someone's prospects for promotion presupposes the institutionalisation of a more general normative work-practice of taking the quality of staff interactions into account and a system of personnel files in which deviations from these norms can be lodged. The 'limited' applicability of this management policy is not a function of a singular private–public distinction. It is as inapplicable to a sweatshop or a small bakery as it is to sites outside the workplace. And similarly, as we shall see in Chapter 5, sex discrimination legislation covering sexual harassment is as inapplicable to the high-street as it is to the home.

But surely, given that the law has belatedly come to recognise the offence of rape-in-marriage, is there not a similar case for extending the legal category of sexual harassment to cover a man's harassment of his wife in the home? It hardly needs stating that many women lack the opportunity, knowledge, confidence and rhetorical capacities to protest this behaviour informally. But would it be any easier to make a complaint to a human rights commission than it would to initiate divorce proceedings?

Limited extensions of the purchase of law on sexual harassment beyond the workplace are nevertheless not only conceivable but already part of existing legislation and case law, for example in respect to landlord–tenant relations. Similarly it is incorrect (as we will see) to assume that all forms of workplace harassment which do not have an explicitly sexual component (and hence do not count as sexual harassment) would fall outside the range of EEO (sex-discrimination) legislation. It would equally be a mistake to ignore all the mutually supportive links which exist between legal and personnel management action and which have the potential to be built upon. However, whilst there is scope for extending the scope for official and informal action against sexual harassment, and, above all, for improving existing mechanisms, the political-pluralistic context in which any such measures have to operate militates against the law's covering every angle.

Suspicions about the complicity of EEO policies in a 'male protection racket' were based on their supposedly reducing the issue of sexual harassment to a question of manners, this being in and of itself a sign that something was amiss. In 'Kant, rhetoric and civility', the practice of derogating manners was given a history. The fact that manners today lack ethical significance and political seriousness in many people's eyes was linked to the early-modern association of manners with rhetorical perspectives on ethical matters. These in turn were linked to patriarchal, aristocratic and disciplinary ways of exercising power which came to be the subjects of a morally charged political attack in the name of Enlightenment-rationalist and romantic principles, including those emanating from feminism. I now want to go on to fill out that argument on manners by suggesting that the alleged archaism of manners is premised upon ignoring the governmental inventions of the absolutist era.

The process of 'courtising' warrior-aristocracies (as Elias called it) is evidently a segment of that history of governmentality. Suppose we apply the hypothesis of a transactional relationship between 'political-ideological' and governmental dimensions to the history of courtly manners. Such a hypothesis might help to make sense of the fact that this history is associated with a newfound respect for upper-class women's bodily integrity and intelligence. One reason we need to adopt this dual viewpoint on the history of courtly manners is in order to account for the fact that, from its inception, the court society was the subject of 'an anti-courtier trend'. Not only the vices and abuses but the very virtues which courtiers were supposed to cultivate came under 'principled' attack (Smith, 1966). The contradictory role played by Christian values and ethical practices in this history is particularly germane to our concern to disrupt the conventional contemporary association of manners with an unsavoury patriarchal and aristocratic past.

Not surprisingly, Christianity figures as a source of moral-political criticism of courtly manners on account of their 'impurity' from the standpoint of the Augustinian strain in Christianity. Yet it seems equally to have been the case that variants of the ultra-ascetic, anti-sensualist element in Christianity played a key role in the *origins* of the courtly ethos. This asceticism was embodied in the decorous figure of the 'courtier-bishop', embodying all the courtly virtues which Elias associates with Renaissance court society. By as early as the tenth century such men had been trained in the German 'cathedral schools' of Otto the Great for the life of a state administrator (Jaeger, 1985). There is thus no basis for identifying manners with an unalloyed aristocratic mentality and monarchical form of political rule: courtly manners are equally part of a history of Christian and administrative (self-)governance. This multidimensionality may also help us to acquire a more balanced perspective on the patriarchalist associations of manners.

It will be recalled how measures against sexual harassment which in some sense entail a policing of manners (of the sort to which, for instance, Gutek's 'goal of preventative medicine' is clearly dedicated) are frequently lambasted. Whatever success they may enjoy is said to be predicated on their complicity with the patriarchal misrecognition of the behaviour as an indecorous transgression against gentlemanly respect for women's chastity, modesty, etc. by a few 'rogue' males. Bularzik's rather patronising criticism of her nineteenth-century sisters and MacKinnon's (1979, p. 173) attack on contemporary proposals to oppose the 'sexualisation' of the workplace operate on these premises.

Bularzik's view of the social purity movement (and the language in which women reported offensive speech and behaviour directed at them) as sexually unliberated and in league with male Victorian attitudes has not passed without criticism in feminist social history. The movement's campaigns against male 'lust' and on behalf of continent 'psychic' love are now more likely to be seen as a defence of female 'bodily integrity' and capacity for sexual independence in the face of brutal male sex-practices and their appalling economic and medical consequences (Jeffreys, 1985, pp. 5, 40).

But even where sexual or bodily manners *are* connected to what nowadays would be regarded as prudishness, it is difficult to see how any unequivocally patriarchal significance can be attached to this connection. Sexual prurience, including virginity, is not an ethical demand that has been addressed exclusively to women, certainly not within the world of the Christian sects, orders and priesthood (Brown, 1988). For example, recalling the place of Christian *ascesis* in the history of manners, one might cite Jaeger's (1985, p. 128) discussion of the style-setting status of the bodily decorum expected of the medieval courtier-bishop in the course of officiating at baptism ceremonies.[13]

Jaeger's point is of course only a special case of the fact that the intended beneficiaries of medieval and renaissance courtesy literature and training in respect to manners were mainly men. This is not a problem but rather an asset for my argument. The expectation that a well-mannered woman will always defer to others' wishes (especially men's) is surely a product of a transformation undergone by discourse on manners during the eighteenth century, with the rise of etiquette books aimed specifically at wives and daughters (Curtin, 1985). Their literary precursors, the courtesy books, represent a discourse on manners and self-fashioning which certainly calls for the cultivation of self-control. However, their purpose is not to teach deference but to *empower* their (mainly male) readers. Why shouldn't a régime of manners be equally useful for women today? One should take the term 'empowerment' not only in its political sense but also in a 'social' one.

'Civil' manners remain necessary to the institutionalisation of the principles of citizenship at stake in sexual harassment. But they are also about how to move through a status-filled world without tripping oneself up: not about deference therefore but rather about maintaining dignity.[14]

In respect to combatting sexual harassment informally, it was suggested in Chapter 2 that, far from being synonymous with responding quietly to aggression, the idiom of manners embraces the ability to calculate when it is proper to be rude or malicious to offending parties. *Men* who wish to stay out of trouble in this regard no doubt have to learn to 'watch what they say' (Ramazanoglu, 1987, p. 66). But the same might be said about recipients of sexual harassment – victory in ethico-rhetorical confrontations with a perpetrator of sexual harassment may require a more controlled *and* controlling response. To judge from the range of advice on possible ways of personally responding to it found in the management policy literature (see Chapter 6), there is reason to doubt that the policing of inequitable male manners in the workplace requires women to turn the other cheek.

Conclusions

'Manners', writes Catharine MacKinnon (1987a, p. 46), 'are often taken more seriously than politics'. Adherents of the sociological-structural critique offer the invidious choice of treating sexual harassment as either (primarily) a moral or a political issue. By contrast, the aim of my approach is to capture the aspects of sexual harassment which most pertain to the possibility of lodging and handling it as a problem of *government and ethical culture*. To treat it as such *is* to lower the political-ideological temperature. Barbara Gutek's recommended régime of 'professional manners' is hardly calculated to 'politicize' the corporate personnel at whom it is mainly aimed, let alone the bulk of the working population. But so what? The purpose of this partial depoliticisation is not to relieve politicians of the obligation to do something about sexual harassment. Quite the contrary, it is a condition for political governments' and private organisations' doing anything about it. Only a régime of liberal government (both central and dispersed) possesses the prerequisite ethical and technical means and the legitimacy (in the context of a pluralist culture) to act with a view to withdrawing the old cultural licence to practise sexual harassment.

For MacKinnon this dependence of liberal government on instituting a régime of inequitable manners could only certify its insufficiency in respect to a system of male supremacy whose 'genius' lies in the fact that 'the strategies it requires to survive it from day to day are precisely the opposite of what is required to change it' (MacKinnon, *ibid.*, p. 16). What is required to change this system is not only the institutionalisation of a principled feminist vision into the legal system, but also something like the advent of a magic (political-therapeutic) moment of collective politicisation when a critical mass of the female citizenry 'experience' the totality of the economic disadvantages, vulnerabilities to sexual violence, etc. to which they are prey as no longer acceptable (*ibid.*).

MacKinnon's wishful thinking is only the logical outcome of the evaluative grid employed in the radical critiques which this essay has sought to challenge. In the black squares sits a 'liberalism' characterised, of course, solely as a *political* philosophy; occupying the white squares is a transformative feminist philosophy. To judge from the texts examined so far, this philosophy or 'theory' creates an unbridgeable gulf between a feminist political stance and the institutional and policy-oriented terms of reference through which currently conceivable modifications of women's work experiences can take place. What is missing from this evaluative grid is a sense of the governmental dimensions by which, like it or not, both liberalism and feminism have been historically driven: a 'depoliticising' array of concerns with the health, living standards and quality of life of national populations. The modifications in morals and manners envisaged in the working-life regulations of an EEO management policy may not be calculated to 'politicise', but they do latch onto mainstream norms and values which sexual harassment flouts, including and especially polite respect for other people's 'personal space', their mental and physical health, and their occupational competences. These norms and values are calculated to win cultural recognition for the problematic status of this sexist behaviour not only from 'the converted' but also from sections of the population who may not identify with feminist (or, in some cases, even liberal) philosophy.

This is not to say that the issue should be expunged from the political register. The stakes of citizenship and self-determination involved inevitably make it a feminist-political issue, even if there are no final 'democratic' solutions. But feminist thinking, I have suggested, does not only originate in (post-)Enlightenment political philosophy and popular struggle. It is also a daughter of governmentality. The consequences of that claim remain to be explored.

4 Social Theory and Legal Argument

Introduction

Amidst the string of defeats and declines of the Reagan years, progress in respect to the justiciation of sexual harassment in the workplace stands out as one of the few beacons of hope in Catharine MacKinnon's otherwise bleak assessment of 'fifteen years of trying to change the status of women by legal and every other available means' (MacKinnon, 1987a, p. 1). Starting with the decision in *Williams v Saxbe* (413 F.Supp 654 DDC, 1976) 'ten years of steady progress in the lower courts' (MacKinnon, *op. cit.*, p. 231, n. 7) were capped by a unanimous confirmation in the US Supreme Court that a broad range of workplace sexual harassment constituted unlawful sex discrimination (*Meritor Savings Bank, FSB v Vinson* (91 L Ed 2d 49, 106 S.Ct. 2399, 1986)).[1]

Crucial to this success, asserts MacKinnon, was the contribution made by feminist jurists and lawyers alert to the lures of legal 'protection' for women.[2] MacKinnon's personal role is exemplary. Drafts of her (1979) *Sexual Harassment of Working Women* were in circulation back in 1975, a critical year where case law was concerned (MacKinnon, 1979, p. xi). Her arguments and categorisations have helped to shape legal judgements both in the US and abroad.[3] She herself helped represent Ms Vinson in the 1986 Supreme Court hearing (MacKinnon, 1987, p. 104).

MacKinnon (*ibid.*, pp. 112–16) insists that this 'success-story' has to be heavily qualified. Still, the existence of a modicum of step-by-step progress in bringing the law to bear on the problem of sexual harassment seems incontestable. What part do bodies of feminist sociological knowledge and moral/political ideologies play in making this socio-legal progress regarding sexual harassment possible? Or, alternatively, in retarding it? How are these forms of thought used *strategically* (or tactically) in framing demands for legal remedies and, especially, in shaping actual legal arguments and decisions? Finally, returning to the question of 'success', how might the perceived *limits* of these legal remedies be interpreted?

Behind these questions lurks the claim that legal strategies cannot be 'read off' from the theories or ideologies by which they are supported. Taking Catharine MacKinnon's arguments on law and sexual harassment as its object, the purpose of this chapter is to provide a working illustration of arguments against the practice of regarding legal categories and arguments as founded upon the social theories (or ethico-political doctrines) with which they are explicitly or implicitly associated (as though identifying the theoretical or ideological 'presuppositions' of legal materials sufficed to determine their value and use). To anticipate, in case this anti-foundationalist point be thought too obvious to be worth reiterating,[4] its heretical implications in this instance are that both the currently depleted reputation of feminist sociologies of 'gender' or 'sex-roles' and received opinions about the patriarchal significance of common law torts pertaining to 'sexual invasions' may need to be reconsidered.

A systematic empirical study of the strategic limits, uses and reception of feminist social theories in legal argumentation lies beyond the scope of this essay, which merely suggests a few lines of attack and terms of description. In so doing, the essay also finds itself engaging with intersecting debates about whether, or if so how, feminists should pursue the pathways of legal reform and about the usefulness of general theories of women's subordination. Whilst such general theories do not uniformly rule out working for piecemeal reform it will be agreed that the two are apt to collide.

Few writings enact this tension more dramatically than those of Catharine MacKinnon. In a study restricted to her legal and political approach to sexual harassment, however, it is not so much the oscillations in MacKinnon's views on these matters[5] as her rigorous and seemingly successful attempt to synthesise social theory and a strategy of legal reform which provides a more appropriate focus of attention. As such, MacKinnon's argument may be read as a riposte to the criticism that general feminist theories of women's subordination ignore the diversity of ways in which women are constructed and positioned in a social order which is neither uniform, nor uniformly oppressive;[6] and, consequently, are prone to an indiscriminate suspicion of institutions such as the law which militate against serious engagement in working for their reform.[7]

Can this claim about the practical consequences of general theories be sustained in the face of MacKinnon's intervention? *Prima facie*, it is framed by a general theory which links a systematic explanation and social critique of sexual harassment to a technical-legal strategy for enhancing the possibilities of litigation, *via* a feminist vision of social change. However, examination of the linkages between theory, ethico-political vision, and legal strategy will indicate that her most telling socio-juristic arguments establishing the discriminatory character of sexual harassment may not depend upon that theory quite as much as she supposes. These reservations about 'reading-off' MacKinnon's legal approach from its theoretical supports apply with equal force to her critique of both orthodox legal definitions of sexual harassment and traditional tort remedies by reference to their respective underpinnings in sociological role theory and patriarchal ideology. MacKinnon's failure to take adequate account of their practical uses can be linked to a problem associated with the visionary ingredient in her theoretical approach. This vision, I suggest, also has an unfortunate effect on the way she represents the potential, the limits and the ethical-political significance of legal remedies for sexual harassment. MacKinnon's representation of the potential of law seems to preclude the possibility of establishing a broader network of regulation than that afforded by litigation alone.

Sociologies of Law

Targeting both a legal and general audience, MacKinnon's *Sexual Harassment of Working Women* (1979) sought both to modify and to reinforce existing legal interpretations of sexual harassment at work as unlawful sex-discrimination within the meaning of Title VII of the Civil Rights Act (1964).[8] If this legal interpretation is to overcome the initially successful defences mounted in lawsuits filed during the 1970s, argued MacKinnon, it must have built into it a feminist sociological understanding of the causes and scope of sexual harassment. As already foreshadowed, this understanding takes off from a critique of the prevailing 'differences approach' to equal opportunity law. At the heart of this approach, she maintains, lies an 'underlying vision of the reality of sex in American society' (MacKinnon, *ibid.*, p. 4), which she identifies with the sociology of sex-roles and a related liberal ideology of equality (*passim* but cf. especially pp. 149ff, 178–82). The differences approach views sex-discrimination as a failure to respect men's and women's equality *qua* persons, by 'arbitrarily' differentiating on the basis of their gender between individuals 'similarly situated' as regards their occupational statuses, roles and capacities (MacKinnon, *ibid.*, pp. 107, 144, 192).

As a vehicle for interpreting discrimination at law, argues MacKinnon, this doctrine is often fatally dependent on the establishment of 'reasonable comparability'. It must show that a woman possessed exactly the same qualifications for promotion as a man, but was denied some employment benefit on the 'arbitrary', i.e. non-pertinent, ground of her sex.[9] But what if women and men regularly 'present non-comparabilities' (p. 5), whether, as in *Gilbert v General Electric* (1976, 429, US, 125), due to biological differences or to socially enforced ones?[10] It was partly on this basis that the initially successful defences in the 1970s cases were mounted: non-comparability supporting the argument that disparate treatment was not the unlawful result of women's differential attractiveness to men. Such defences have generally fallen on appeal (Baxter, 1985). However, the differences approach is said to be made vulnerable to those defences by its implicit representation of sexual harassment as 'an unfortunate, irrational, outmoded, superficial' irruption into an otherwise non-discriminatory workplace environment in which men and women are otherwise treated as 'undifferentiatingly human' (MacKinnon, *op. cit.*, p. 120).

By contrast, MacKinnon's 'inequality' approach 'sees women's situation as a structural problem of enforced inferiority that needs to be radically altered' (*ibid.*, p. 5). Every case of sexual harassment is 'but one example' and 'an integral part' of an institutionally grounded system of social stereotyping (*ibid.*, p. 180, 122), which disadvantages women not simply as individuals but as a group. On the one hand, the differences approach ignores the extent to which, in supposedly objective organisational norms and routines, 'in the guise of setting a single standard for persons, women are measured by the standards of men' (MacKinnon, *ibid.*, p. 144). On the other, it understates the regularity with which, in order to 'qualify' for employment, women are required to meet quite different standards: sexual attractiveness, an obliging, flattering, even seductive demeanour, etc. These sex-based 'qualifications' may require a projection of potential sexual compliance and entail complicity with sexual harassment. A structural sexualisation of the division of labour thus locks women into a double form of subjection which promotes sexual harassment as not an exception but the rule:

> Sexual harassment . . . presents a closed system of social predation in which powerlessness builds on powerlessness . . . Working women are defined and survive by defining themselves as sexually accessible and economically exploitable. Because they are economically vulnerable they are sexually exposed, because they must be sexually accessible they are always economically at risk. In this perspective, sexual harassment is less epidemic than endemic. (*Ibid.*, p. 55)

Locating the problem, as it notoriously does, at the level of a distorted, hence arbitrary, stereotypical *image*, the sex-role sociology embodied in the differences approach underestimates not only the institutional bases of sexual harassment but also those psychically located yet socially determined *pathologising* dimensions of the system of male supremacy.

It is this social pathology of the normal male which makes predatory behaviour towards women something men in general are conditioned to perform *quite unconsciously* and therefore to regard as natural:

> Most men do not sexually harass women with an intent to injure the female sex . . .   That sexual harassment can be so much of a habit, so much part of the definition of normalcy and so unconsciously done is part of the pathology that requires legal intervention . . . (*Ibid.*, p. 199; see also p. 114)

If sexual harassment is the manifestation of an all-pervasive and deeply embedded system of male dominance, then under what conditions can it be appropriate for women to look for redress to *law*, which according to many feminist theorists (e.g. Freeman, 1989, pp. 51–55) has traditionally provided one of the most powerful instruments and conduits of this system? MacKinnon agrees that, traditionally, the law (tort law in particular) 'has never in fact protected women's dignity or bodily integrity', its ostensible protections being 'both condescending and unreal' (MacKinnon, 1987, p. 104). Nevertheless, if only with respect to employment conditions, the equality provisions of the Fourteenth Amendment and 'Title VII' together provide a window of opportunity for women's gaining at least some redress from sexism. Two radical ethico-political transformations are sought.

One objective is to make what she variously calls the 'shadow world' or 'abstraction-machine' of legal claims against sexual harassment as adequate as possible to its victims' raw *experience* of 'pain and stifled anger' (MacKinnon, 1979, p. 57; MacKinnon *et al.*, 1984, p. 34); or to put it the other way around, to ensure that this experience of sexual harassment is 'written into its legal definition' (MacKinnon, 1987, p. 105; see also p. 116).[11] Relatedly, 'the purpose of discrimination law is to change the society so that this kind of injury need not and does not recur' (MacKinnon, 1979, p. 172). The underlying 'social realities of sex' which systematically engender sexual harassment, including its socio-pathological implications, cannot be altered without bringing about 'a transformation of conscious-ness'. Thereafter, sexual harassment would only be committed by the odd, clinically sick individual (MacKinnon, *ibid.*, p. 199). A dialectical process of social transformation is envisaged. The equality provisions lodged in the law are accorded a radical political meaning, basically functioning as a prefigurative vision of a truly egalitarian society. Then, if the law can be held to its supposedly radical word (Stanley and Wise, 1987, p. 52), a new legal concept of sexual harassment incorporating not only women's immediate experiences, but also its structural determinations, will then provide a stepping stone towards this new world (MacKinnon, 1979, p. 57).

However, the juristic argument through which the structural, critical, and visionary dimensions of her analysis are to be built into its legal definition seems at some remove from the dialectical trajectory of legal reformation envisaged in these more elevated statements. The starting-point of the legal argument, she says, is 'not the point at which existing legal cause or action for sexual harassment unravels but the point at which the less good legal case can be scrutinised for its social truths' (MacKinnon, *ibid.*, p. 55). This statement inaugurates a more modest task: to identify *typical* incidents of sexual harassment which were prone to fall into a legal grey area, and then to reconsider the legal categorisation with both legally unambiguous and ambiguous cases in mind. This is a strategy for extending the purchase of existing law on workplace harassment in determinate, limited ways. In order to prepare the ground for my argument on the likely legal reception and utilisation of MacKinnon's theoretical perspective on sexual harassment, some examples of how this 'inequality approach' is fed through into definite recommendations for extending the scope of justiciable actions (Title VII Discrimination) will now be outlined.

Legal Arguments

Firstly, MacKinnon (*ibid.*, pp. 32–40) argued that the 'Title VII' requirement to prove some disadvantage in respect to 'compensation, terms, conditions or privileges of employment' as a consequence of being sexually harassed must be interpreted as covering not only *quid pro quo* situations but also (under the heading of 'conditions of employment') detrimental effects on the quality of the working environment. In the *quid pro quo* legal setting, the price of refusing (or accepting) a sexual advance is the loss or gain of a 'tangible' benefit of employment, dismissal, promotion, wage increase, etc. Attansio's (1982, p. 24, n. 152) statistical breakdown of the causes of action in sexual harassment suits filed during the seventies and early eighties confirms that this sexual bargain was the only kind of sexual harassment situation for which in the US legal opinion of the time a 'good case' could be made.[12] Yet, notoriously, many of the most commonly experienced forms of sexual harassment – lewd remarks, unwanted sexual touching, leering, pin-up displays, etc. – frequently neither require the active cooperation of the harassed woman nor, if resisted, result in some tangible detriment to employment benefits. Sexual harassment behaviour may well be disavowed by its perpetrator even as it is going on; or passed off as flattery or fun. There may thus be no explicit unwelcome 'advance' to be refused. Protests are ignored or victims are 'coerced into tolerance' (MacKinnon, 1979, p. 40).

The 'social truths' yielded by the inequality approach, which justify extending Title VII discrimination definitions so as to cover this hitherto 'less good legal case', can be readily predicted. Women's generally subordinate and economically vulnerable position in the sexual division of labour leads to a prediction that this sort of intimidatory workplace atmosphere would be endemic.

Secondly, the combination of the unconscious, social pathological component of sexual harassment and the probable economic power relationship between the parties may be shown to have implications for decisions as to the burden and thresholds of proof. The victim may fear for her job if she protests the harassment. At law, of course, this poses the question of guilty intent. Did the respondent know (or could he be reasonably expected to know) that his advances were unwelcome and unreciprocated? If the harassed woman feels unable to refuse sexual intercourse, does this mean she voluntarily consents to it (MacKinnon, 1987, p. 110)? If sexual harassment emanates from socio-pathological, unconscious attitudes towards women, then the need to prove *mens rea* by demonstrating the existence of an unambiguous refusal must be waived: 'The intent requirement would be difficult to meet, for the wrong reasons . . . Why should unconsciousness of its sexism exempt a practice when (this) is integral to the easy disregard that has so long sanctioned women's oppression?' (MacKinnon, 1979, pp. 199, 114).

In confirming the trend of US case law in the 1980s that 'so-called "hostile environment" (i.e. non-*quid pro quo*) harassment violates Title VII' (*Meritor Savings Bank v Vinson*, 1986, L Ed 2d, 106 S.Ct. 2399, 59), Justice Renquist is virtually taking the words out of MacKinnon's mouth. Some, if not all,[13] the implications of her emphasis on the 'unconscious' bases of much sexual harassment have also been upheld in the Supreme Court's rejection of the legal defence that sex-related conduct in such cases was 'voluntary' ('in the sense that the complainant was not forced to participate against her will').

Sociologies in Law

Let us grant MacKinnon's success in persuading judicial authorities to incorporate elements of a feminist perspective in adjudications of sexual harassment. But how much and to what extent do these successful socio-legal arguments depend, *especially at the point of their judicial reception*, upon the theory (including its critical and visionary components) by which those arguments are ostensibly framed? The answer to this question cannot be independent of the results of putting a parallel question to what is said to be the generator of the differences approach: the sociology of sex-roles. To compare the 'persuasive' (forensic) force of invoking the particular way of knowing sexual harassment yielded respectively in the inequality and differences approaches may be more productive than to assess them at the level of their theoretical implications.

Certainly, there is no reason to assume that the legal intelligibility of these socio-legal strategies rests upon assent to any or all of the sociological theoretical arguments or assumptions which underpin them. The intelligibility or pertinence of *differences* between these theories in the legal context cannot be taken for granted either. For example, it is doubtful if the debate over whether sexual harassment ought to be located at the level of stereotypes or institutional and/or structures would be legally intelligible or relevant. What if the theoretical differences between the differences and inequality approach had little or no legal pertinence? In other words, suppose that incorporation of the inequality approach into US legal understanding of sexual harassment in the determinate respects suggested by MacKinnon involves acknowledging something like the following minimal set of statements in connection with its regular incidence. Extrapolating from pronouncements on the need for such extensions in the main US judgements of the 1970s and early-to-mid 1980s (especially the enormously influential *Bundy v Jackson* (1981, 641 Fed R 2d 934), it looks as if what the law has to take into account is the existence of an *element of culturally sanctioned regularity* in the occurrence of sexual harassment. This regularity is related to a *discernible pattern of disadvantage* suffered by women, as a social group, in a variety of sites both within the workplace and without. The chances are that superordinate/subordinate relations in the workplace will be gendered in favour of men. However, irrespective of their officially authorised power over women, men as a social group are in many cultural circles invested with a 'cultural license' to pursue women sexually (Farley, 1978) to a degree which justifies the law's treating sexual harassment as enacting a problematic social power relationship, and not simply as the exercise of one individual's preference in respect to the other.

Is there any reason to suppose that a socio-legal argument capable of demonstrating a *pattern of disadvantage* of this sort, regardless of its cause, would not be sufficient to justify legal recognition of sexual harassment and legal reform along the lines of the specific recommendations associated with MacKinnon's inequality approach? In *Bundy*, for example, a passing reference to women's being 'inferior in the employment hierarchy' is the closest we get to any concept of a *structure* of oppression (Bureau of National Affairs, 1981, p. 60). On this line of argument the modest task of a (pro-) feminist juristic argument is simply to build up a picture of elements of typical sexual harassment situations which the law is currently failing to acknowledge. In other words, adapting MacKinnon's words, cited earlier, the task is to shift the criteria of recognition such that what appeared a weak or hard case comes to be seen as a standard one.

Why shouldn't even the blandest of multi-factorial sex-role sociologies be adequate to this task? In order to establish the existence of patterns of disadvantage suffered by women at work and elsewhere, it is not necessary to demonstrate that this social pattern of sex-related disadvantage is *consistent* throughout the social body or that it derives from a single (deep) *structure*. Consider the precocious example of an inequality perspective outlined in *Sail'er Inn v Kirby* (1971, 5 Cal 3d 1; 485 p2d, 529). Here, refusal to hire a woman as a bartender was disallowed on the grounds of disabling women as such 'from full participation in the political, business and economic areas' and relegating 'the whole class of women . . . to an inferior status without regard to the capabilities or characteristics of its individual members' (cited MacKinnon, 1979, p. 116). The judgement undoubtedly evinces awareness of persistent disadvantage to women as a group consequent upon discriminatory hiring policy. It does not, however, so clearly evince 'the understanding that sex discrimination is a system that defines women as inferior to men' (*ibid.*), as though whatever places women at a disadvantage consistently emanates from a single structural cause. The rhetorical power of invoking this pattern of regularity derives, perhaps, less from the logic of structural explanations than from the *ethical and administrative logics of statistical investigations and sociological surveys.*

After all, for some time now these governmental forms of social investigation have played a major role in establishing certain kinds of individual and group conducts as 'social problems'. The surveys and sociological analyses which, during the 1970s, did so much, alongside popular protest, to highlight sexual harassment as just such a problem stands in that nineteenth-century tradition of social statistical investigation which works by identifying 'moral topographies' of social evils and anti-social behaviours in the city.[14] One presupposition for mapping the social incidence of sexual harassment numerically in this way is the existence or establishment of a grid of behavioural norms pertaining to particular institutional sites against which deviations can be registered. The framework of role-theory may be more serviceable both in this general regard and for purposes of legal argument than that of those structural theories which aspire to transcend it.

For in contrast to the indeterminate concepts of subjectivity and experience around which MacKinnon's model revolves, role theory embodies a functional conception of the person as a bundle of normative roles and statuses.[15] On the one hand, this conception accords well with – it may well be partly derived from – managerial ways of thinking about and acting on organisational life. Managerial sociologies of sexual harassment at work such as those of Gutek (1985) and Myer *et al.* (1981) demonstrate how readily this conceptual framework lends itself to being translated into an ethos, a pedagogy ('role models') and a policy of 'human resources' management with respect to this problem which are surprisingly extensive in scope.

On the other hand, it is equally translatable into the similarly fragmentary legal concept of the person as the locus of imputation of rights, duties, standing to sue, etc. From this standpoint, the problem for the differences approach raised by MacKinnon concerning cases of discrimination (e.g. *Gilbert*), where women present 'non-comparabilities', ought not to be insuperable. As MacKinnon (1979, p. 193) concedes, even in cases of female discrimination around unique biological characteristics such as pregnancy, it remains possible to establish some points of comparability – pregancy being a consequence of human sexuality, a characteristic shared by men and women. It is no more difficult in sex-role sociology than it is in law to conceive of people as bearers of a given status such as equality for some purposes but not for others.

Sex-role sociology may not be very exciting or theoretically satisfying (Connell, 1987). But the main prerequisite for a social theory, for the purposes of socio-legal argument, is its capacity to establish a plausible ethical imperative and a sociological/statistical demonstration of its non-observance on a massive scale. Knowledge of this order may yield what many will regard as only the most superficial knowledge of the nature and causes of sexual harassment. But this very superficiality may be the source of the usefulness of sex-role sociology in tying sexual harassment down to something definite (a demonstrable breach of a norm of expected conduct) which is actually actionable at law or in other regulatory régimes.

To conclude, it would seem to follow that the differences approach is not *founded* on any sociological theory. The sociology of gender-roles on which this approach draws is part of an administrative technology. The knowledge which it yields is not objective in the sense of being value-free. Its objects, its very field of vision cannot exist independently of (re-) calculations and standards of appropriate conduct in particular or more diffuse social sites. However, it was not only 'Weberian' managers and administrators but also, and perhaps mainly, the organised opinion of the 1970s women's movement, including feminist sociologists of gender, who furnished the law with new categories of conduct such as sexual harassment which it would henceforth have to learn to treat as a breaches of legal norms. The differences approach may well stand in need of amendment along the lines recommended by MacKinnon if it is to take into account a range of sex-related differences in work and surrounding social conditions. But there seems to be no clear reason to suppose that in order to persuade either legal authorities or the public at large of this need for reform, a theoretical displacement of the 'sex-roles' idiom is required. The connection between anti-discrimination law pertaining to sexual harassment and sex-role theory is more in the nature of an historical accident than one of fatal theoretical dependence.

Tort and Taboo

Just as the brunt of MacKinnon's attack on the differences approach was borne by the theory and ideology on which it is said to have been founded, so too, her attack on tort law is mainly directed against its 'underlying' patriarchal vision of women (MacKinnon, 1979, p. 172). In taking issue with MacKinnon's view of the place of tort law in justiciating sexual harassment, I do not dispute her contention that sex-discrimination law offers a better pathway to legal redress for women. But in MacKinnon's eyes, tort remedies are not merely a second-best resort. The values, purposes and the very language of these torts are subject to a far-reaching critique which, as we shall see, has implications for not only legal but also non-legal measures.

In all this MacKinnon displays an instructive consistency. Law, she maintains, is generally given over to enhancing male supremacy. One way of achieving this end is through tortious actions at common law. These, it is said, are driven by a paternalistic concern to protect wives' and daughters' sexual integrity. By contrast, anti-discrimination law acknowledged, for the first time in legal history, the principle of equality between the sexes *qua* persons (MacKinnon, 1987, pp. 104, 105, 116). So, between anti-discrimination law, pointing forward to women's equal personhood, and sexual torts, pointing backwards to patriarchy, there can only be a radical discontinuity (MacKinnon, *ibid.*, pp. 104–105). However, this argument that sexual torts are essentially patriarchal and discontinuous in respect to sex-discrimination remedies is difficult to sustain.

To begin with, it is a statistical fact that the great majority of 'Title VII' sexual harassment claims are *supplemented* by tort claims for punitive, exemplary or emotionally consequential damages, over and above compensation for lost wages and other tangible job-opportunities (Attansio, 1982). Even more damaging to the assumptions of antipathy and discontinuity, however, is MacKinnon's own mindfulness of the contemporary value of these torts as precedents in legal argument. The first and broadest positive lesson of the case law pertaining to 'torts of sexual invasion' is that

> Women's bodies, particularly the conditions and consequences of men's sexual access to them, are not a novel subject for the law. The law of torts historically provided civil redress for sexual invasions at a time when social morality was less ambiguous in defining a woman's sexuality as . . . capable of compensable damage . . . the examination of tort shows that the law is quite accustomed to treating cloudy issues of motive and intent, the meaning of ambiguous acts, the effects of words on liability for acts and the role of excessive sensitivity in determining liability and damages, all in a sexual context. These issues have arisen before. They have not been thought so subtle as to preclude a judicial resolution once a real injury was perceived to exist. (MacKinnon, 1979, pp. 164, 170–71)

Sexual touching, for example, including kissing without consent, has been considered under the torts of assault, battery (extending to 'a touching of the mind' by placing the person in a state of fear) and the intentional infliction of emotional distress. Much of what is now captured by the designation 'sexual harassment' could even figure as criminal acts under the antiquated headings of *criminal conversation, loss of consortium, insult, lewdness, fornication,* and so on. In *Craker v The Chicago and Northwestern Railway Co.* (1895, 36 Wis. 657, 17 Am. Rep. 504,), the employer of a railway conductor who repeatedly grabbed and kissed a Wisconsin school teacher was successfully sued for $1000. A further feature of this judgement which argues in favour of tort analogies is its incorporation of a distinction between 'negligent' and 'intentional' harms and its insistence that the former, no less than the latter, amounts to injustice, vexation and degradation and is therefore compensable. Considerations such as the irrelevance of *mens rea* required by a feminist perspective were already envisaged in the 'bad old days' of sexual torts. These are just as capable, in some circumstances, as anti-discrimination law of discounting (men's) 'experience' where appropriate. Relatedly, the criteria of emotional distress do much to meet the standard defence that the victim of sexual harassment reacted 'over-sensitively' (MacKinnon, 1979, p. 167). MacKinnon also points out an instructive affinity between the tort of inflicting emotional distress and the modern concept of 'stress' in health-and-safety regulation.

In general, therefore, it cannot be said that MacKinnon fails to appreciate any of the advantages of these torts. What does not seem to be appreciated is the extent to which these advantages redound to the discredit of her overall critique of tort law and of her overall conception of how and to what extent sexual harassment should be regulated (by law). One problem in this critique can be traced to a rather crude view of the meaning of 'liberal' distinctions between private and public domains and their bearing on women's subordination. MacKinnon's main caveats against tort law remedies, it will be recalled, went to the difficulty of registering sexual harassment as a 'social' injury and as an *employment*-related issue. Tort law construes it, by contrast, as a 'moral' injury, in the liberal sense. Liberalism is here of course identified with a philosophy or ideology of individual (negative) liberty which furnishes a justification for demarcating certain areas of life as private zones of personal discretion, moral (or immoral) choice, etc. and which are *ipso facto* not open to state intervention. It follows that to characterise sexual harassment as a 'moral problem' in this sense is to assume that it is essentially a private issue of personal morality and individual responsibility. In making this assumption, tort law 'rips . . . injuries to women's sexuality out of the context of women's social circumstances as a whole' (MacKinnon, 1979, p. 171). In order to capture the 'social injury' of sexual harassment, this 'moral' assumption must be written out of its legal definition. The progressive possibilities of anti-discrimination law are seen as a simple function of the extent to which it transfers the problem from the private to the public sphere.

This line of argument suffers from a tendency to reiterate rather than to challenge simplistic 'liberal' philosophical or ideological suppositions of a neat division between private and public realms of human existence. True, this categorisation is assigned to the realm of ideology – women's place does not reflect any natural abilities or dispositions of sexes; private relationships do in reality have political dimensions and repercussions, etc. However, for MacKinnon, to categorise an activity or domain as private is to imply that it is non-social and not subject to regulation; and that if a space can be shown to be crossed by regulation, power-relationships, resistance, etc., then this signifies that really it has no private dimension at all. 'The private is the public for those for whom the personal is the political. In this sense *there is no private*, either normatively or empirically. Feminism confronts the fact that women have no privacy to lose or to guarantee' (MacKinnon, 1987, p. 100 – my emphasis).

It hardly needs stating that this breathtaking generalisation[16] ignores evidence of significant diversity in the forms, purposes and above all impacts on women of public-private differentiations (e.g. Brown, 1980, Rose, 1987). To dichotomise 'the private' and 'the social' is to ignore the extent to which, especially in a liberal style of *government*, as distinct from the simplistic *ideology* with which MacKinnon identifies liberal morality, arenas, agents or relationships are designated as private for some purposes but not others. They may also function as both effects and instruments of public regulation. This may range from state regulation, through a series of intermediate (e.g. advisory or voluntary) bodies, to self-regulation. There is therefore no *necessary* incompatibility between construing sexual harassment as a 'social' problem whilst simultaneously regarding its regulation, to a greater or lesser degree, as the responsibility of some 'private' body, such as the management of a corporation. The one construction does not cancel out the other. With this suggestion in mind, let us now return to MacKinnon's contention that it is difficult if not impossible in tort law to register the *social* and *employment-related* character of sexual harassment in the workplace. Is MacKinnon right in conflating these two things and counterposing them to the category 'private'?

If to categorise an offence as a matter for private law is to exclude the possibility of treating them as employment-related and/or of 'social' concern, then what has been described as 'one of the principal features of private law in recent years' becomes hard to account for:

> ... the dramatic increase in the variety of circumstances in which courts are willing to hold that one party owes a duty of care in tort to another .... the view that categories of relationship attracting duty of care is immutably fixed by precedent, to be extended only by legislation is now seen as quaint. (Logie, 1989, p. 115)

As if in direct support of this contention, MacKinnon herself has drawn attention to the decision in *Monge v Beebe Rubber* (1974, 316 A2d 549 NH). There, dismissal from employment based on the employee's rejection of sexual harassment was judged in breach of the 'duty of care' imposed on employers in the vicarious liability provisions of the employment contract. Again, MacKinnon's passing mention of affinities between tortious conceptions of emotional distress and the modern medical/psychological concept of work-induced stress will be recalled; together with her suggestion that sexual harassment could be seen as falling under the provisions of health-and-safety legislation or labour contracts.

Even where insistence on the private dimensions of sexual harassment is linked to an alleged harasser's defence – as in the initially unsuccessful

1970s cases – this need not entail denying that the incident constituted either an ethical or a legal offence. In *Tomkins v Public Service Electric and Gas Co.* (1976, 422 F Supp 553), the defence successfully sought to characterise plaintiff's sexual harassment as 'a physical attack motivated by sexual desire', and her dismissal as due to her having refused his offer of an affair, not because she was a woman. Differentiation on that basis, it was argued, could happen to 'similarly situated' individuals of either sex and therefore fell outside the Title VII definition of sex discrimination. Apart from this exploitation of the differences approach, it was also argued that what occurred was a sordid (inter-) *personal* confrontation: 'Title VII . . . is not intended to provide a federal tort remedy for what amounts to a private incident which happened to occur in a corporate corridor rather than a back alley' (*Tomkins*, p. 556). Consequently it was not 'Title VII' discrimination.

How is the appeal to plaintiff's uncontrollable urges and the private/personal character of the incident actually functioning? According to the generalised view of the function of the private–public distinction, to characterise the offence as private and personal ('an unhappy and recurrent feature of our social experience', *Tomkins*, *ibid.*) is to make its offensive character ethically and legally invisible. Whilst that may be the defence's *aim* in offering the excuse, in *Tomkins* it actually functioned as a reason for questioning the *area* of law – i.e. tort – to which the offence, if there was one, should be assigned. As we have seen, in tort law such an excuse would not, on past precedents, *necessarily* be an acceptable defence. In short, denying that the act was discriminatory, employment-related and of public interest did not entail that no sexual harassment took place. Moreover, characterising it as a private incident did *not* prevent the court from treating its repercussions as an employment-related issue. If, according to this original decision, Ms Tomkins had no right to action, it was simultaneously held that, nevertheless, her employer had no right to fire her; on the contrary, he was obliged to investigate her complaint. Not to do so was to exhibit a conscious preference for a male over a female employee (*Tomkins*, p. 554). This 'sex-based' corporate attitude evidenced by her dismissal was therefore something for which the employer was vicariously liable (*Tomkins*, *ibid.*).

This is the view of a judge who is indulgent about the 'fact' that sexual attraction plays a 'subtle' part in most personnel decisions (*Tomkins*, p. 557). Having shown that in even this 'worst case', to attribute a private and moral dimension to sexual harassment does not preclude regarding it as a social and employment-related issue, it now remains to consider MacKinnon's generalised objection to the *language* of sexual torts. The basic objection is of course to the fact that the protections for women afforded by all the sex-related torts are founded on a set of patriarchal attitudes about the ideal structure of household authority and conjugal relations; attitudes which are manifested in the moralising idiom of these torts (MacKinnon, 1979, p. 172). The effects of this ideological foundation are manifested, for example, in the tortious treatment of sexual insult. This is only compensable, claims MacKinnon, because a woman's chastity was regarded as defining of her virtue and her virtue defining of her value to her husband, to whom such invasions would amount to 'loss of consortium'. All torts of sexual invasion 'blended the enforcement of moral standards with protection for men's possessory interests' (MacKinnon, *ibid.*, p. 169).

But is it not more by virtue of assertion than argument that MacKinnon assimilates all torts of sexual invasion, such as intentional infliction of emotional distress, to explicitly patriarchal family-related sexual torts? In contemporary resorts to them in legal characterisations of the injury to women entailed in sexual harassment, translations of the intent of anti-discrimination law into the language of tortious injury do not always carry the suggestion of paternal-proprietal attitudes to women. Observe the implicit reference to notions of bodily integrity and dignity in an influential legal decision in favour of legal recognition of sexual harassment's constituting a discriminatory, hostile work-environment: 'Surely the requirement that a man or woman run a gauntlet of sexual abuse in return for the privilege of being allowed work . . . can be as *demeaning and disconcerting* . . . as the harshest of racial epithets' (*Henson v Dundee*, 1982, 682 F2D 897, 902, emphasis added). *Bundy* (Bureau of National Affairs, 1981, p. 59) makes substantially the same point, adding that sexual harassment 'always represents an intentional assault on an individual's innermost privacy'.

The same reasoning underpinning MacKinnon's reluctance to countenance a positive role for torts in anti-discrimination suits also underlies the way in which she conceives the overarching purposes and above all the *limits* of the regulation of sexual harassment. Here is MacKinnon's response to a proposal for *non*-legal regulation:

> Inventing special rules of morality for the workplace would institutionalise new taboos rather than confront the fact that it is women who are systematically disadvantaged by the old ones. Resistance to sexual harassment is less an issue of right and wrong than an issue of power. Women are in no *position* to refuse, which is what makes refusal so moral an act . . . the reason these acts can . . . recur . . . is not the

breaking of a code of good conduct but the relegation to inferiority
for which they stand. To see sexual harassment as an injury to morality
is to turn it into an extreme case of bad manners. (MacKinnon, 1979,
p. 173)

If this objection merely went to the idea of 'special rules' concerning
men's treatment of 'ladies' – according to which sexual harassment
would be banned alongside, say, swearing – then this statement might be
unexceptionable. However, MacKinnon's general derogation of 'manners'
would seem to have the effect of extending her critique of torts of sexual
invasion to *any* conceptions of sexual harassment which are articulated in
the tort idiom; that is to treat it as involving a moral affront to individuals'
bodily integrity. It follows from this general anathema on ethical regulation
that management action against sexual harassment is out of the question. If
sexual harassment is to be regulated it will be by anti-discrimination law or
not at all.

The Limits of Law

This inference is confirmed by the absence of any reference in MacKinnon's
arguments to the strategic role of management policies in institutionalising
non-sexist norms of conduct in the workplace. The incentive to employers
to take such initiatives which is built into the vicarious liability provisions
of the Civil Rights Act goes unnoticed. MacKinnon's main references to
these provisions (MacKinnon, 1979, pp. 93–94, 211–13, 237–38) are
exclusively directed at underlining the *justice* of incorporating them in
the legislation and of invoking them in civil suits.[17]
    A failure to think strategically about the possibilities of 'infra-legal'
regulation also comes through in her more recent reflections on the
limitations of current sexual harassment law. Women's reluctance to
undertake proceedings casts a shadow on her generally affirmative verdict.
One reason for this reluctance, she argues, is their (accurate) anticipation
of the fact that 'first-person' reiteration of a sexual harassment episode
in court is likely to cast its victim in the humiliating role of a player
in a pornographic vignette (MacKinnon, 1987, pp. 111–15). Is this a
case of masculinist rituals of adjudication failing to do justice to, indeed
exacerbating, women's experience of injury? Or are these problems an
unintended consequence of an adversary system of legal process which,
among other things, normally requires that all the relevant facts of a case
be publically read into the record? If the pornographic effect of testimony
is the result of its public, ceremonial character then that might be one reason

to look to alternative judicial or semi-judicial processes. For instance, to anticipate the discussion in Chapter 5 below, in the public tribunal hearings at which sexual harassment complaints may be heard under Australian sex discrimination law, where the plaintiff is likely to be seriously embarrassed by verbally rehearsing the details of the harassment, the proceedings at that point may be conducted in camera. The conciliation phase which proceeds (and typically precludes the need for) the tribunal is of course also confidential.

No doubt MacKinnon would have problems with this way of doing things too. The point of adverting to this 'Australian way' of addressing the problem of personal testimony is not to offer a specific alternative (from a very different legal culture, moreover) but simply to draw attention to MacKinnon's silence concerning alternative dispute resolution. What seems to be lacking is any sense that limits to the law's potential might reflect anything other than the entrenchment of structurally reinforced male interests. There are surely quite legitimate reasons to doubt whether law can or should be made to bear the radical weight of responsibility which in her vision of equality she wishes to place upon it: namely that of serving as the fulcrum of radical social and personal transformation.

This vision of radical social transformation, it could be urged, leads her to place an exaggerated trust in the commanding status of law and concomitantly, in the consciousness-raising impact of legal publicity. It is as if, once the law can be remade so as to embody a feminist structural understanding of what gives rise to sexual harassment; to approximate women's experience of the injury it imposes; and to foreshadow a radical alternative set of relations between the sexes, then its traditional majesty could be invoked in order to provide an Archimedian point of transformation. No wonder MacKinnon has no time for privately conducted alternative dispute resolution procedures. Well-publicised legal cases have an undoubted impact. However, it is unlikely that any impact they might have can be sustained if the significance of sexual harassment law is conceived solely in terms of the exercise of a legal *sovereignty* over sexist conduct. In a liberal political milieu such as the USA, sex-discrimination law is *neither* capable of dramatically changing society either by commanding obedience or by changing hearts; *nor* limited to the provision of just remedies to individuals and to symbolising the general social unacceptability of sexual harassment. The Civil Rights Act under which it is unlawful is not only an instrument of justice but also an anti-discriminatory social policy and form of governance. The preventative-policing function served by the vicarious liability provisions of the legislation, for example (as an incentive to corporations to initiate their own sexual harassment policies, including complaints procedures), cannot be understood solely in terms of the symbolic, exemplary and commanding powers of law. Here the effective working of the social policy objectives of the law itself is contingent upon the establishment of 'infra-legal' regulatory apparatuses located, not inside the state, but rather in 'civil society'. They may receive a charter from the law and serve as a means of relaying it but they are not its direct instruments. In this way all sorts of sexual harassment might be addressed which might well slip through the net where full civil litigation is the only avenue of complaint.

In addition to a code of conduct accompanied by a complaints procedure and a range of sanctions and preventative measures, a management policy on sexual harassment may also offer encouragement, training and advice aimed at encouraging employees in some circumstances to confront it personally and informally. With or without that assistance, where women employees, individually or as a body, take matters into their own hands, this too may be seen as part of the subjection of sexual harassment to a kind of policing.

MacKinnon's assumption that in targeting inequitable and gross manners, management-based attempts to modify the ethos of the workplace would *necessarily* have no effects on the power relations which encourage sexual harassment is certainly not based upon anything like an examination of the range of measures involved in such attempts. They are not bound to be effective. But does the mere fact of their affinities to the language of torts or their failure to tackle structural causes guarantee that such measures will be to no avail?

Conclusion

If one were to formalise the difference between MacKinnon's conception of the progressive potential of law and that hinted at in these paragraphs, one might say that she tends to view law as a *ceremonial and coercive expression of state sovereignty* rather than as one regulatory vehicle among others of a *strategy of liberal social government*. From this latter perspective, the political virtue of anti-discrimination and supporting affirmative action legislation resides in their providing the *legal environment*, including legislation, supportive case law and sanctions, within which a variegated network of *both* legal measures *and* 'infra-legal' initiatives could be instituted and supported. These may be located in enterprises, government departments, educational institutions, and possibly, within limits, other feasible sites too. These 'government' milieus cross-cut the divisions between state and society, private and public. Even within the realm of litigation, anti-discrimination legislation need not be seen as a law unto itself. Legal argument on the substance of the offence particularly with respect to its compensable aspects may be nourished rather than stultified by reference to the law of torts.

As impressive as MacKinnon's socio-legal intervention has undoubtedly been, it is precisely such a nuanced view of the indispensible yet limited place of law in liberal social reform which her anathematisation of a 'moral' approach to sexual harassment seems to preclude. Two likely problems have been identified. The first problem concerns her exclusive emphasis on the role of law in regulating sexual harassment; the second, her conception of the purpose of legal reform as one of bringing the law into line with a contentious vision of equality. The two casualties of this approach considered (and hopefully redeemed) in this essay have been the sociology of sex-roles and tort law. In view of the strategic purposes to which sociological role theories lend themselves in legal arguments on sexual harassment, they may appear just as good as, if not occasionally better than, more far-reaching accounts of the purchase of 'masculinism' on the social structure and the sexually-differentiated psyche. Just as sex-role sociology cannot be judged on the basis of its theoretical claims and assumptions so, too, torts of sexual invasion are not premised on any single, patriarchal ideology. On the contrary, they furnish useful supplementary ammunition to lawyers and litigants in pursuance of anti-discrimination remedies against sexual harassment.

To conclude, the *imprimatur* placed by the Supreme Court in *Meritor Savings Bank v Vinson* on the possibility of justiciating sexual harassment does not have to signify the end of the (qualified) success-story recounted by MacKinnon. It might also be taken to signal the *start* of a different story of a broader, infra-legal government of sexual harassment operating in the capillaries as well as the legal capitals of the social body. This is a liberal tale, to be sure, but one which does not simply recapitulate that classical liberal perspective according to which, in the words of John Locke, 'the care of every man's soul . . . does not belong to the magistrate . . . but . . . is to be left unto himself' (Locke, 1667, 1956, p. 139). A liberal governmental policy needs not content itself with legal measures aimed at providing remedies to aggrieved individuals. What is needed is a broader infra-legal policing of manners aimed at empowering women and producing forms of conscientiousness on the part of men. The business of good 'social' government cannot be left up to *either* 'the individual' *or* 'the magistrate' alone.

5 Second Principles of Social Justice

Introduction

How far is it possible to regulate sexual harassment by legal means? Drawing for the most part on the Australian federal (rather than the Australian states') sex-discrimination legislation and its accompanying instrumentalities; on a range of both federal and state tribunal cases; and on a series of informal interviews with practitioners, I approach this question by postulating certain *ethical conditions* for its current and continuing justiciability. A motley set, these conditions do not readily lend themselves to being assembled under the rubrics of *philosophical (or political-ideological) justification* through which legal and ethical concerns are usually brought together. Thus the principal candidate for this status, equality between the sexes, I suggest, forms but one of these conditions and may also be open to a non-philosophical interpretation. The unlawful status of sexual harassment hinges on considerations of 'good manners' and bodily integrity, honour and shame, natural justice, vicarious liability, and judicial judgements concerning 'character'. These 'secondary' considerations also involve matters of principle. Contrary to what is often thought, equality is not the 'first' or the only principle at stake.

Whilst these ethical considerations justify its legal regulation, they do so in ways which are not independent of positive legal reasoning in the way moral principles in law are usually thought to be – in some instances they are built into the very wording and technical *modus operandi* of the law. They are not only 'conditions' but also 'constituents'.[1] Conversely, these ethico-technical factors are not purely internal to law. They also constitute political and cultural conditions for the public acceptability of making certain sorts of sexual harassment unlawful. Politically and culturally acceptable to whom? it will be asked. A case will be made that a plurality of variously overlapping, conflicting or simply disconnected constituencies may need to be taken into account: women, the electorate as a whole, the legal establishment and profession, as well as the diverse strands of both organised feminist opinion and even to a certain extent anti-feminist opinion.

To some feminist critics of the legislation, this patently liberal argument

90

may sound like a recipe for arriving at a neutered law predicated on a politics of the lowest common denominator and rendered powerless to address a problem overwhelmingly affecting a particular 'constituency', namely women. But anti-feminist opponents of the legislation are no more likely to be satisfied by the limited, *tactical* recognition accorded to (some of) their concerns. True, I attempt to fend off radical criticism of current sexual harassment law from both feminist and anti-feminist quarters; moreover, this is done partly from a liberal point of view. For all that, the argument is no stock exercise in 'liberal fence-sitting'. It is both a defence of the law, pro-feminist components and all (though not as something beyond improvement) and a defence of a 'liberal point of view' which aims to accommodate certain basic feminist concerns about liberal philosophy.

Finally, amongst that plurality of relevant concerns and constituencies, none is more important than those pertaining to the jurisdiction and *cultural* environment of the common law. Attention to the array of 'second principles' at work in sex-discrimination law calls into question the frequently expressed perception that the traditional common law is an unmitigated obstacle to making sexual harassment justiciable.

Outline of the Commonwealth Legislation

Sexual harassment is defined for the purposes of the Australian Commonwealth Sex Discrimination Act (1984, henceforth SDA) as any unwelcome conduct (including 'statements') of a sexual nature, rejection of, or objection to which disadvantages the other person's employment, or in the case of educational institutions, their studies (ss.28–29). A provision for combating sex discrimination with respect to 'the provision of goods, facilities and services and accommodation' (section 3(b)) makes sexual harassment by an employer or an employee against a customer in a bar or restaurant, by a landlord against a tenant or even by the employer against their domestic help also unlawful. Sections 14 and 105–106 build in employers' or educational institutional authorities' vicarious liability for harassment by employees unless the former are able to show that they have taken 'all reasonable steps' to pre-empt such incidents.

A pre-existing statutory corporation, now called the Human Rights and Equal Opportunity Commission (HREOC) is responsible for implementing the legislation.[2] The Act invests commissioners with the powers and responsibilities, firstly, to receive and process complaints. Secondly, having judged that a complaint is not *prima facie* 'frivolous, vexatious, misconceived, or lacking in substance' (s.52(2)(d)), an initial phase of investigation and negotiations aimed at securing voluntary settlement must be initiated. These are conducted under strictly confidential conditions by aides known as 'conciliation officers'. Thirdly, if conciliation fails (a judgement which carries no imputations of fact or guilt) the complaint (unless withdrawn) must go to a public tribunal hearing. This is constituted as a (non-criminal) civil enquiry, presided over by either the president of the commission or one of the commissioners (barring the one involved in processing the complaint thus far). The commission is also entrusted with an *educational* brief 'to promote recognition and acceptance within the community of the principle of the equality of men and women' (s.3(d)).

The tribunal enquiry, asserts the statute, 'is not bound by the rules of evidence': it is to be conducted as informally and expeditiously as compliance with the requirements of the Act permit (s.77(1)). The tribunal is thus not strictly speaking a court of law. Its powers are nevertheless considerable. It can (a) compel the attendance of both the parties to the dispute and any material witnesses; (b) obtain any relevant documentation; and (c) if the complaint is substantiated by the enquiry, make a 'determination'. These outcomes may include enjoining the 'respondent' to apologise to, re-employ, promote, or financially compensate the 'complainant'. This compensation is calculated according to criteria ranging from loss of earnings to compensable detriments to mental and physical health. At the discretion of the commission, parties to the dispute are entitled to legal representation. Should the commissioners' 'determinations' not be complied with (since they are not an exercise of the Commonwealth's judicial powers), they are 'enforceable' in the federal court (section 82, ss.1). There, however, the case must be reheard in its entirety.[3] In spite of the statutory license not to be bound by the rules of evidence most tribunals do in fact proceed on the basis of criteria of evidence approximating the civil ('balance of probabilities') standard of proof which the federal court is obliged to use (Ronalds, 1987, p. 183).

States with anti-discrimination legislation already in place contribute both precedents and personnel for the implementation of the federal legislation (Ronalds, 1987, p. 176). Where state and federal legislation conflict, or where a state lacks an anti-discrimination law, federal law prevails (*Viskauskas v Niland* 1985, 57 ALJR 414). Like any federal legislation, its constitutional validity depends upon its provisions falling under one or more of a number of the 'heads' of Commonwealth powers over the states embodied in the Australian Constitution. In this case the external powers provision (section 51, *placitum* 39) was invoked. Commonwealth authority for the legislation over all states, in particular those with no anti-discrimination legislation of their own, was established through the device of invoking Australia's having become a signatory to an international covenant, the United Nations Convention On The Elimination Of All Forms Of Discrimination Against Women which was ratified by the Commonwealth government in August 1983. Giving effect to 'certain provisions' of this convention is the first stated 'object' of the Act (s.3(d)).

Two Shoals of Criticism

Mostly emanating from the 'new right' end of the political spectrum, anti-feminist criticism of sex-discrimination and related equal opportunity law tends to hinge on its alleged deviation from the time-honoured spirit and methods of the English common law. On one side we have a tried and trusted model of 'gradual social change through the determination of individual disputes . . . Draw[ing] upon precedents embodying the public morality developed over the ages . . . For the express purpose of defining, protecting and enforcing human rights', on the other, an alien equity programme aimed at engineering changes in public morality by legislative fiat, enshrining rights for a fanatical feminist minority which 'can be effectively enforced only at the expense of traditional liberties' (Cooray, 1985, p. 34).

Australian sex discrimination law, it is asserted, provides a charter for arbitrary quasi-judicial tribunals run by ideologically driven political-administrative agencies. In support of this thesis, Chipman (1985) invokes the SDA provisions that HREOC tribunal hearings need not be bound by the rules of evidence (s.77(1)); and that the right to legal representation is subject to the permission of the commission. Why, he asks (ignoring the difference between civil and criminal law), should a complaint of sex-discrimination require less supporting evidence than a charge of shoplifting? In keeping with the 'totalistic language' of the UN Convention by which it is authorised (Levin, 1984, p. 62), the educational brief of the Commission is a license for the 'totalitarian' propagation of a particular ideological viewpoint under the auspices of the state, and funded from public revenue. It is alleged that irrespective of the legal qualifications of commissionary staff, it is their track record of feminist activism which most qualifies them for appointment (Chipman, *ibid.*, p. 27). The ultimate aim of this 'thought-police' is to make sexist thoughts and attitudes inexpressible (*ibid.*, p. 26). Sex and race discrimination law override common law rights to 'offensive free speech' and 'private' acts of discrimination on the part of an employer ('having regard to his personal likes and dislikes') with respect to his employees (Cooray, 1989; 1985, p. 92).

The capacity of this 'common-law-libertarianism'[4] to serve as an echo-chamber for widely-held fears, feelings and concerns should not be under-estimated. Moreover, these criticisms occasionally pick out possibilities of malpractice and arbitrary decision-making and the occasional irregularity which, if generally realised or not corrected, would give friends of civil liberties cause for concern. No matter if it persistently trades on ignorance, distortion and misogyny, common-law-libertarianism is a viewpoint which supporters of sex-discrimination law ignore at their peril.

The feminist lines of criticism questioned in this essay mirror the common-law-libertarian critique in two ways. Whereas common law lib-ertarians complain that sexual harassment law goes too far, their feminist counterparts insist that it fails to go far enough. To define sexual harass-ment as 'unwelcome conduct of a sexual nature' likely to 'disadvantage the other person's employment' (SDA 1984, section 28(3)(a)) is to legitimate comparable sexist behaviour occurring both within the workplace and without (Stanley and Wise, 1987).

A second kind of general argument will link this allegedly arbitrary limitation on the scope of equal opportunity law to a 'liberal-patriarchal' strategy which is simultaneously manifest and concealed in the philo-sophical concept of the 'civil individual' on which all such legislation is said to hinge (Pateman, 1988). The recognition of women as individuals under liberalism places them at a double disadvantage. Not only does the feminine tend to be excluded from the public sphere on the basis of being identified (through a 'fraternal sexual contract') with the private dimension of civil society. Women who do work are also, like men, subject to a common condition of 'civil slavery' which is ideologically occluded by the formal equalities and freedoms established in the con-tract of employment. Whilst liberal rhetoric provides some bases for pushing equal opportunity policies in subversive directions, in general they are irredeemably mortgaged to a 'catch-up' logic which at best allows a few women to participate (on men's terms) in the world of work. 'Equal to' in this liberal-contractual universe means the 'same as' men, who lose nothing by it, since relevant sexual differences in opportunities are excluded from consideration by that work of calculated abstraction which consists in treating people as 'individuals' (Game, 1984).

In this expansion of the arbitrary limitation hypothesis, yet another parallel to the common-law-libertarian critique can be glimpsed. Albeit in different ways, both the feminist and anti-feminist critiques work by exposing equal opportunity laws as the expression of an ideology, which is either identified with the principles of liberal philosophy or identified as an

equally damning failure to apply them. For the common-law-libertarian, the
ideological bogeyman determining legislative provision and tribunal procedures is liberalism's popular-democratic-egalitarian stripe, generalised to
a totalitarian degree, that is to the point of transgressing the liberal principle
of individual liberty. For his feminist counterpart, the ideological significance of the law lies in its commitment to an implicitly ('masculinist')
abstract individualism and its consequent failure to carry the ostensible
liberal commitment to equality and individual self-determination to their
logical conclusion. In Pateman, this ideological meaning of women's
legal construction as civil persons in contract law is directly inferred
from a reading of the liberal principles of liberty, equality (and, secretly,
fraternity) associated with *philosophical* contract theories. In both cases a
similar principle of critical interpretation is in play.

Whilst these radical critiques might well furnish grounds for opposing
all legal measures, they also carry conviction amongst some feminists who
assume the need to engage with legal and social policy processes from
within. Amongst the more specific institutional and procedural obstacles
to effective laws pertaining to sexual harassment identified in this more
'reformist' feminist literature are included: reliance on the adversary
system and the resulting pressures of cross-examination; the advantages
accruing to respondents able to afford expensive legal representation;
inappropriately stringent rules of evidence; the insistence on a 'subjective' test of the respondent's intentions; reluctance to apply vicarious
liability provisions to employer bodies or to compel them to establish
in-house policies and procedures; opportunistic invocations of natural
justice requirements; the preference for conciliating complaints privately
over bringing them to a public hearing.[5]

These criticisms run in different directions. Some object to the
unnecessarily stressful and stringent nature of the legal process.
Others complain of a reluctance to bring the full weight of the
law to bear on alleged offenders. One of the tasks of this essay is
to ask whether these concerns may be disentwined from the sweeping
claims of the anti-liberal feminist critique. Without attempting to meet
it head-on, I will venture to suggest that the price of sexual harassment laws operating within a 'liberal' framework is not necessarily a
blindness to the sex-specific nature of the problem; that the equali-
sation in status promoted by legal action against sexual harassment
need not be premised upon 'male' definitions of the problem and
the norms from which it deviates; and that the forms of legal
action currently available are not entirely inappropriate to dealing
with it.

Philosophical Idealisations and Ethical Culture

I have advanced the hypothesis that not all the ethical constituents of
sex-discrimination law can be captured by adverting to the moral or
political philosophy by which it is supposedly underpinned. Let us once
again rehearse the 'anthropological' conception of ethics informing this
hypothesis; only this time, with special reference to its legal bearings.

It begins with the proposition that principles and related forms of idealisation such as those embodied in the egalitarian intent of discrimination
legislation are only *one* component of *some* ethical cultures, and not always
the most important component at that. Ethical cultures also include the
'examples' (model forms of conduct, demeanour, life-histories, etc.) through
which ethical conduct is actually taught; and the not entirely edifying
forms of sensibility on which ethical training depends (e.g. honour and
shame). They have an important technical dimension too: the successful
performance of an ethical action or judgement depends not only or even
necessarily on its rational justification, a good will or unspotted intentions,
but also upon a set of capacities which are by no means innate or evenly
distributed amongst all human beings.

Ethical judgements and actions can come unstuck in so many ways:
they can be indiscriminate, inappropriate, moralistically worded or staged,
or lacking in moral authority. Techniques of effective ethical judgement
and action include the 'casuistical' capacity to 'square' principles not only
with other principles but also with an understanding of the circumstances
surrounding a particular case; the 'character' and associated capacities of
individuals involved; and the amoral or even immoral exigencies which are
inseparable from particular social activities. Ethical culture thus includes
ways of shaping oneself in such a way as to be ethically competent. And
it includes the more or less localised or specialised *milieus* in which one
acquires those competences: physical and architectural arrangements which
dispose individuals to make, or become the subject of, certain kinds of
ethical judgement (as we will see shortly, equal opportunity commission
offices are an 'ethical milieu' in this sense).

To conceive the ethical as a hybrid realm of material culture is not to
deny that first principles may play an important role in it. In civilian
legal cultures, for instance, ethical-political principles enjoy something
like a socially defined approximation to a foundational status, albeit not
to the extent that civilian legal philosophers pretend (David and Brierley,
1985, pp. 124–25, 143–45). Nor is this conception of the ethical predicated
upon seeing it as being more a matter of custom and feelings than about
'reasons'; as though styles of reasoning were not themselves habitual.

The analysis of 'cases' in medicine and, closer to our concerns, in the common law itself, are two of the main institutional models on which this casuistical conception of ethical judgement is based. The fact that it does not take the form of deductions from general principles does not *always* preclude it from drawing upon *any* general considerations (as long as the cases to which they are applied are sufficiently similar to the 'paradigm cases' from which the general considerations were drawn). One doesn't have to be a born-again common-law libertarian to see that the casuistical form assumed by ethical judgement according to this model of ethical culture does not preclude the possibility of arriving at appropriate, fair and *equitable* judgements (Jonsen and Toulmin, 1988, pp. 256–59).

Given the proverbially casuistical form of 'the common law mind' and the fact that Australian sex-discrimination law has somehow to be made to work inside a common law legal system, there is surely something to be said for bringing this approach to ethics to bear on an investigation of the ethical constituents of that law. To begin with, what is the status of the principle of equality deployed in this legislation?

Equality and Ethical Culture

Along with the elimination of sexual harassment, the stated 'objects' overarching the federal legislation include the promotion of a general principle of equality between the sexes (SDA, 1984, s.3). Its abstraction from sex-based specificities make this principle an irresistible target for both feminist and anti-feminist criticism. But is it appropriate to treat it as the cornerstone of the legislation and hence as that on which it either stands or falls? Equality may be the most important principle at stake, but is it the only one? What sort of mundane forms of equality can it be expected to yield in practice? The need to take sex-based differences in material circumstances and needs, status, desires, etc. into account in cashing out principles of equality is not in dispute. However, in order to do so is it necessary to develop an equally general, feminist concept of equality as a substitute for the bogus liberal one?

Rather than dwell on attempts in feminist jurisprudence to supply this lack (e.g. Littleton, 1987), let us examine a practical example of the dialectics entailed in such a project in the document which furnished the justification for Australian federal anti-discrimination legislation covering sexual harassment: the *U.N. Convention On The Elimination Of All Forms Of Discrimination Against Women*. It has been criticised for its liberal-individualist assumptions (Burrows, 1986). Yet, in its declamatory opening paragraphs, a vision of 'full equality' between the sexes is outlined which turns on an organicist philosophy of society and human personhood. Equality means 'full development of the potentialities of women in the service of their countries and of humanity' as well as through the exercise of the (negative) individual liberty which is their human birthright. To accord equal personhood to women in this dialectical way is hardly to assimilate them to a flat individualist abstraction concealing an inventory of 'masculine' possibilities.

However, this attempt to truly universalise the principle does not prevent these declarations from being both excessively and insufficiently determinate in content. The Convention endows the principle with too much content to the extent that it identifies anti-discrimination policies with a substantive vision of 'full equality', female autonomy and social integration. The problem for any government of a (would-be) liberal polity intent upon giving effect to the Convention is that this vision and those values are contestable and hence breach the liberal criterion of political neutrality in respect to competing substantive visions of the good life (Larmore, 1987, ch. 3). That is why, to the extent that sex-discrimination legislation lends itself to interpretation as being *founded* upon the principles of sex-equality in the convention, it lays itself open to those common-law-libertarian depictions of its legislators as having thrown their weight behind one ideological point of view for the purpose of dragooning 'the rest of society' into conformity.

Signatories to UN conventions are not obliged to follow their recommendations to the letter. Consequently, no general inferences can be drawn about the Australian legislation from the totalitarian implications of the Convention's rhetorical flourishes. Yet to ignore the ammunition which the Convention in places provides for opponents of the legislation would be equally mistaken. Appeals to 'full equality' could be taken to provide a charter for extending the purchase of legal regulation to cover every conceivable kind of sex-inequality, irrespective of the benefit to women of so doing or of the public discredit it is likely to bring on sex-discrimination legislation.

For instance, one may have no liking for the practice of aiming to increase the numbers of female customers in discotheques by discounting the cost of entry to female customers. But to categorise it as unlawful discrimination may lend credence to the common-law libertarian's interpretation of the legislation as a harbinger of a totalitarian nanny-state. *Tully v Ceridale* (1990, EOC 92–319) established that this discounting practice did constitute unlawful sex-discrimination in the provision of goods and services. No woman was disadvantaged by it and the male complainant suffered no social injustice. Yet, after initially dismissing the complaint as trivial, the HREOC was obliged to process it, finding that it did constitute 'disparate treatment' within the meaning of the act. The key to this decision, affirmed the presiding commissioner, was the principle of equality as set out in the associated UN declaration.

The case also illustrates how subsuming sex-discrimination legislation under a general principle of equality renders its object *insufficiently determinate*. That object was set out in unmistakable terms by Justice Stephen in the landmark Victorian sex-discrimination case, *Ansett Transport Industries v Wardley* (1984) 92–003, 75, 271:

> the question . . . resolves itself, in the end, into a search for legislative intent. The act (i.e. The Equal Opportunity Act, 1977) *gives legislative effect throughout the Victorian community to a broad social policy concerned with the status of women* in that community. (my emphasis)

In other words, state (and federal) legislation cannot be read as an attempt to give legislative effect to a universal principle of equality between the sexes which is abstract to the social problems currently faced by women in particular. In *Aldridge v Booth* (1987), with a view to challenging the SDA's constitutional validity, the respondent's defence sought to exploit the seeming generality of the principle of equality by driving a wedge between s.28 of the SDA (on the unlawfulness of sexual harassment) and the UN convention which authorises the Commonwealth legislation. The consequences of the former's dependence on the latter (via the External Powers provisions of the Australian Constitution) is to make it 'improbable' (despite the gender-neutral terminology of sections 28–29 of the Act) that all men can secure protection from sexual harassment under the Act.[6] The defence claimed that this restriction 'confers on [women] an advantage not enjoyed by men'. This is inconsistent, it was said, with Article 1 of the Convention, which stipulates that the purpose of eliminating sex discrimination is to promote equality between men and women. Justice Spender's response is worth quoting at length:

> the argument of the respondents assumes that one cannot promote the exercise and enjoyment of rights "on the basis of equality with men" by prohibiting discrimination against women. There is in this argument a necessity for a legislative prohibition of sexual harassment of men to be in existence . . . . If this argument of the respondents be right, legislation prohibiting the killing of young girls would be inconsistent and contrary to the terms of the convention, unless there was in existence legislation prohibiting the killing of young boys, even though in fact,

the killing of young girls was widespread, and the killing of young boys
non-existent or rare. The fact that the legislation . . . does not address
sexual harassment of men in the workplace is irrelevant . . . (*Aldridge
v Booth*, 1987, s.22, 30)

Justice Spender's judgement is not a once-and-for-all endorsement
of the fact that section 28 of the SDA does not afford remedies for
all men. Some men may be vulnerable to sexual harassment. Under
state sex-discrimination legislation (and under certain circumstances, in
Commonwealth legislation too) they would be entitled to protection. Even
in states without such legislation they may be covered in other ways. If a
sexually harassed man cannot secure legal redress then that might be an
argument for reform.[7] *Not* to frame the provisions of the federal legislation
relating to sexual harassment in gender-neutral terms would be to invite
injustice. However, in arguing the case for doing justice to men who are
sexually harassed, we are talking about a secondary consequence of there
being such a law. The *social* problem which necessitated it overwhelmingly
concerns the treatment of women.[8] Yes, justice *tout court* must be served
(complaints proceedings must respect the demands of legal order). But
the legislation may also unashamedly present itself as an instrument of a
social policy aimed at redressing the disadvantages suffered by women as a
social group. Along with the HREOC's educational remit, the judgements
of Justices Stephen and Spender suggest that this social justice objective
corresponds to the intent of the legislation. To that extent, the legislation
goes some way to meeting feminist concerns about liberal legislation on
the grounds of its dependence upon abstract principles which are indifferent
to the sex-specific nature of the problems which the legislation is meant to
remedy.

However, one cannot argue that point without conceding the existence
of a measure of tension between the social justice intent of the legislation
and the general principle of equality between the sexes upon which *prima
facie* the legislation is founded. Whether a formula for the principle of
sex-equality could be found which was immune to the twin dangers of
rendering it either too determinate (too committed to controversial socio-
political values), or insufficiently determinate (abstract to the social policy
objectives of the legislation), may be doubted. The tactical need for *some*
general principle of sex-equality is clear enough (on account of the UN
warrant for legislative action). But how much importance should be given
to it? Perhaps a more promising basis for anti-discrimination arguments is
furnished by the more specific claims to equality of treatment found in the
UN convention, such as the demand that signatories make provision for

women's maternity and other equal employment opportunities (art. 11) or 'accord to women in civil matters a legal capacity equal to men' (art. 15). For at these points the document is pointing to irredeemably undialectical, piecemeal 'civil' legal statuses, such as the right to sue and be sued, which certainly do not owe their existence to any general ideal of full equality.

These forms of 'civil capacity' correspond of course to one of the four types of citizenship status distinguished by T. H. Marshall (1949). Suppose one were to downplay the teleological significance which he attributed to citizenship (according to which citizen-statuses may be interpreted as steps to an ideal republic) in favour of attention to the more administratively attuned sides of his arguments (see Chapter 7). On this interpretation, sex-discrimination laws offering protection (*inter alia*) against sexual harassment may be seen as intended to place women on a basis of occupational equality only within highly determinate work categories, statuses and calculations. Considered as an 'industrial citizenship' status in Marshall's sense, treatment as an occupational equal for this purpose carries no *necessary* implications for any other conceivable equalisations in, across or beyond work environments.[9]

In this respect, the equalities of status associated with anti-discrimination law need not be seen as qualitatively different from the sorts of occupational equality (insufficient though these may have been) which women enjoyed before the advent of sex-discrimination legislation. For instance, the confirmation of women's 'right to work' (as set out in the Sex Disqualification (Removal) Act, 1919) in *Nagle v Feilden* (1966, QB) disconfirms the common-law-libertarian's claim that, unlike sex-discrimination law, the common law can always be relied upon to construe individuals' likes and dislikes, however unreasonable, as constituting a 'private' realm of negative liberty which the law must safeguard at all costs.[10]

Summing up, it looks as though the general philosophical principle of sex-equality set out in the UN declaration cannot tell us very much about which practices of equality in the workplace are worth fighting for and defending; and which practices of inequality are too frivolous to make a 'federal' case out of them. In order to reinforce the argument for a more modest view of the kind of equality at stake in sexual harassment law, a series of *non*-egalitarian ethical bases for its successful operation and legitimacy will be reviewed.

Bad Manners and Bodily Integrity

The first task is to restate the case for seeing one of the objectionable elements in sexual harassment which provides a basis for its establishment as a legal category and a social problem as consisting in a breach of *manners*. To see sexual harassment in this way means equating it to a breach of sexual etiquette and interpersonal 'social' protocols *which are not always sex-specific*. Thus, sexual harassment may be likened to a more general class of inconsiderate behaviour or gross impoliteness which is commonly, but not exclusively, directed by men against women. It includes standing too close to another, presuming an inappropriate familiarity, staring at strangers, gate-crashing another's sphere of activities, and putting them in a position of having to say no.

But, surely, it will be objected, acceptance of these analogies is equivalent to saying that sexual harassment is only a superficial matter. And aren't gentlemanly codes of manners in regard to 'ladies' one of the most important ways in which women's subordination is accomplished in 'patriarchal' societies? [11]

On any reckoning, sexual harassment involves an invasion of a woman's personal space. In most analyses its invasive aspects are understood in terms of their representing a transgression of personhood. However, the history of European absolutist 'court societies' sketched in Chapters 2 and 3 suggests that this invasive aspect of the behaviour we call sexual harassment was called into question long before the advent of universalistic valorisations of 'the person'. Rather, it was in the newfound respect for both the bodily integrity and intellectual capacities of aristocratic women which accompanied the transformation of late-medieval and Renaissance warrior-aristocracies into courtiers that the conceptual equivalent of what *we* now call 'personal space' achieved a restricted cultural distribution in European 'court societies'.

Historically, the notion of bodily integrity involves constructing individuals, both men and women (originally, of course, mainly the well-born), as bearers of a 'dignitary' space extending over the contours of the body and extending beyond and around it in such a way as to prescribe and symbolise appropriate measures of social distance, and hence polite respect or self-restraint for those who occupy this status. However, it is because the repertoire of good manners (staring, bodily proximity, familiarities . . .) *continues* to include the very means by which the boundary-lines of personal space (in the sense of bodily integrity) are drawn by both sexes that the judgements of superficiality, aristocratic archaism and patriarchal condescension so often levelled at the language of manners are misplaced. A policing of manners is on the contrary an indispensible concomitant of a democratic political culture. 'Correct' conduct towards a woman worker is thus a token and prerequisite of respect for her status as a working colleague, and hence of respect for the work she does. In

T. H. Marshall's terms, it is a practical concomitant of equal 'industrial citizenship'.

Equipped with this historical, ethical-cultural perspective on manners and bodily integrity, and their possible compatibility with a feminist perspective on women's industrial citizenship, the next question is whether and to what extent common law torts of sexual invasion which we encountered in Chapter 4 are hospitable to these notions where they crop up in Australian sexual harassment law. One explicit attempt to link contemporary sex-discrimination legislation to traditional common law protections of bodily integrity occurs in the recent landmark sexual harassment case, the federal court rehearing of *Aldridge v Booth* (Qld g22, 1987). At one point, Lynette Aldridge's case against her employer turned on establishing the fact that his behaviour had created a 'hostile environment' for her. To that end, it was suggested that one intention behind s.28 of the Sex Discrimination Act is to give effect to one of the specific purposes of the UN convention already mentioned: namely, that more localised citizenship status referred to as 'the right to health and safety in working conditions'. And how is this phrase to be interpreted? As nothing less than 'the right to personal and physical integrity'. The psychological aspect of this integrity, it was contended, has long been written into that part of the common law known as the law of trespass: '. . . It is the mental element of the apprehension of battery which constitutes the tort'; the evil which Article 11 seeks to remedy then being tortuously defined as 'the mental element of the fear of invasion of one's person' (*Aldridge v Booth*, transcript, first day, pp. 67–68) – i.e. one's body and/or 'personal space'.

Ms Aldridge's counsel's attempt to construct a pedigree for sex discrimination law in torts of sexual invasion is no 'one-off' improvisation. In another tribunal hearing, the Victorian Equal Opportunity Board likewise linked the 'benefit of employment' represented by a non-threatening environment to the concept of bodily integrity and hence to the issue of sex discrimination and harassment:

> The court further held that it is an act of discrimination to deny an employee a benefit connected with employment that accrues to other employees. A benefit of employment is quiet enjoyment, that is, freedom from physical intrusion or from being harassed . . . *Hutchinson and Smirlis* (1986, EOC 92–152, 76, 502).

It must be stressed that the relationship between anti-discrimination law and torts posited in this case is analogical rather than one of identity.

Neither in this nor any other Australian case I know of has sexual harassment been found to constitute a tortious injury.[12] Nevertheless, in view of these connections between disparate treatment and 'personal space' invasions, it is unsurprising to find that, following a positive finding of unlawful discriminatory conduct, the question of appropriate compensation is discussed primarily in the language of torts: chiefly, injury to feelings, pain and suffering and loss of enjoyment of life.

What has this legal relationship between sexual harassment, sex-discrimination and bodily integrity got to do with the realm of manners? Basically, reference to a regime of manners is made wherever the question of the *norms or standards* of non-discriminatory conduct is raised. Legal equations between sexual harassment and breaches of common politeness abound; as for example in *Kiel v Weeks'* (1989, EOC, 92–245) references to 'boorish behaviour'. The link between such anti-discriminatory norms and 'the civilising process' is made explicit in a particularly horrific case, *Queen v Equal Opportunity Board, Ex Parte Burns* (1985, V.R.). There, Justice Nathan characterises the acts of 'fingering' the complainant whilst she was forcibly restrained as 'offending the standards of right and decent behaviour between members of opposite sexes' and, by dint of that offence, discriminatory: 'Less favourable treatment' ('the substantive phrase of this Act') occurs if the ordinary standards of acceptable conduct for one sex are not extended to the other. 'Fingering' falls outside acceptable conduct' (1985, V.R. 322).

Justice Nathan's judgement permits the question of whether sex-discrim-ination law is implicated in a patriarchal 'protection racket' to arise in the sharpest possible way. For in characterising the respondent's conduct as 'unacceptable' in this way, he refers to Lord Denning's judgement in a case brought under the British Sex Discrimination Act (1975), *Peake v Automotive Products* (1978, QB). That complaint was directed against the traditional practice of allowing the (minority of) women who worked in the plant to stop work for five minutes before the men at the end of the day in the interests of safety. Rejecting the complaint, Lord Denning refused to interpret the 'less favourable treatment' clause of the Act in such a way as to 'obliterate the differences between men and women or to do away with the chivalry or courtesy which we expect mankind to give womankind (. . . and which) we have been taught to believe is right conduct in our society' (*Peake*, p. 238).

The assumption is of course that the weaker sex is paid this chivalrous respect in the common law, and where more so than in respect to tortious injuries? *Peake* seems to confirm MacKinnon's (1979) view that such legal discourse is mortgaged to those traditional good manners which symbolise and reinforce women's subordination, such as gallantry. Yet Lord Denning's invocation of chivalry as lawful discrimination cannot be interpreted as representative of 'the common law view'; it was subsequently overturned in *Ministry of Defence v Jeremiah* (1979, 3 All. ER 833). In any case, not all acts of sex-discrimination are 'averse to either sex' (*Peake*, p. 240). The SDA (s.30) itself lists unobjectionable grounds on which discrimination is lawful, such as protection against body searches by a member of the opposite sex. Above all, the *use* of Denning's opinion in *R v. Equal Opportunity Board, Ex Parte Burns* consists in placing his views in the service of an explicitly sex-neutral conception of the ordinary standards of civil conduct at issue. Contravention of these standards falls under the SDA insofar as it represents a disparate treatment on the basis of sex (since the acceptable conduct in question cannot legitimately be applied to one sex and not the other).

Egalitarian, anti-sexist principles and norms of conduct at issue in sexual harassment at work may, then, be confirmed at law through their assimilation to a taken-for-granted aspect of mainstream ethical and legal culture, namely, standards of 'civilised manners'. Many of these standards of 'civility' have been and continue to be hostage to patriarchal attitudes. But is all considerate behaviour of this order? Polemically, these anti-discriminatory references to manners may be used to remind those who see sex discrimination legislation as alien to common law liberties of the common law pedigree of some of the protections furnished by such legislation. If the protection of working women from unwanted sex-based 'invasions' conflicts with men's right to offensive free speech or behaviour, as Cooray implied, then this is simply one more instance of the need to weigh conflicting common law rights and liberties in the legal balance. Why should it be legitimate to limit free speech on the grounds of its being libellous but not when it jeopardises the right to 'quiet employment'? Or, when it jeopardises 'the right of a man (*sic*) to work at his trade without being unjustly excluded from it' (*Nagle v Feilden*, 1966, 2 QB 644)?

It would be a pity were the undoubted advantages of sex-discrimination law over private tort actions from a feminist point of view to blind its advocates to the sorts of supportive cross-references assembled in the last few pages between anti-discrimination law and common law protections of individuals' rights to bodily integrity and peaceful employment.[13] The breach of norms of polite and professionally respectful conduct which I have here sought to suggest constitute part of the 'ethical substance' of sexual harassment in the eyes of the law provide a useful key to understanding those affinities and their importance. They are both operational (as we have seen in *Aldridge*'s case, these affinities are successfully mobilised in legal arguments) and a hitherto underexploited resource for 'legitimating' sexual harassment law. In general, Australian sex-discrimination law might be seen as an attempt not to displace but to remould and supplement older (and mostly ineffective) common-law provisions for the protection of women's bodily integrity, by instituting a legal basis for a wider reform of 'inequitable manners'.

Honour and Shame in the Conciliation Process

The *conciliation* of complaints is inseparable from dispositions towards oneself and others associated with *honour and shame*. Two statutory requirements of the conciliation process permit these less than egalitarian considerations to come into play: its confidentiality and its designated objective – the statutory requirement in the 1984 Act (s.73) that the commission 'endeavour' to effect 'an amicable settlement of a complaint'. The conciliator is expected to investigate a complaint and play a neutral, 'ring-holding' role. Any settlement reached through conciliation must therefore be, in the words of the current HREOC 'Conciliation and Complaints Procedures' brochure, 'voluntary and mutually satisfactory'. Given these terms of reference, it is not surprising to find that the achievement of settlements sometimes depends upon not driving the respondent into a humiliating corner.[14] For instance, the price of eliciting an admission of fault and reparations from the respondent may well be to allow him the benefit of a benign but misunderstood, 'honourable' intention. Considerations of honour and shame may also operate to foreshorten both the fact-finding and mediating processes of the conciliation procedure itself. Irrespective of either his culpability or the strength of the case against him, a well-off respondent may well pull out his cheque-book at the outset. A private and confidential settlement avoids the potential damage to the respondent's reputation which might result from the complaint's going beyond the conciliation stage to a public hearing.

In a contemporary ethical climate in which honour and shame have come to appear in a questionable light, it is only to be expected if these concomitants of conciliation are found worrisome:

> Conciliation . . . means . . . compromise . . .   The culture and habits of conciliation officers are such that they will seek to communicate the common ground between the parties – that often being synonymous with the lowest common denominator. Settlements are usually produced on this basis even if the strict legal requirements of the legislation are flouted. (Cited in Ellis, 1988, pp. 144–45)

The implication of this report on the workings of the English anti-discrimination law is that the intentions of the legislation are bound to be defeated by the very nature of conciliation. Either conciliators will idealistically strive to attain communicative transparency between the conflicting parties; or, more likely, failing this, they will settle for a shabby, 'face-saving' compromise.

In this perspective, the heart of the legislation consists in its recognising women's basic human right to participate in the workforce on the basis of equality with men. This right should not be treated as a bargaining chip at a negotiating table. If it is simply a question of one party's being in the right and the other in the wrong then what is there to negotiate about? Conciliation is a mendacious 'fraud' against women which casts a shadow over the whole current legislative strategy for making sex-discrimination justiciable. If anything, conciliation works to consolidate the inequalities of power in society by failing to bring perpetrators of discrimination to public account and to bring down a clear conviction (Gregory, 1981; Scutt, 1986, esp. pp. 10ff.).

Social and legal justice for women *may* be compromised by the heavy accent placed on conciliation in the Australian legislation. But are these the only ethical considerations to be reckoned with? Equally questionable is the moral-rationalist antipathy to the *negotiatory* element in conciliation implicit in this critical perspective. Negotiation inhibits the strict allocation of guilt and responsibility in accordance with the demands of reason and justice. From this Kantian perspective the component of honour and shame entailed in the conciliation process must appear especially problematic, with its tolerance of mixed motivations (e.g. concern for public reputation), and its tinge of mendacity.

But to what extent does the practice of conciliating sexual harassment complaints in Australia correspond to these philosophical terms of criticism? If either of the parties does not desire to confront the other in person, then separate 'conferences' may be held. The attention of both parties is drawn to the formal (and unnegotiable) legal basis of a complaint, to determining the legally relevant facts and setting them before the parties (Ronalds, 1987, p. 177). Thereafter, the conciliation style may vary (Ronalds, *ibid.*, p. 175). As for mendacity regarding the harasser's intention, if, as Ronalds (*ibid.*, p. 118) also points out, the harasser's 'subjective' intention is not germane to the determination of unlawful sexual harassment in a federal tribunal hearing, then why should the question of honourable intention never be allowed to 'float', so to speak, in conciliation conferences?

Even if some respondents do become genuinely upset and remorseful about their behaviour, purgative, self-transforming outcomes lending to reconciliation can hardly be the officially designated criterion of a successful conciliation. Should the unreconstructed attitudes of a respondent who wants to put the episode behind him as expeditiously as possible, by apologising or paying up, be of legitimate concern to a conciliator? This leads back into the more general problem of the criteria on which it is decided that a complaint cannot be conciliated and hence to the question of the desirability of conciliated settlements from a 'social justice' point of view.

In a recent discussion paper aimed at reviewing the Victorian Equal Opportunity Act, competing arguments on these issues were considered. Debate was no doubt occasioned by the fact that, at least during the mid-1980s, approximately 97 per cent of complaints in that state were settled at the conciliation stage.[15] On the one hand, it was suggested that such private settlements might be the result of parties' being pressured into unfair settlements and that they save the respondent from the (possibly) harsher results of the complaints being adjudicated at a public hearing. Moreover, it was felt that unless a significant proportion of complaints were referred to a public tribunal, 'the community' would not receive a loud enough signal concerning the unlawfulness of sexual harassment. Should certain complaints be so referred 'because of their potential for a wider effect'? it was asked. On the other hand, the inappropriateness of the equal opportunity board's pressuring complainants into participating in test cases was also noted.

To this dilemma might be added the difficulty of placing a single, comparative value on conciliation outcomes. For example, from the point of view of what complainants want out of the process, the significance of a 'mere' apology varies. Many complainants, it seems, would prefer winning an apology to financial compensation, either as a matter of principle or out of sensitivity to speculations about their motives in making the complaint.

The point of rehearsing this debate on the merits and demerits of conciliation is not to take sides but merely to suggest that in its very detail the question cannot be decided by reference to philosophical principles of social justice. Where a complainant wishes to settle at the conciliation stage, for example, calculations and feelings of honour and shame may, as we have just seen, run contrary to the social justice and educational policy aims of the legislation. However, it would be difficult to argue in the name of egalitarianism that the woman's preference for an 'honourable' settlement (or her reluctance to put herself through the distressful experience of a hearing) should be overridden. As in our discussion of manners, so in the case of honour and shame, the assumption that the essential 'ethical substance' of sexual harassment from the legal perspective is the question of (general) social and personal equality between the sexes founders in the face of evidence that other, and in this case sometimes discrepant ethical considerations are at stake in the process of implementing the law.

Anti-discrimination Law, Sexual Harassment and Natural Justice

One reason to be cautious about suggestions that the HREOC or its equivalent state bodies ought to promote more public hearings of sexual harassment complaints is the possibility that it would entail placing conciliators or the statutory body itself in a relation of advocacy to the complainant and hence in breach of natural justice requirements. The ethical and technical complexities involved in deciding on the applicability of the rules of natural justice suggest a need to reconsider two assumptions about the *limits* to the realisation of principles of social justice for women imposed by the exigencies of administering laws governing sexual harassment. The first assumption is that observance of natural justice is little more than a matter of regretful necessity, a concession to a legal ploy cynically aimed at preventing socially just outcomes. The second assumption is that its observance is simply a routine professional obligation. Whilst neither of these assumptions are without substance, both underestimate the ethical and political significance of regard for natural justice. Examine it not only as a matter of principle but as a component of an ethical and legal culture, and a case arises for regarding it as neither (entirely) a cynical nor a routine matter.

Within the common law, 'natural justice' signifies a well-known double duty of 'fair play'. Its first component is *the right to be heard*: the obligation to inform the subject of any decision in which their 'interests' are at stake and to afford them the opportunity to present testimony on their own behalf. This principle underpinned the reprimand handed down to the Victorian Equal Opportunity Board in the preliminaries of the previously discussed sexual harassment case *R v Equal Opportunity Board and Anon; Ex Parte Burns and Anor* (1985 Vr, 317). An allegation of sexual harassment against one of the respondents had been ventilated at an open hearing of the EOB in the absence of the respondent and without informing him of the nature and particulars of the complaint . The second principle is that no one ought to be a judge in their own cause; this is the subject-of-decision's right to be heard before an *unbiased* decision-maker. The bearing of this second principle, *nemo judex in sua causa*, was illustrated in *Koppen v Commissioner for Community Relations* (1986) EOC 92–173.[16]

The inapplicability of the *right-to-be-heard* rule in *Hill v Water*

Resources Commission (1985, EOC, 92–127), however, seems less straightforward. Here 'the respondent' was deemed to be not the personnel actually involved in (most of) the discriminatory behaviour but the employer body itself. Subsequently, complaints of a denial of natural justice were voiced in the press (Wyndham, 1985). The argument was that not having been joined as co-respondents to the complaint, the names of those actually involved were 'bandied about' in the hearing, charges of misconduct being made about them, without their having been given a right of reply. This complaint went no further, yet received qualified endorsement in a statement by a former deputy commissioner on the Victorian Equal Opportunity Board (Friedlander, 1985).

In this case, a non-specialist will hesitate to do much more than to note the existence of this concern about the applicability of the rules of natural justice. The circumstances in which the rules of natural justice are applicable has been an especially vexed issue in the field of non- or quasi-judicial administrative decisions (Hartley and Griffith, 1981, pp. 330–46). If counsels for respondents in anti-discrimination tribunal hearings are found ritually claiming that natural justice has not been observed in their client's case, that is only to be expected. And it is this practice which provides the basis for the first of the two attitudes to its constraints which I wish to discuss: namely that the invocation of natural justice is seldom anything but a cynical manoeuvre aimed at rendering anti-discrimination complaints procedures inoperable – especially when such appeals are made at every point in the investigative stages (Atkins and Hoggett, 1984, p. 38).

If only on tactical grounds, such generalised impatience with concern for natural justice in sex discrimination complaints seems difficult to justify. Even if there is reason not to dismiss this cynical view altogether, it surely stands to be corrected in the light of the following more commonsense angle on natural justice drawn from an EEO legislation handbook:

> The role of the conciliator also means that she or he must not appear to be acting in a way that favours one party to the detriment of the other. Some respondents may assume that, by the nature of their employment and the area they work in, conciliators will be biased against them. This is an unfortunate confusion of the role of the conciliator. They are professional bureaucrats in a position of administering a statute and hence their actions and decisions are determined by the wording of the statute and not by any personal beliefs or prejudices. (Ronalds, 1987, p. 177)

This assertion about the conciliator's professional obligation to maintain a neutral, 'ringholding' posture is constantly echoed in staff training manuals and tribunal judgements. It goes hand-in-hand with the provision that the investigating commissioner and the one who presides over the public hearing cannot be the same. If a reservation might be expressed about Ronalds's characterisation of natural justice constraints as a routine professional obligation, it is not so much about its correctness as about its matter-of-fact tenor. It is implied that there is no cause for any respondent in a sex-discrimination complaint even to *suppose* that in this area, natural justice principles would not be automatically applied in fact. Erroneous they may be, but are such preconceptions entirely adventitious ('an unfortunate confusion')?

One indication to the contrary is suggested by the way in which the Victorian equal opportunity apparatus has chosen to underline the stipulation that a commissioner presiding over a tribunal hearing shall not have been involved in investigating the complaint brought under it. The public hearing is held under the auspices of an 'equal opportunity board' which plays no part in the investigation and conciliation proceedings at all. Along with educational work, these initial phases in the processing of complaints are the responsibility of the 'Equal Opportunity Office', located on a separate floor of the building and separately staffed. Presumably 'walling off' the different facets of EEO commissions' work in this way is making some kind of public statement. Were there no question of the neutrality of the commission in the public's mind, this ethical-architectural statement would be unnecessary.[17]

Irrespective of whether this suspicion has any basis in fact, the social policy objectives of the legislation signalled in its authorising UN Convention, in judicial interpretations, and in the HREOC's educational brief can easily lend weight to it. Commissionary staff may be professional bureaucrats but it would be odd if the women or men who are drawn to such work lacked feminist sympathies. The charge that feminist commitment is the only important qualification for equal opportunity positions may be a slur. But *that* such commitments form *one* of the necessary qualifications for these positions – routinely built into job-descriptions – is a matter of public record (Eisenstein, 1990, p. 90). No impropriety need be involved. However, the professional-ethical balancing-act sometimes involved in occupying such a position (e.g. as a conciliator or tribunal commissioner) again calls into question Ronalds' diagnosis of certain respondents' 'confusion' about the attitude of the Victorian Equal Opportunity Board. For it is not simply a question of the tension between natural justice requirements and the intrusion of EEO practitioners' 'personal' beliefs and prejudices. Yes, the latter must be held in check. Nevertheless, it cannot be denied that the beliefs in question here are likely to chime in with the legislation's social policy commitments and are indispensible for performing (non-judicial) aspects of the practitioners' job. In other words, what may be at stake is not a conflict between professional and unprofessional behaviour, but rather a 'casuistical' balancing-act between two *bona fide* obligations.

To what extent is it possible to draw a clear line of demarcation between lines of action on the part of the HREOC (or equivalent statutory bodies at state level) which can be legitimately taken in direct pursuit of those commitments and those which outstrip the limits to such actions laid down in the legislation or in subsequent judicial judgements? The education work of the commission is a clear example of the former, the conciliator who assumes an advocacy role in respect to complainants a clear example of the latter. But were that line between the educational-cum-ideological and the judicial to be breached, would the demarcation be quite so clear?

Certainly, circumstances can be envisaged in which such a breach might occur. Take the issue of inequity in the respective access of parties to a sexual harassment case to legal representation. Tiffin (1984, p. 4) has shown how in *O'Callaghan v Loder* (1984, EOC 92–024, 75, 509) this issue arose in the most dramatic and unacceptable way. Suppose that her accompanying proposal (Tiffin, *op. cit.*, p. 11) that a state-or federally-funded 'public counsel' expert in anti-discrimination law, be made available, *gratis*, for representing women without the necessary financial resources were to be taken up. This would be an example of a line of action, directly in pursuance of the social justice objectives of the legislation, which certainly touches the semi-judicial as distinct from educational work of such bodies. If the HREOC were made responsible for this arrangement, it *might* be seen as playing an advocacy role *vis-à-vis* the complainant. Might this not involve a breach of natural justice and hence create a public image of partiality? Or the risk of promoting a public perception of partiality? On one view, resort to a 'walls-within-walls' policy within commissionary institutions ought to suffice to re-establish the proper limits of this advocacy role and preempt legal or public objections to an equitable legal representation and funding policy. Yet in the recent discussion paper on possible reforms to the Victorian legislation, commissionary assistance to needy complainants was rejected precisely on the grounds that it could compromise the commission's conciliatory role (Law Reform Commission of Victoria, 1990, p. 25).[18]

The lesson is clear. There are certain circumstances in which conflict may arise between the judicial and 'progressive' social policy wings of commissionary activity in the area of sex-discrimination; in which case the precise scope of professional obligations to respect natural justice in such work is not something that can be taken for granted.

In arguing, more generally, that observance of natural justice is a vital element in the procedures and in the ethos of those who administer them, it has not been my intention to lecture EEO practitioners on their known professional obligations, but rather to suggest why the place and ethical significance of these obligations in the ethical 'make-up' of such a practitioner might be more than a merely routine one. Sexual harassment law is, to reiterate, an instrument of a liberal social policy. This policy is to be implemented by state officials in a pluralist society in which the pro-feminist ethico-political objectives of the law are not universally shared and in which only a limited 'enforcement of morals' through social legislation on the part of the state is possible. In these circumstances, the ability of commissionary staff to respect natural justice in processing complaints cannot but be a major test of legitimacy.

There is thus no room for moralism and accordingly my argument faces two ways. If observance of natural justice holds more than routine ethical-political significance, there may also be good reason to treat it as less than a moral absolute. If it is an extremely serious matter, it may also be that a *degree* of cynicism about its scope of application is a mark of ethical intelligence. Without accepting that it offers a basis for a *critique*, it is time to give this cynical view of natural justice its moment. In this way it becomes possible to underscore the ethical as well as practical and political/ideological bases for decisions, such as *Hill v Water Resources Commission*, which set limits to its scope.

To this end, it is necessary to question a conventional bifurcation in the meaning of the term 'natural justice'. On the one hand, it is a precise piece of legal terminology with a limited, technical reference. On the other, it is usually identified with the 'basic' moral principle of fair-play. Given this bifurcation, the temptation to regard observance of natural justice as a categorical imperative, in Kant's parlance, is understandable. On this view, there is no place for cynicism. However, suppose natural justice principles were to be viewed as an artefact and instrument of an ethical culture which is not so readily detachable from legal, political, commercial cultures. The price of identifying the ethical meaning of natural justice with its most abstract, discursive form is a more or less studied ignorance about the conditioning, shaping effects of the legal and political circumstances, the technical meanings, and the practical effects which constantly attend the often 'ritual' enunciation of natural justice claims in actual legal settings. Are these 'lower orders' of social existence extrinsic to the ethical force of appeals to natural justice?

Examples of the conditions surrounding the applicability of its principles lie readily to hand. There may be variation in the circumstances under which its two different limbs (*the right to be heard* and the right to an *unbiased* judgement) are applicable (Hartley and Griffith, 1981, p. 330). In turn the 'right to be heard' cannot be claimed prior to its being lodged in some definite institutional forum. In Hartley and Griffith's words: 'the exact content of the "hearing" and the procedural rights that go with it will not be the same in all cases' (*ibid.*). The practical scope of natural justice principles will therefore vary accordingly.

The very fact that the general 'ideal' of natural justice is identified with 'fair play' may be read as an echo of its practical origins in an adversarial legal system. Legal actions in such a system will always be to some extent a 'trial' of rhetorical strength, a battle for the moral (as well as legal) high ground. There is therefore nothing *un*fair about the 'cynical' invocation of natural justice considerations by counsel for the respondent in a sexual harassment case. Nevertheless such appeals do point to a dissociation between this counsel's 'agonistic' motive for safeguarding natural justice (to get the client off) and the motive driving the quasi-judicial tribunal process which consist in the search for truth and the provision of remedies against injustice. This dissociation opens up a space for setting legitimate limits to the circumstances in which rules of natural justice apply on practical, legal–administrative grounds *which are themselves ethically driven.*

For example, in *Hill v Water Resources Commission*, the decision not to seek to join those involved in the harassment seems to have been partly based on the impracticality of attempting to make out a separate case against each and every one of the numerous men involved and (in keeping with vicarious liability provisions in the New South Wales state legislation) the persistent failure of management to act against them (Friedlander, 1985). Whether or not the decision was justified, the *ethical* point at issue is that the choice involved was not between respect for a legal principle and the pursuit of ideological objectives. Where there is a *prima facie* case of unlawful conduct, there is an obligation to find a technical form of tribunal hearing in which the case can be conducted as expeditiously as possible. Both sides may be moved (and constrained) by considerations of an ethical nature. As de Smith's *Review of Administrative Action* (1980, p. 239, cited in *Koppen*, pp. 76, 673) notes, respect for natural justice does not equate to a license to short-circuit the practical and evenhanded administration of justice. There is thus a place for a degree of cynicism about routine invocations of the 'principle' of natural justice on the part of both critics and practitioners. Its observance is not a categorical imperative but a matter of prudential legal decisions.

Thresholds of Proof and Evidence of Character

Only one of the 'ethical conditions' relating to evidence will be examined in any detail: a certain judicial investiture of an 'ethical-rhetorical' capacity to make judgements about 'character', together with its implications for the levels of legal formality required by tribunal hearings. What follows is purely illustrative and suggestive of a wider argument which, were it to be corroborated, would have to be played across a range of evidence-related issues.[19]

Few acts of sexual harassment take place in front of witnesses. If tribunal hearings take an ungenerous view on the range of evidence they are prepared to accept, feminists are entitled to draw their own conclusions about the level of judicial determination to do anything about the problem. There is after all a long and dishonourable tradition of judicial pronouncements around women's alleged propensity to lie about sexual offences.[20] However, some feminist criticism of current evidential thresholds evades the question of precisely what alternative standards of proof ought to apply, by equating the very asking of the question with judicial misogynism (Morgan, *op. cit.*, pp. 157–58). Not only does this view underestimate the corrigibility of misogynistic decisions.[21] It also assumes that (female) complainants are *incapable* of lying, and implicitly treats (male) respondents as nothing but ciphers of a patriarchal power-structure rather than as legal subjects entitled to justice.[22]

The question of alternative standards of evidence in tribunal hearings is also apt to be avoided in complaints about the practice of interpreting the legislation as entailing that tribunals 'may' be bound by rules of evidence (*Aldridge v Booth*, g22 1987). As Ronalds (1987, p. 183) puts it: 'the tribunals are hardly distinguished from courts'; and nowhere more so than in regard to its *adversarial* rituals and values (Tiffin, 1984, pp. 8, 11).

Perhaps gruelling formalities imposed by the adversary system, such as cross-examination or unduly onerous requirements of proof might be dispensed with. Perhaps the tribunals may have failed to take up the opportunity to develop innovative methods of conducting enquiries created by the liberal stipulations of the legislation (Ronalds, 1987, p. 183). Even so, why should all desirable reform run in the direction of greater 'informality'? Tiffin's critique of the adversarial climate of the tribunals is accompanied by a proposal to introduce 'an inquisitorial panel of members eliciting evidence from all parties' (Tiffin, *op. cit.*, p. 11). This is a call for a different kind of court, not for something that doesn't look like one. How *much* informality is consistent with retaining the support of a conservative legal profession? It can hardly do any harm to the legitimacy of these tribunals if it is recorded that contrary to the 'common law–libertarian view', these tribunals *are* steeped in 'the spirit and methods of the common law'. Are *all* the evidential criteria and procedures open to question?

Emphasis on evidential obstacles may also produce an unduly bleak picture of what sexually harassed women can expect to achieve in the current tribunal system. In the case most frequently cited in support of this emphasis, *O'Callaghan v Loder and Anor* (1984, EOC, 92–024), Justice Mathews was not convinced that, on the balance of probabilities, the complainant's evidence had satisfied what she took to be the onus in such cases 'to make her unwillingness [to have sexual contact] known to the employer' (1984, EOC 92–024, 75, 514). Whilst Justice Mathews conceded the difficulties of so doing imposed by the power-relationship between complainant and respondent, she would not accept that this relieved the female complainant of 'some obligation to make known to her employer (especially in this case where no "job-related consequences" were allegedly threatened by him) that his attentions are unwelcome' (pp. 75, 516). As Ronalds (1987, p. 117) has argued, the consequence of this decision is 'to perpetuate the power-relationship which is crucial to sexual harassment – that the harasser can make the objective decision about whether the advances were unwelcome' (*ibid.*, p. 118). Justice Mathew's introduction of a 'subjective' test of consent (the respondent's belief that his advances were welcome) into its definition is inconsistent with the New South Wales legislative definition and makes 'the onus of proof carried by the complainant . . . extremely high' (*ibid.*). But does this decision really 'portend' a far more general failure of 'male-dominated legal practice' (Scutt, 1985, p. 125)? The 1984 Commonwealth legislation specifically plugs this gap (and in effect provides a basis for disapproving Mathew's opinion in this regard) by introducing an 'objective' test of unwelcome conduct which, in Ronalds' (*op. cit.*, p. 118) words, 'is not specifically tied to the view of the harasser but incorporates the concept of a reasonable person'.

It has been suggested that neither the spectre of misogynism nor the promise of greater informality can justify indefinitely deferring the question of which evidential thresholds must be met if a complaint of sexual harassment is to be upheld; and that the general emphasis on how *much* evidence is required for a complaint to succeed may lead to underestimating the potentialities of the current legislative framework (including its existing capacities for change). To reject this emphasis *in toto* would be a mistake. However, it is also worth recording how *little* 'hard' evidence has in fact been prerequisite to a number of recent successful tribunal complaints.

Since the judgements in question nevertheless satisfy common law 'civil' standards of proof, one is driven to ask whether these standards are as inflexible (i.e. devoid of 'informality') as the critical emphasis on the odds against complaints succeeding sometimes implies.[23] Of particular interest here is the legal force of the *ethical categories and forms of judgement* which are operative in these cases.

Whilst few acts of sexual harassment take place before witnesses, the mental state of the victim after the event may be known to others; the events themselves may have been systematically logged; there may be objective detrimental after-effects (loss of employment, sick leave, etc.); and in general a range of testimony as to the likelihood of the events in question having occurred is potentially available. At the risk of overgeneralising, over and above the 'hard' evidence of eyewitnesses, medical reports etc., there are two other inter-connected criteria of evidence on which successful complaints have turned, which seem to possess a definite ethical component: (i) inconsistencies in the testimony of the parties or their respective witnesses and (ii) judgements about 'character' pertinent to the credibility of testimony.

In the federal rehearing of *Aldridge*, Justice Spender, for instance, grounded his decision in favour of Lynette Aldridge to a significant extent on his having formed a favourable impression of her verbal truthfulness and of the accuracy of her diary in which unwitnessed incidents had been logged. In *Hutchinson v Smirles and Co.* (1986, EOC, 92–152, 76, 501), the presiding commissioner comments favourably on the lack of hesitation and forthright manner in which the complainant delivered her evidence. In *Boyle v Ishan, Ozden and Ors* (1986, EOC, 92–165), what shifted the balance of probabilities in favour of the complainant were inconsistencies in the evidence of the respondent (the manager of the food shop where she worked) and in that of the relatives he called as witnesses (e.g. could they have been present on all the occasions in question?); and once again the commissioner's favourable impression about the 'character' and 'credibility' of the complainant and her evidence. Finally, in a New Zealand case, *H v E* (1985, EOC, 92–137, 76, 355), credibility and consistency are conjoined in the commissioner's judgement on the *narrative and characterological improbability* of the respondent's wife's story of having sacked the complainant, when by her own account she had offered the complainant tea and sympathy on the following day (p. 76, 355). Thus in cases where more material evidence is lacking, 'solomonic' *judgements of character* may be decisive. It seems somehow in keeping with the law's being (as we have seen) a repository of under-appreciated ethical categories such as civility, honour and shame that it should also prove so hospitable to this equally 'old-fashioned' and related concept of character.

Less apologetically, it could be suggested that this type of judgement is only 'old-fashioned' from the standpoint of ethical and psychological theories which are premised on a romantic-humanist concept of the (indeterminate) whole *person* (Williams, 1985, pp. 92–94). These ways of conceiving human individuals spurn the more deterministic concept of character, with its suggestion of definite limits to individual capabilities. A further characteristic of the concept of character is its inseparability from a *moral* psychology. Every judgement about a person's character is in part a moral judgement. From the standpoint of modern Enlightenment or post-Enlightenment humanist theories of the person, this is a problem. For it makes the 'adequacy' of this judgement inseparable from the authority of the one who judges. This authority is in turn linked to a 'capacity' (simultaneously cognitive, rhetorical *and* status-related) to make such judgements. Commissioners' judgements about the character of parties and witnesses to sexual harassment complaints are thus predicated upon their being invested with a certain *ethical status*, a licence, so to speak, to exercise this kind of ethical-rhetorical skill.

This interpretation of character-judgements rebounds on the debate about the excessive formality of tribunals in two contrasting ways. On the one hand, judgements involving estimations of parties' and witnesses' character and consistency clearly depend on investing the proceedings with a certain judicial *gravitas*. They could hardly be made sitting around a coffee-table! On the other, these judgements are not lacking in a certain *informal* quality. They enjoy little codified, technical status. It looks as if a simple call for 'more informality' not only fails to designate any single direction for the reform of the tribunal process, but also threatens to undermine a vital condition – at once formal and informal – of the existing arrangements' capacity to work as well as they currently do.

Contractual Responsibilities

Lying at a tangent to these evidence-related conditions, the final non-egalitarian ethical condition on the agenda concerns (all too briefly) employers' legal responsibilities and obligations towards their employees. The 1984 Act (s.105) provides that 'a person who causes, instructs, induces, aids, or permits another person to do an act that is unlawful (under the Act) shall for the purposes of the act be taken also to have done the act'. Vicarious liability in the common law derives of course from the development of 'master–servant' law. It remains a 'duty of care' attendant upon a legal contract of employment and is sometimes seen as an extension of the 'good neighbour principle'. In the light of criticism of sex-discrimination legislation as 'toothless' on the grounds of its failure to compel managements to develop internal EEO policies (Probert and Wootten, 1984), it is worth noting that the legal force of this duty of care is not limited to the vicarious liability clauses of the legislation. For example, the Victorian Equal Opportunity Board has interpreted section 105 as having created a privilege for the Commonwealth Employment Service (CES) to exercise this duty of care in cases where complainants were first recruited by that agency. Whenever the CES hears about sexual harassment from victims forced out of their jobs and returning to the service in search of new employment, liaison between the CES and the Victorian Equal Opportunity Office takes place. If a complaint is lodged with the latter, then the CES routinely refrains from listing any vacancies arising in the harassed women's previous place of employment, pending a satisfactory resolution of the case.[24]

Limited though it is (employers are free to advertise vacancies else-where) this measure exemplifies once again (as in Chapter 4) how, in quite localised ways, making sexual harassment illegal *can* work more generally to provide both a supportive environment for, and one of a number of minor prods to, non-legal *managerial* or other official initiatives in developing an anti-sexual harassment policy in particular companies.

Provision for the employer's duty of care is also vital to the possibility of proving *constructive dismissal*, in circumstances of sexual harassment where, without being dismissed by her employer, the complainant felt constrained to leave her employment. In *H v E* (1985, EOC, 92–137, 76, 349) it was decided that there was no need to prove that, as a consequence of a sexual harassment incident, the employer *intended* to repudiate the employee's contract. Citing Denning's characterisation of the duty of care as an employer's duty to be 'good and considerate towards his servant', the conduct in question was found to entail a breach of the 'relationship of confidence and trust . . . implied as a normal incident of the relationship between an employer and employee' (*ibid.*, pp. 76, 358–59).[25]

More broadly, the fact that employment relations are governed by a wage contract, with its concomitant of a duty of care, is arguably vital to the possibility of regulating sexual harassment in this domain; and conversely, to the impracticality of extending this regulation to cover similar conduct no matter where it occurs. In other words, the current limits to the applicability of sexual harassment law may not be entirely arbitrary.

This contention will seem especially contentious to those radical critics referred to at the outset, such as Pateman, who will not fail to suspect the fact that regulation is restricted to the *public* dimensions of civil life and who will not fail to point the finger at the relations of subordination implicit in these contractual duties of care. To the first objection, it may be replied that it is probably no more feasible to seek to regulate sexual harassment (where it falls short of physical violence) in a public thoroughfare than in private adult domestic sexual relations. The problem of making sexual harassment in a thoroughfare legally actionable is clearly not that it is not public. But can an action lie when the relations between the parties (and indeed possible witnesses) are characterised by 'accidental propinquity' (Baker, 1979, p. 347)? Passers-by have no legal obligations towards one another analogous to the duties of care inscribed in an employment contract – citizens are under no legal obligation to go to the assistance of someone in distress. In a firm with an effective sexual harassment policy in place it would be unacceptable for not only someone in a supervisory capacity but even a fellow employee to disclaim any responsibility or interest were they to take part in or to witness an act of harassment.

With respect to domestic sexual relations, the required relations of legal obligation linking the parties are either absent or relatively vestigial, compared to non-legal normative constructions of adult intimate and domestic relations. The existence of voluntary, emotional bonds between the partners articulated in psychological discourses is probably more important to the legal delineation of the relationship as a going concern than formal obligations. As a token of the importance of contractual obligations in making sexual harassment actionable, we might note the possibility that harassment of a domestic help would be unlawful under the 'goods and services' provisions of the Commonwealth legislation.

The second objection seems to turn on a utopian denunciation of *all* social relations involving subordination of any kind (how else could Pateman's characterisation of the modern wage contract as a charter for 'civil slavery' be interpreted?). To protest the language of paternalism deployed in contract law is one thing. But unless one has an unshakeable faith in the desirability (let alone possibility) of a perfectly hierarchy-free democratic society, what is the point of making the mere existence of an hierarchical element in social relations an occasion for criticism?

Conclusions

A series of positive and negative ethical constraints on how far legal action against sexual harassment might be expected to go in securing effective remedies and in educating the wider community have been outlined. These ethical conditions seem to me to be crucial to both the acceptability and efficiency of current legal measures.

Whilst these 'second principles' are not limited to articulating legal concerns about equality between the sexes, sexual harassment law has to be seen partly as an instrument of an egalitarian social policy targeting the disparate treatment of women. The industrial citizenship-status established in the legislation cannot be reduced to a general principle and need not be seen as contributing to a general politics of 'full equality'. To see the status in this way would be inconsistent with the liberal political logic of the legislation. However, this political logic is not purely derivative of liberal political principles. Rather, it is an instance of a liberal form of *governance* which sanctions interventions directed at specific problem-groups of the population. These social-governmental interventions cut across the hallowed private–public distinction of liberal philosophy and are not bound by a formal principle of equal treatment which is blind to substantive inequalities. The SDA and its operational workings go some way to accommodating the feminist view that sexual harassment is not a 'uni-sex' phenomenon. Whether it is politically possible to make the law more congruent with radical feminist political-egalitarian aspirations is more doubtful. In a pluralist polity, the political and cultural acceptability of a progressive social policy will tend to hinge, it has been claimed, on its capacity to be represented (and operated) in a way that is compatible with a politically neutral attitude on the part of the state towards contested ideologies, including those of feminism.

It is this need to represent and attack the problem of sexual harassment in a (partly) ideologically neutralised way which justifies locating the problem of sexual harassment and its legal governance partly in the mundane realm of manners. There is no ideological basis for objecting to policies aimed at securing respect for employees' bodily integrity. This respect is predicated not on women's 'ladylike' qualities but on their occupational competences. The 'principle' at stake is one of 'equitable manners'. The same need to take the problem outside the combat zone of ideological politics also explains the attention warranted by other non-egalitarian ethical considerations involved in making sexual harassment justiciable: considerations of honour and shame, natural justice, the ethical skills involved in judgements of character and the ethical obligations arising out of the contract of employment.

One way in which these ethical conditions serve the cause of making sexual harassment justiciable is by serving as a series of vital bridges between the traditional common law and a modern liberal-egalitarian law and social policy. The sorts of equality sought by the law do not necessarily conflict with ethical dimensions of the common law which lay emphasis upon the value of individual liberty (notably, natural justice constraints) or relations of subordination (e.g. vicarious liability provisions, the unlawfulness of constructive dismissal). It is incumbent on opponents of sexual harassment law to show that the freedom of individual thought and action by which they set so much store is more important than women's freedom from threats to their bodily integrity.

If there is reason to doubt the wisdom of seeing the industrial citizenship stakes in sex discrimination law as (for better or worse) part of some sweeping egalitarian programme, how else might it be seen? Let me conclude with a speculative suggestion which I shall attempt to substantiate shortly. It is that the regulation of sexual harassment be seen as a minimal ethical and political condition in a democratic culture for members of a workforce to be willing and able, ethically speaking, to *subordinate themselves* to the demands, interests and hierarchical relations of modern economic institutions; and to do so knowingly and honourably, not because they have been ideologically duped. A work-place in which organisational subordination was made more dignified, congenial, mobile, and equitable might not be everyone's idea of utopia; but as an ethical and political objective it is not to be despised.

6 Managing Without a Politics of Subjectivity

Introduction

In the conclusion to 'Femocrats, official feminism and the uses of power' Hester Eisenstein (1990, p. 103) registers her 'persistent impression that theory lags radically behind practice'. Feminists' recent experience in government bureaucracies, trade unions and electoral politics,[1] Eisenstein claims, 'provides data for a reconsideration of a lot of what has been said in the first round of theorising about gender difference, and its relation to organisational structures and work-experience'. Needless to say, this hypothesis is open to a variety of interpretations and tests. The Equal Employment Opportunity (EEO) management policies with respect to sexual harassment in the workplace outlined (and interpreted) in this chapter furnish the basis for one such test. How well do these policies stand up, it will be asked, in the face of an influential feminist critical challenge which revolves around the supposition of a general antipathy between sexually-differentiated realms of subjectivity and 'modern bureaucratic culture'?[2]

What is called in question, on account of its supposedly 'masculinist' basis, is not solely state bureaucracies but the whole organisational mentality of the modern workplace – irrespective of who owns it or of its function (industrial, commercial, administrative). EEO management policies are suspected of an inadequacy bordering on complicity with respect to the subordinating effects of bureaucratic culture on women. If feminist interventions into bureaucracy are to have more than token results, they must attempt to subvert and transcend the limits of existing EEO policies. A strategy aimed at bringing the subjugated subjective dimensions of organisational life to the forefront of analysis and action – in short, a theory and politics of sexed subjectivity – is required.

In the course of critically returning this challenge, I shall draw attention both to details of contemporary EEO policies on sexual harassment and to the broader historical aspects of 'bureaucratic culture' which this critique cannot easily accommodate. The circumscribed definitions, procedures and normative régimes which, from the standpoint of the critique are most suspected of being superficial, arbitrary and limited, are seen on my

123

interpretation as positive preconditions for gaining regulatory purchase on the problem of sexual harassment. To think of the problem in this way is not to ignore all the 'systemic' cultural factors encouraging sexual harassment. Rather it is to be forced to reckon with their diversity and to focus on those aspects of the problem which are open to practical modification, both procedurally, and at the level of a broader social policy aimed at modifying the ethical climate of the workplace with respect to women.

However, there is reason not to see this confrontation between feminist theory and (pro-) feminist bureaucratic practice entirely in black and white terms, ending in the ruination of the 'theoretical' party. Not all feminist theories are equally subject to the difficulties urged against the critique of modern bureaucratic culture. To take only one instance, at certain points some versions of the critique draw on feminist-psychoanalytical arguments. The *general* utility of this approach for a sexual harassment management policy may be questioned, it will be concluded, without ruling out the possibility of its usefulness in certain contingencies.

To this qualification of the claim that existing 'theory' lags behind 'practice' must be added a caution about the very terms of this contrast, a reservation which will serve to clarify the relationship of the argument on managing sexual harassment to the concerns of a social and cultural policy. It is not enough to expose the theoretical failings of the anti-bureaucratic critique and its consequent disutility for putting the nuts and bolts of a workable sexual harassment policy in place. For this would be to leave untouched the fact that theory in this instance functions less as a guide to policy than as a guide to conscience. The main philosophical task of this essay is to suggest that 'theory', ethical considerations, and the details of EEO policies may be configured in different ways. It is not to disparage theoretical work or the importance of ethical attitudes in favour of exclusive attention to 'getting the procedures right'. The need for broader strategic perspectives on the problem of sexual harassment goes without saying.

But how are these broader perspectives to be conceived? Not only in radical criticism but in mainstream progressive analyses of equal opportunity policy, arguments typically revolve around a utopian dichotomy between limited, technical, 'specific reforms' and a general reformation of 'the norms, language and culture of administration' (Wilenski, 1986, p. 165). A line of argument aimed at cross-cutting both poles of this dichotomy is possible. On the one hand, examination of current management policies on sexual harassment suggests possible linkages between procedural remedies and a broad array of equally specific, affirmative action measures. On the other hand, the need for a general cultural reformation is put in question by placing bureaucratic culture in a historical perspective which casts doubt upon the claim about its constitutive masculinism. This supposition will be seen to rest on a romantic contrast between bureaucratic formality and informality which finds paradigmatic expression in stereotyped sociological representations of Max Weber and the history of 'rationalisation'.

In short, this chapter has two aims: to challenge the romantic estimation of bureaucratic organisation and the transformative politics of subjectivity to which it gives rise; and to envisage practical ways of linking specific procedural techniques for managing sexual harassment to a broader EEO social policy aimed at modifying workplace 'ethical cultures'. It is in the failure to take these sorts of linkages seriously that the 'lag' between theory and practice in some recent theoretical writing on EEO issues will finally be located.

A Range of Illustrative Policies

The empirical basis for establishing the existence of this lag in respect to management policy on workplace sexual harassment is furnished by four texts, all of which combine sympathy with feminist goals and principles with preparedness to engage with the work of constructing a policy. Of the two closely related Australian policy documents discussed, one emanates from a trade union, the other from a personnel management body inside the federal public service bureaucracy. For purposes of contrast and comparison, these Australian EEO policy documents are flanked on the one side by a British trade union-oriented handbook, and on the other, by a North American business studies text which combines sociological analysis of sexual harassment with pragmatic advice aimed at liberal-progressive corporate management.

Of the two illustrative trade-union-based handbooks, Hadjifotiou's (1983) *Women and Sexual Harassment* is by far the most radical and combative in its posture towards management. As such it presents both parallels and non-parallels with the most advanced Australian trade-union documentation of the issue, the Administrative and Clerical Officers' Association's (ACOA) handbook, *Sexual Harassment in the Workplace* (1983).

In both texts a socialist-feminist model of sexism as a patriarchal structure is drawn upon to provide the opening characterisation of the issue (ACOA, 1983, p. 34); Hadjifotiou (1983, pp. 23–24). Equally, both texts develop policies which seem to owe relatively little to this framework. For example, according to Hadjifotiou any capitalist, male-dominated management will inevitably be opposed to implementing such a policy. Yet, ignoring the oppositionalist implications of this view, she recommends publicity and grievance procedures which management is to be induced (through collective bargaining) to administer (Hadjifotiou, 1983, ch. 6). For its part, the ACOA document simply uses its preliminary 'theoretical view' as a reason for attempting to build some of the power dimensions of the problem into official definitions and procedural tactics. As well as advice on how to negotiate a policy, both handbooks provide parallel advice to individual union members on how to take both procedural and informal action: who to contact, the need to carefully log harassment encounters, etc. Hadjifotiou's handbook suggests concrete formulations calculated to enlist the support of fellow workers in publicly ridiculing offenders (Hadjifotiou 1983, p. 65). Both handbooks also propose training schemes for union representatives, supervisors and personnel officers. These officers may be required to mediate or negotiate with the alleged offender and the complainant, listen supportively, and provide practical aid to complainants.

Whereas the ACOA handbook concentrates on advocating workable procedures (along the lines of the Federal public service document to be examined shortly), Hadjifotiou's policy proposals have a more scattergun character. Largely indifferent to procedural niceties, her main concern lies in canvassing various ways of placing harassment on the collective bargaining agenda, for example by exploring the possibilities of getting management to see it as a health-and-safety issue (Hadjifotiou, 1983, pp. 161–62). Even where the call is for independent trade union action, the target is the sexism of union officials and the rank and file as well as that exhibited by management. To this end, a campaign of publicity and 'direct action' against visual displays offensive to women is proposed (*ibid.*, pp. 99–106). And the text also offers itself as a primer for trade union officials in preparation not only for complaints about sexual harassment, but also for representations by male unionists who have been sanctioned for sexual harassment and who want the union to mount a case for unfair dismissal on their behalf (*ibid.*, p. 79). Less astutely, perhaps, it recommends compulsory counselling for offenders (*ibid.*, p. 85).

Eliminating Sexual Harassment: Guidelines for Sexual Harassment Contact Officers and Personnel Officers (SHCOs) is a revision of the 1981 Federal Public Service Board (FPSB) guidelines in the light of subsequent anti-discrimination and public service legislation. Owing much to the ACOA's document, and in its most recent edition packaged together with a training kit involving 'Hypotheticals'-type role-play – it is probably the most comprehensive framework of public-sector management policy on sexual harassment in Australia to date.

The manual's theoretical starting-point is a simple statement about the pattern of disadvantage under which women labour as compared to men and the accompanying sexual inequities in workplace power relations. This emphasis on the systemic nature of the act serves to justify an insistence on the irrelevance of the harasser's *intention* (FPSB, 1986, p. 2) and on the vicarious liability of employers to establish an effective anti-harassment policy (*ibid.*). It covers both '*quid pro quo*' and 'environmental' forms of sexual harassment, including offensive visual displays, even in some circumstances the display of 'works of art' (p. 3). However, this concern with underlying causes is not *generally* built into the way in which the problem is conceived for purposes of taking action against it: namely, as a breach of a norm of equitable and professional workplace conduct which is unconducive to women getting on with their job (*ibid.*, pp. 1, 9, 27). A flexible array of remedies to individuals is made available. Informal action by the person affected or by departmental managers or supervisors is one option. Formal channels include either an intra-departmental mechanism for lodging a complaint, investigation, counselling, and disciplinary action (under s.62 of the Public Service Act); or, if the complainant desires external arbitration, either the FPSB's own Merit Protection and Review Agency (MPRA), or resort to the Human Rights and Equal Opportunity Commission's (HREOC) apparatus established by the Federal legislation for handling sex-discrimination complaints.

All told, the policy represents a blend of formal and informal, legal and 'infra-legal' options. Internal departmental proceedings prescribe a sympathetic, supportive and counselling role for SHCOs *vis-à-vis* complainants (*ibid.*, pp. 10–11). However, this supportive role is subject to certain formal constraints: the need for SHCOs to be seen as independent of departmental management (and of the HREOC too, should it be brought in) and of the investigation and resolution of the complaint should it go to the MPRA (*ibid.*, p. 11). As in the ACOA document, much attention is devoted to preserving confidentiality and hence protecting all parties, including SHCOs and related personnel, from defamation proceedings (*ibid.*, pp. 8, 13, 25, 45).[3] The SHCO also has the formal task of ensuring that natural justice is respected *vis-à-vis* the subject of the complaint (*ibid.*, pp. 5, 24, 30). The officer's contact with those accused of harassment is restricted to the task of clarifying rules of proper workplace conduct and complaints procedures.

An array of informal measures is also recommended. Apart from advice to individuals about what they can do for themselves, management is encouraged to take preventative actions, irrespective of whether a formal complaint against an individual has been lodged, aimed at 'a more widespread problem of the general atmosphere' prejudicial to women (*ibid.*, pp. 20–21). On the question of what these preventative measures might involve, the document has relatively little to say.

The relative conservatism of the FPSB document (and the union policies too) in this regard is paradoxically underlined by their more business-oriented North American counterpart. For all the emphasis in the former on the power relations which lend encouragement to sexual harassment, none of them make mention of the desirability of making changes to prevailing structures of authority. By contrast, in Coeli Myer *et al.*'s (1981) text a comparable array of complaints procedures is supplemented by discussion of the likely encouragement or discouragement to sexual harassment afforded by pyramidal and matrix forms of supervision (*ibid.*, pp. 92–93). It also suggests building considerations of sexual harassment into selection and promotion procedures; getting more women into managerial or supervisory positions; and performance-appraisal with a view to detecting problems of harassment by registering fall-off in work performance (*ibid.*, pp. 97–98). Finally, Coeli Myer *et al.* offer an unashamedly 'entrepreneurial' rationale for informal counter-measures on the part of the victims of sexual harassment.

Four aspects of the range of currently available management policy options reviewed here will be taken up in the ensuing discussion: the (ostensibly) marginal role of theoretical analysis; the mix of formal and informal measures; the possibilities of linking anti-harassment measures to various *other* reforms of workplace conduct and organisation and the unpredictable 'political' valencies of these diverse proposals.

With regard to the latter, as we have seen, it is by no means self-evident that it will fall to the public sector rather than private corporations, to unions rather than management, or to political 'radicals' rather than 'moderates' to be the movers and shakers in establishing meaningful policies on sexual harassment.[4] Nor, if the example of the vicissitudes of anti-discrimination policy in the Australian federal public service is anything to go by, is the 'political' picture any clearer as regards actual implementation of such policies. The track record leaves no room for complacency.[5] But how far are these managerial EEO initiatives open to radical criticism from the standpoint of feminist challenges to the bureaucratic mentality as such? And what is so 'romantic' about this challenge?

Romanticism and Bureaucratic Culture

In Chapter 1 romanticism was characterised as a general ethical technique for shaping one's personality and conscience in accordance with a 'dialectical' schema of perfect development. Aspects of the self which, it is assumed, 'society' only permits being expressed in compartmentalised, mutually opposed ways (instrumental reason/emotional expression; duty/desire; work/leisure; head/hand; mind/body; etc.) are to be brought and held together in a simultaneously playful, yet ethically serious, reciprocally transformative interaction. *Political* romanticism involves the use of public affairs and institutions as *occasions* for this way of working on the self. Romantic 'occasionalism' depends upon conceptualising social relations in such a way as to render them into a form appropriate to a romantic ethical play of subjective distantiation and involvement in respect to them. This is the purpose and appeal of all typifications of bureaucracy as giving expression only to the rational side of human nature, i.e. as 'instrumental reason'. From (and *only* from) this perspective, to the extent that bureaucratic routines 'fail' to open themselves up to people's personal involvements and ideals, they cannot but appear as a subject for conscientious objection.

In view of the ways in which antinomies of the 'heart v. head' variety have been gendered, it is not surprising if historically, as a movement, romanticism played a major role in shaping feminist ethical and political attitudes. Only a small proportion of the critical literature on EEO policies in Australia would go all the way with the romantic critique of 'the veritable sexual harassment bureaucracy' put out by the North American Alliance against Sexual Coercion (1982, p. 86), for instance, with its radical rejection of feminist involvement in management or government in favour of communitarian 'direct action'.[6] However, for all their inconsistency with romanticism at the level of concrete actions, practical involvements and even ethical stance, some of these more nuanced and tactical Australian responses to EEO developments are by no means unswayed by the romantic ethos.

For instance, eschewing the option of feminist-bureaucrat-bashing, Lynch (1984) demonstrates the possibility of feminists who are involved in EEO programmes in a managerial capacity performing a balancing act between the constraints of such work (secrecy, power-dressing, career-consciousness, being a 'boss') and the pursuit of feminist objectives in keeping with demands emanating from the 'grassroots' women's movement. Lynch insists on the futility of seeking any grand reconciliation inside a unified political consciousness between the respective cultural universes of radical feminist activists and bureaucratic feminists. Moreover, the ethical juggling act which she enjoins upon feminist bureaucrats is seen as irreducible to a simple conflict between feminist ideals and a male-dominated bureaucracy opposing their realisation at every turn.

Lynch's 'Bureaucratic feminisms' could be read as a *casuistical manual of feminist conscience-formation*. Recent attempts to rehabilitate the discredited arts of casuistry carry the implication that the romantic ethos is not the only available contemporary means by which 'progressive' individuals involved in government can establish a politically conscientious attitude to their work.[7] However, is feminist 'suspicion' of the bureaucratic role as such *always* as 'healthy' as Lynch supposes (*ibid.*, p. 38)? This suspicion of 'femocrats' is premised on a romantic identification between feminism proper and its most personally involving, oppositionalist and communitarian forms of intervention.[8] Even the staunchest defences of the benefits of feminists working in government intermittently treat the terms 'femocrat' or 'feminist bureaucrat' as though they were oxymorons (Summers, 1986, p. 60); as though bureaucratic involvements cannot, as such, qualify as a bona fide *feminist* intervention. This identification of feminism with its 'ideologically soundest' edges is on a par with the related premise underlying the Alliance against Sexual Coercion's (1981) suspicion of corporate management's 'mixed motives' in taking up EEO issues such as sexual harassment. Here, too, the perceived problem is the lack of the right (i.e. motivationally pure) subjective relation to the problem on the part of these managers. Admittedly, not all romantic critical attitudes to bureaucracy are 'rejectionist'. But is the generalised *suspicion* of bureaucratic culture which a romantic ethos is apt to engender any more productive?

EEO Policies and Secretarial Subordination

Back in Chapter 3, we discussed critiques of EEO policy-makers' supposed superficiality in interpreting the problem of workplace sexism as 'unprofessional' breaches of standards of conduct. Underpinning the preoccupation with procedural practicalities, say these critiques, is an assumption that bureaucratic organisation can be analysed without remainder into officially sanctioned, rationally based roles. In keeping with this allegedly 'Weberian' view of bureaucracy, any gender-inequalities in the organisation must be attributed to an adventitious incursion of sex-role behaviour, learned elsewhere, which contradicts the impersonal, hence gender-neutral norms of decision-making and action (functionally specialised tasks, open recruitment and promotion, etc.) prescribed by bureaucratic roles. This state of affairs needs to be remedied by a combination of EEO-based managerial regulation, law and rational persuasion aimed at restoring working women to a status of equality with men. From the standpoint of the critique of bureaucratic culture, any policy based on these assumptions will necessarily fail to adequately address the deep-seated masculinism inherent in both 'objective' structures of managerial authority and procedures and in (frequently unconscious) 'subjective' patterns of feeling, response and interaction, which are located in the informal underlife of the bureaucratically organised workplace.

Recent studies of EEO policies with respect to secretaries by Pringle (1988) and Game and Pringle (1986) exemplify this propensity to see bureaucratic norms and practices as constituting 'a new kind of patriarchal structure' (Pringle, 1988, p. 88). One point of departure for the critique is the attempt by a number of Australian secretarial organisations to improve secretaries' working conditions by professionalising the secretary's job. This is a strategy for attacking its associated disabilities and indignities by writing out the 'personal service' dimensions of the secretarial role. Instead, emphasis is placed upon the impersonal skill-components of the job, such as the inter-departmental or client–office communications and administrative/managerial possibilities opened up by information technologies.[9]

Pringle's objection to this 'professionalisation' strategy turns on its implicitly 'Weberian' view of bureaucracy. Without a doubt, the secretarial role *is* seen in this strategy as an archaic, inefficient and irrational residue of traditional patrimonial relations of authority which bureaucratic rationalisation has historically worked to break down. Pringle (*ibid.*, p. xi) claims that where women's place in the workplace today is concerned, far from representing an anomaly, the secretary is 'everywoman'. In seeking to make the secretary into part of a bureaucratically-run management team, secretarial organisations are falling into a trap. All this 'brisk' talk of skills (Pringle, *ibid.*, p. 99) only serves to repress the extent to which the much-vaunted rationality of bureaucratic systems 'requires as a condition of its existence the simultaneous creation of a realm of the other, be it personal, emotional, sexual or irrational – masculine rationality attempts to drive out the feminine but does not exist without it' (Pringle, *ibid.*, p. 89). These cut-and-dried bureaucratic norms and procedures are the product of a masculinist closure ('a denial of the feminine') which never quite succeeds in its objective (Game and Pringle, 1986, p. 286). 'Phallocentrically' organised sexual difference constitutes the unconscious, sexual meaning of ostensibly meritocratic formalities, subsisting within them as a kind of absent presence which it is the task of feminist analysis to 'deconstruct' (Pringle, *op. cit.*, p. 2). In addition, the liberal-patriarchal bases of the bureaucratic order constantly manifest themselves in the informal underlife of the organisation in jokes, gossip, clothes, looks, conflicts, office 'affairs', both phantasised and real (*ibid.*, p. 90). The 'personal services' dimension of the secretarial role is in consequence only the most visible form of a more ubiquitous sexualisation of the workplace. Boss–secretary relations are seen, then, as being to a great extent secretly organised around heterosexist desires and fantasies ranging from the fetishisation of technology (*ibid.*, pp. 175–6)[10] to sado-masochism (*ibid.*, pp. 51–55).

Hovering between history, theory and even mythology,[11] it is this theoretical conception of the workplace as a site of 'liberal-patriarchal' sexuality which underpins Pringle's suspicions of sexual harassment policies. To seek to establish norms of formal conduct aimed at reducing sexual harassment is to treat it as an exceptional abuse of power for sexual purposes. Such norms serve to cast a legitimising shadow over the 'compulsory' heterosexual relations (e.g. the signs of potential sexual compliance that go with the 'office wife' stereotype) and a whole spectrum of behaviours, attitudes and phantasies through which men attempt to assert power over women, but which fall outside EEO criteria for sexual harassment (Game and Pringle, 1986, p. 290). Further, even where other anti-discrimination policies relate sexual harassment to more pervasive forms of 'male power', such policies restrict their view of the *ways* in which such power is asserted to the mode of coercion. This is to exclude the régime of *pleasures* operative in the power-relations of bosses and secretaries; such as masochistic phantasies in which the secretary is placed in the role of a nanny figure, cajoling and caring for her infantilised boss (Pringle, *op. cit.*, pp. 51–55). Even if the secretary is ultimately disadvantaged by this sexual/familial phantasy, it may be initiated with the complicity of both parties.

Forms of 'resistance' aimed at exposing and subverting this masculinist régime canvassed by Pringle include: informal protest actions, mimicry and other minor acts of insubordination which draw on the resources of 'women's culture' (*ibid.*, pp. 287); a 'postmodern' exhibition consisting of pastiches of secretarial stereotypes (*ibid.*, pp. 102–103); or pedagogical interventions into the 'charm school' (dress, deportment, beauty treatment, etc.) side of secretarial training (*ibid.*, p. 152). Policies on sexual harassment should not be boycotted, but instead used as opportunities for women to expose those subterranean heterosexist power relations which anti-sexist bureaucratic norms fail to touch (Game and Pringle, 1986, p. 290).

It is not difficult to recognise the outlines of the romantic ethos in Pringle's generalised view of bureaucracy as a one-sided expression of a masculinist instrumental rationality which can only sustain this identity by attempting to drive out or dominate its 'other', the feminine, the emotional, the sexual; in its demand that bureaucracy and sexuality always be thought of together (i.e. dialectically) rather than as merely contradictory modes of authority (Game and Pringle, 1986, p. 286); in its 'occasionalist' [12] posture towards EEO norms and procedures and in its conviction that the ostensible 'objective' rules of the bureaucratic game merely mask the secret, subjective means by which power is exercised.

Yet inside this framework quite different arguments are deployed. Eclectic borrowings from work by Michel Foucault and Herbert Marcuse which caution against identifying the exercise of power with coercion are allied to a feminist–psychoanalytical exposé of heterosexist desire. Not all of these arguments are equally tied to a romantic ethico-political perspective. It is the general 'post-structuralist' argument on bureaucratic culture and the 'deconstruction' of its conflictual subjective underlife that I will now attempt to challenge by means of a brief detour into the conceptual history of this cultural form.

The Iron Soul of Weberian Bureaucracy

Liberal feminists' failure to take the 'subjective underlife' of the workplace into account in the formulation of EEO management policies, it has been claimed, testifies to the power of the Weberian model of bureaucratic rationality, which remains at the heart of orthodox personnel management thinking and organisation studies. Pringle places her critique in a longstanding tradition of sociological critiques of this model dating at least from the 1960s. If, in the face of these critiques, it remains a cornerstone of managerial orthodoxy, then the reason for its tenacity, she feels, must lie in the ideological work it performs (Pringle, 1988, pp. 85–86). Her contribution to this critical tradition consists in demonstrating the masculinist ideological rationale of Weber's emphasis on 'the separation of the public world of rationality and efficiency from the private sphere of emotional and personal life' (*ibid.*, p. 86) as the defining mark of 'bureaucratic' existence.

Goodsell (1989) illustrates the extent to which the romantic character of this tradition has been exposed from within the fields of administration, business management, and public policy. However, faced with the romantic criticism that the 'instrumental' rationality of bureaucracy stultifies individuals' 'free' development, moulding them in the image of 'organisation man', Goodsell's 'case for bureaucracy' basically evades the fact that, as romantic critiques recognise, historically bureaucracies *did* need to remould the 'character' of their staff. In order to meet the charge that 'Weberian' bureaucratic norms are founded on a masculinist fantasy, we may profit from a recent shift in ways of reading Weber emanating from German scholarship. The conventional picture of the grand, sociological theorist of 'social action', 'modernity' and its rationalisation of existence has given way to a rather different picture of an historical anthropologist, economist and intellectual political activist whose polymathic interests are linked by a set of ethical-cultural concerns.[13] This revisionist reading of Weber yields a concept of bureaucratic culture as an historically localised and variable 'life-order' (*Lebensführung*) informed by an ethos consisting of not only ideal purposes and a code of conduct, but also ways and means of conducting oneself.

Bureaucracy is more than a vehicle for moulding rational character. Yet it is arguably within this ethical-cultural dimension that the historical variability in what *counts* as (ir)rational, and in *the reasons for cultivating a rational attitude*, which Weber builds into his conception of 'rationalisation', manifest themselves most clearly. Thus it is not necessary to assume that this ethical-cultural dimension is all-important, merely that it is significant, in order to conclude that once it is taken into account then the general case against bureaucratic culture collapses.

As we have seen, the critique assumes that according to Weber, bureaucratic organisational norms are premised on the separation of reason and emotion, procedure and psyche, public and private. It is further assumed that these separations are (hitherto) coterminous and historically invariant, and that the rational attitude expected of bureaucrats or bureaucratically organised personnel is ethically as well as emotionally vacuous. There are undoubtedly passages in Weber which lend support to such assumptions; where, for instance, bureaucratisation is seen as equivalent to a general process of dehumanisation involving the replacement of 'all personal, irrational and emotional elements which escape calculation' by the personally detached and strictly '"objective" expert' (Weber, 1968, I, p. 975). But in such instances it has to be said that Weber is ignoring his own constantly reiterated warnings against ironing out the diverse ways in which 'the various departments of life' in the modern world have been rationalised, and the motivations for these developments, into some singular, creaseless logic (Weber, 1930, pp. 77–78).

In a well-known swipe at the stereotype of bureaucracy as inimical to individual self-realisation held by the romantically inclined 'litterati', Weber insists on the historical specificity of the 'rational' imperatives of bureaucracy in the following terms:

> The bearing of this thesis may be disregarded here – decisive is that this freely creative administration would not constitute a realm of free arbitrary action and discretion, of *personally* motivated favour and

valuation such as we find among the pre-bureaucratic forms. (Weber, 1968, I, p. 973)

The 'objectivity' required of the model bureaucrat and bureaucratic decisions entails setting aside the partialities of *patronage*. What is excluded as irrational ('arbitrary'), is a repertoire of 'private' group prerogatives and interests (family, friendship, aristocratic status, etc.) which (within limits) used to be regarded as quite legitimate.[14] The reference of this 'Weberian' norm of bureaucratic rationality is thus quite specific. For example, it would not necessarily extend to a demand that bureaucrats ought never to work to advance the interests of their nation, or corporate executives the interests of their company, whether or not the ensuing actions are 'rational' according to some more global point of view.

Nor do the norms of bureaucratic rationality entail the exclusion of all *sentimental* considerations. As the cited passage from Weber goes on to insist, 'the rule and pursuit of "objective" purposes' is inseparable from the cultivation of a spirit of loyalty and vocational 'devotion' in respect to those purposes (Weber, *op cit.*, I, p. 979). As Pringle (1988, p. 86) would quickly remind us, loyalty is directed to the office not to a personal superior. However, the early-modern humanist *concept* of person in question here – the person as a notable personage, a bundle of prestigious statuses – bears little relation to the modern Romantic 'emotive' concept entailed in Pringle's characterisation of the distinction between offices and their incumbents. Like his critics, Weber himself and his supporters, too, occasionally exaggerate the generality of its 'impersonal' requirements, e.g. in Moore's (1962, p. 87) evocation of the ideal of 'a society of cooperative strangers'. Such characterisations obliterate the fact that, as Moore himself avows (*ibid.*, pp. 83–95, 109), bureaucracy holds no *general* antipathy to relations of friendship beyond the point at which it opens up the possibility of 'jobs for the boys', indulging incompetence, or betrayal of confidentiality. The supposition of an essential normative antipathy between bureaucracy and informal relations such as friendship hinges on a romantic identification of such relations with freedom from normative compulsion, spontaneous attraction, intimacy, and free choice. A single historical example will serve to suggest why both this opposition and the philosophical fantasy concerning friendship on which it rests may be unsustainable. It concerns the bureaucrat's capacity for preserving *confidentiality*.

For good or ill, modern belief in open discussion makes the value placed on confidentiality in bureaucratic culture appear questionable. Yet we can also appreciate its value. Confidentiality acquired this ambivalent value at the point at which, partly under the impress of a nascent democratic culture, bureaucracy came to be implicated in a problematisation of 'Machievellian', absolutist-monarchical representations of government as the administration of state secrets (Meinecke, 1924, 1957; Goldberg, 1983, ch. 2). One indication of the ethical *status quo ante* is a text on 'The parts, place and office of the secretorie' appended to Angell Day's (1599, 1967) letter-writing manual *The English Secretorie*. This appendix is a prime example of a text in the conduct-book genre aimed at the formation of a high Renaissance bureaucrat (a 'secretorie' at that time being 'a man who writes for his lord'). Curiously, one of the qualities of character deemed especially appropriate to the *secret-keeping* essence of the 'secretarial' office is the capacity for a certain kind of friendship with one's superior. Not only is the relationship of friendship *explicitly* codified (it's not a secret to be uncovered by a critique), it is also a constituent, semi-formal part of the habitus of a Renaissance 'bureaucrat'. We simply cannot make sense of these early-modern proto-bureaucratic relations if we continue to think in terms of general equivalences between informality, friendship and the unsuccessfully repressed underlife of bureaucratic culture.

The general point is clear: the demands for rationality and objectivity entailed by the bureaucratic ethos and culture cannot be interpreted as embodying a claim to objectivity in an *epistemological* sense. The cultivation of an 'objective', rational attitude should not be seen as a vain attempt to acquire a general capacity to take, in the English moral philosopher Henry Sidgwick's phrase, 'the point of view of the universe', a general capacity for impartiality which operates through a general normative exclusion of the subjective dimensions of existence. Hegel's (1821, 1967) phantasy of bureaucrats as representing 'the universal class' in a perfectly ordered ethical post-liberal-democratic, corporatist state may stand as a monument to this epistemological-political phantasy. It is not a phantasy to which Weber subscribed.

It begins to look as though critiques of bureaucratic thinking along the lines of Pringle's suspicion of anti-discrimination policies for secretaries are radically misdirected. At least to the (limited) extent to which they have come to be grafted onto a democratic culture, bureaucratic norms today are incompatible with the preferences, liberalities (and discrimination) of patronage. No matter how rife patronage may be in some workplaces, or which gender it may benefit, patronage has now become difficult to justify. However, there is no reason to define such norms through an opposition to a generalised sphere of the personal or private, still less to identify women with them. 'Bureaucratic culture' can only be constitutively masculinist on condition of there being some overarching, institutionally embodied cultural spirit of 'instrumental reason' in which masculine values and habits are inherent. The purpose of the historical argument against the radical sociological critique of Weberianism has been to deny that proposition. Only by a sleight of hand (exemplified in Pringle, 1988, pp. 85, 87, 89; cf. also Franzway *et al.*, 1989, p. 143) can the delimited historical senses in which Weber speaks of bureaucratic rule as precluding 'personally motivated' actions, be extended from their intended reference to patronal prerogatives to signifying the exclusion of *the* personal and private realms. It is in these moments at which bureaucracy is flatly equated to the separation of the rational from the emotional that the political-romantic basis of the critique is most apparent.

This identification of bureaucratic culture with an unrealisable model of instrumental reason also falls victim to its assumption, noted earlier, that it restricts what counts as rational to 'formal' calculations about 'means', to the exclusion of 'substantive' goals and commitments. As Charles Larmore (1987, pp. xiii–xiv, 144–45) notes, Weber's distinction between formal and substantive rationality has to be read in the light of the two different but equally ethical outlooks respectively informing them. In 'Politics as a vocation', Weber (1947, pp. 120–287) characterised the ethos appropriate to forms of substantive rationality as 'the ethics of ultimate ends' (*Gesinnungsethik*). This consists in a set of convictions which individuals commit themselves to put into practice irrespective of the consequences of so acting. The ethos associated with the cultivation of a formal rational attitude is indeed premised upon cultivating indifference to certain ultimate moral ends. But this indifference is historically based on learning to take cognizance of the incompatibility between a plurality of passionate convictions about ultimate moral ends – especially religious convictions – and hence the possibly heavy cost of pursuing one of them at the expense of the others. To that extent, formal rationality is not predicated on an amoral instrumentalism but on a liberal-pluralist 'ethics of responsibility'.

The attribution of a 'masculinist' essence to bureaucracy may, therefore, be questioned. But this does not preclude the possibility of identifying specific ways in which norms, values, habits of conduct and bodily demeanours associated with masculinity historically lodged themselves in the ethos of bureaucratic organisation. Our reconstruction of Weber's view of bureaucracy provides for precisely that possibility. For example, one classical locus of a 'masculine' outlook is *stoicism*. Paralleling both Weber's argument on the ethical culture of bureaucracy and the genealogies of discipline and ethics associated with Michel Foucault, Gerhard Oestreich (1982) has provided an illuminating account of the part played by seventeenth-century reworkings of this classical ethos in 'the spiritual, moral, and psychological changes' (*ibid.*, p. 26) which 'social discipline' must have wrought in the personnel of the new standing armies and administrative apparatuses established in the course of the seventeenth century by the European absolutist monarchies.[15]

According to Oestreich, the effectiveness of the new armies and bureaucracies depended upon soldiers' and officials' subordination of not only their traditional kinship and friendship loyalties (as stressed by Weber) but also their religious convictions and warmongering ways of conducting themselves to the rigorous new order of monarchical discipline, and its 'reasons of state'. To anyone accustomed to compliance with the will of another only on the basis of traditional bonds of reciprocal obligations and favours, how strange the relations of automatic obedience to commands required by the new ideal of public service must have seemed! From a political-romantic perspective, personal subordination is unimaginable except as the result of either coercion or ideology. It may be less anachronistic to see the new sort of obedience and 'reining' in of personal aspirations required of a Renaissance administrator or soldier as involving the cultivation of an *ethical skill*. What had to be (re-)learned from ancient Roman models was how to obey in a dignified fashion and how in turn to give orders which would not demean a subordinate's standing. An art of survival under a ruthless superior was also needed. How were these 'ethical skills' acquired?

One reason for the success of the neostoic 'art of living' in assisting individuals to accommodate themselves to these new relations of subordination was the 'manly' severity of its *rhetoric*. At the level of tone and sentence structure, for example, arguments and prescriptions written in the clipped 'baroque' style, for which Justius Lipsius, the most influential of the European neostoic theorists and programmers of this new ethos, was so renowned, were 'martialled' in the Lipsean text after the manner of military troop movements. Rhetorical appeal by means of imagery is also made to seamen and merchants (Oestreich 1982, pp. 29–30, 61, 67–68). A rhetorical ethic of this sort is based less on principle than on precept. It was transmitted not only, or mainly, through treatises but also through the ancient Roman 'examples' furnished by the *vitae* of pragmatic soldier-statesmen such as Agricola, as related in the writings of Tacitus.[16]

In sum, the 'objectivising' or rationalising imperatives of early modern bureaucratic cultures were born out of a contingent mixture of exigencies and imperatives. These can hardly be reduced to an unconscious desire to exclude women; not even, or especially where, as in the case of the problematisation of patronage and kinship networks and the attempt to depoliticise religious faith, bureaucratic culture entailed 'privatising' matters of personal significance. Further, the new institutions did not in principle exclude, but positively required the cultivation of 'subjective' qualities (loyal and confidential friendship, the sense of vocation). There may be connections to be drawn between these historical targets of bureaucratic rationalisation and the equally historical reasons for early-modern administrative organisations' assuming the trappings of 'a man's world' – as one means by which certain *classes* of men (soldiers, seamen, merchants, aristocrats) bred to a different way of life might be persuaded to make public service their new vocation. But only by evacuating *both* the objectivising imperatives *and* the gendered aspects of early-modern bureaucratic cultural mentalities of their limited historical meanings in favour of a romantic-historicist allegory is it possible to reduce the former to the latter.

Historicising the category of bureaucratic culture in this manner suggests that the presence of 'masculinist' attitudes in an organisation does not, *ipso facto*, undermine the validity of its commitments to impersonal standards of decision-making. Moreover, once the distinct sources of its objectivising and man-centred aspects are acknowledged, then the way is open to understand *why* certain forms of masculine identity which have become ensconced in bureaucratic organisations lose their erstwhile justification. Only when men have come to expect 'desk jobs' as a matter of course do displays of warrior-like masculinity at work become a suitable subject for feminist pastiche. From this perspective, to register the archaic character of secretaries' personal services to their male bosses does not mean that the sexist lease on secretarial work might not be in the process of being renewed on some different basis. Bureaucratic cultures may acquire a 'male' colouration in new, but always limited ways.

Moreover, registration of the historical specificity of masculine forms of identity need not be thought to foreclose on the possibility of limited *continuities* in the gendered aspects of bureaucratic cultures. For example, one reason why early-modern bureaucratic culture might have appeared demeaning to a man of aristocratic birth may remain a factor in organisational life to this day: namely, the *feminine* connotations of rational order and discipline. The critique of bureaucratic culture makes much of stereotypes identifying rationality with masculinity. Their prevalence, however, should not blind us to the existence of a contrary series of images: the earth mother of mythological reknown (see note 11 above); the 'social mother' of nineteenth- and twentieth-century family reform policies; the 'phallic mother' of psychoanalysis. In these representations women are identified with a 'heavy' penchant and capacities for overseeing, stabilising or even repressing the more creative, free-floating tendencies of the male.

Michelle Le Doeuff's insistence on this diversity in the ways in which sexual difference and rationality are mapped onto one another is all the more salutory insofar as she links suppression of this diversity to a tendency (encountered in Pringle's argument) to overestimate the importance of *philosophical* versions of this relationship:

> The zone of influence of the division produced by philosophy is a very limited one. This idea of woman as sphynx and chaos is no doubt only current today in a certain fraction of the dominant class. In the popular strata of society, the woman is seen rather as a force for order, 'rational' – indeed a killjoy, it being assumed that the pole of imagination and carefree fancy is the province of masculinity. (Le Doeuff, 1980, p. 150, transl. and cited by Morris, 1987, pp. 173–74)[17]

Leaving aside for the moment any question of the effects of such stereotyping, at this point such a possibility can stand as an augury of the obstacles to women's equal opportunity in the workplace presented by, not formal-official but *informal*-official constituents of modern management policies.

Informality, Bureaucratic Culture and the Cultural License for Sexual Harassment

In the course of querying romantic stereotypes about bureaucratic rational-ity, early-modern bureaucratic culture was seen to have been characterised by a kind of informal ('off-the-record') yet codified 'friendship'. Forms of informality in 'bureaucratic' settings need have nothing in common save their involving some contrastive reference to a prior or current 'rule' in respect to which some divergence or relaxation has taken place. The paradigm 'Weberian' case of formal rules, of course, are those inscribed in written codes of practice, functional divisions of labour, official channels of communication and fixed, hierarchical chains of authority. Moore (1962, p. 94) offers a useful reminder of the *diversity* of phenomena loosely amalgamated under the definitional rubric of informal organisation ('a basket of unwritten scraps'). For instance, some informalities may run counter to official rules ('grapevines' as opposed to official channels), others may be quite routine yet too task-specific to be codified.

Furthermore, far from always conflicting with formal rules, informalities may represent a *deliberate* relaxation of rules. No exception to the rule, a history of 'informalisation' (Wouters, 1977) is characteristic of domain after governmental domain of twentieth-century 'Western' cultures, including and especially work cultures. Nikolas Rose (1990) has drawn attention to a proliferating tradition of personnel management literature which links productive industrial relations not to the repression of personality, but rather to a 'programmed' ethical intensification of subjective elements of working life:

> . . . a subjectification of work, involving the saturation of the working body with feelings . . . wishes, the transformation of work . . . into matters of personal fulfillment and psychical identity, in which the financial exchange is significant less for the cash reward it offers than for the identity it confers on the recipient. Hence the convergence of an entire discourse upon success and failure in jobs . . . the costs and benefits of employment and unemployment conducted in therapeutic rather than economic terms . . . (Rose, 1990, p. 244)

Whilst it would be unwise to overestimate the significance of this 'subjectification of work', equally, it cannot be written off as a peripheral tactic of capitalist social control. Its significance for my argument lies both in the problems it potentially presents for EEO policies on sexual harassment and in its more damaging implications for the critique of bureaucratic culture.

Some of these problems detract from Clare Burton's otherwise astute arguments on the obstacles confronting affirmative action policies and how these might be overcome through EEO policymakers developing 'a politics of skill' (Burton, 1986). This would set out to challenge existing definitions of merit, efficiency and competences, and introduce new organisational practices, incentives and rewards. One candidate for such a challenge noted by Burton might be the informal 'homosocial' conduits (after-work drinks, etc.) for transmitting skills to new appointees (from which women may be excluded by virtue of either their sex or their domestic responsibilities). An EEO policy might be envisaged which sought to make effective mentoring (however it was accomplished and irrespective of the sex of the appointee), a public expectation and a criterion of managerial competence.[18] Where formal criteria of efficiency favour an overly aggressive managerial style which women are likely to find alienating, these are more appropriate targets for reform than measures aimed at redressing women's 'weaknesses' (Burton, *ibid.*, pp. 303–4). With these contentions I have no dispute. However, when cast in the mould of the critique of bureaucratic culture, Burton's analysis runs into difficulties. In targeting frequently unconscious subjective motivations (*ibid.*,

p. 296) and the informal underlife of the workplace, are feminist EEO policymakers really making an unprecedented assault on the organisational mentality? Are *all* 'universalist' criteria which abstract from sexual difference automatically suspect (*ibid.*, p. 301)? Burton maintains that in arguing for the institutionalisation of more 'supportive, facilitative, interpersonal and collaborative' organisational styles, feminists are up against a bastion of male rationalism uniformly committed to an impersonal model of authoritarian management. Conversely, the alternative management style is seen as more in keeping with feminine values and self-image.

Surely the history of twentieth-century management thinking is replete with counter-examples to all of these assumptions.[19] One could dwell on the more benign 'democratic' management tradition (e.g. Tead, 1945), with its emphases on affording space for the realisation of non-standardised forms of talent. But a more telling counter-example might be furnished by a text on the 'personal qualifications' required to be a good executive, which not merely owes nothing to feminism, but is awash in sexist imagery. 'Choosing an executive, like choosing a wife, is a difficult thing', begins Meadows (1957, p. 178). In this instance, the assumption as to the sexual denomination of a senior executive goes along with an valorisation of 'subjective' executive capacities such as a 'sympathetic' understanding of others, respect for their individuality or 'graceful' acceptance of difficult situations, as well as more technical and assertive qualifications. Even at its most sexist, managerial science seems comfortable with the idea that the work of executive personnel requires a range of 'soft' qualifications along the very lines of Burton's alternative. This is not what one would expect from a homosocial society of strangers.

Perhaps 'the politics of skill' would be better off hitching its wagon to the star of the subjectification-of-work trend. However, if there are disadvantages to women accruing from the sexist assumptions built into the deployment of some 'formal' procedures and 'impartial' criteria of evaluation in EEO policies, there are also potential disadvantages associated with the planned 'informalisation' of workplace relations. Let us grant the existence of something like a cultural licence (Farley, 1978, p. 13) for the sexual harassment of women, and that the widespread currency of this disposition on the part of men to treat women as 'fair game' can be linked to patterns of assymetrical relations of power between the sexes. It does not follow, however, that every factor which contributes to this cultural licence to harass women can be derived from those patterns of sexist subordination. A case can be made that in some respects planned informalisation of workplace relations may have precisely this effect. Informalisation, in other words, may promote sexual harassment to the extent that it lowers the threshold of social distance between people at work, and *ipso facto* between the sexes, which the norms of conduct associated with professional respect in the more formal administrative model of organisation work to establish.

The informalisation of corporate culture is not of course purely a function of new personnel management strategies, yet they are clearly vital to it. Martin and Murphy (1988) draw attention to a statistically documented increase in sexual relationships (as distinct from the old-fashioned 'office-affair') between corporate working colleagues in North America. This trend they attribute to the growth of women in managerial and professional jobs involving teamwork, combined with a steep decrease in leisure time as employees' lives become more work-oriented. Martin and Murphy *implicitly* link this sexualisation of the workplace 'in a decade (the 1980s) that blends personal development and professional achievement so seamlessly' to precisely the programmatic subjectification of work traced by Nikolas Rose; and *explicitly* link it to a concomitant exacerbation of the problem of sexual harassment of women.

Similarly, Pringle (1988, p. 93) herself calls attention to the way an atmosphere of 'compulsory jocularity' in a legal practice lent encouragement to readily deniable sexual harassment in the form of a constant and controlling stream of sexual innuendo. Programmed informalisation moreover, is not, of course, confined to the corporate workplace. A further example of a way of managing superordinate/subordinate relationships which again is not itself sexist but which could be part of an institutional licensing of sexism, is the (unsuccessful) alibi recorded by a poetry professor in a North American university report after a charge of sexual harassment had been laid against him:

> . . . his teaching style is deliberately personal and intense . . . [he] believes that his success as a teacher is due largely to his ability to develop close personal relationships with his students, and to drive them to include everything in their lives in their poetry. The intensity was part of the course's appeal. I do want to underscore the difficulty faced by even the most well-meaning instructors in striking a balance between personal interest [in their students' 'emotional' make-up], and professional distance. (Dziech and Weiner, 1984, p. 32)

An absurd alibi, no doubt. Yet, the example may not be such a special case. Unwillingness to assume responsibility for their authority over students amongst academics is not unknown. Emphasis on suspension of conventional former proprieties and openness to personal response has long been a characteristic of modern literary studies. My point is not, I hasten to add, to suggest that one category of students is more at risk than another; but rather that the currency of cultivated informalisation may have something to do with the relative ineptitude of even the more liberal tertiary educational institutions, by comparison with the public service or corporations, in systematically addressing the problem of sexual harassment. Certainly for Dzeich and Weiner (*ibid.*, pp. 146, 181) one reason for its prevalence and why institutionalising dependable complaints-mechanisms and sanctions have proved so difficult lies in the reluctance of many academics to exercise or subject themselves to 'formal' managerial or administrative authority (e.g. to reprimand colleagues).

If there is a lesson to be drawn from these examples it might be this. Like Pringle, but for a different reason, I maintain that if women are disadvantaged by being identified in terms of 'personal' characteristics, this may not invariably be interpreted as a residue of outdated social organisation. Rather, the dissemination of subjectivising management techniques and the informal working relationships which they (intentionally and unintentionally) bring about open up a new porthole through which certain kinds of contemporary 'men's culture' and habits are able to establish themselves. However, as a management strategy, this informalising development is not simply the unwished-for obverse of a formalistic male rationalism incapable of existing independently of the 'other' aspects of existence which it attempts to exclude.

Rather, the psychologisation of work is merely another development. It does not undercut (at most suggesting a need to qualify) EEO evaluations of secretaries' personal services as archaic and out of place. Programmed informalisation takes a variety of forms and is not based on any single set of gendered values. In some respects, it renews a cultural licence to sexually harass women. However, there can be no question of its representing a general licence to make a problem out of formality as such. There is no reason why the existence of normative constraints on the subject-matter of jocular exchanges should be experienced (by men) as placing a general 'dampener' on an otherwise informal workplace atmosphere. All informality, 'programmed' or otherwise, is conditional upon rules. Men's 'locker-room' humour is no stranger to the idea of constraints upon the subject-matter of jokes. All this should sound a warning about the dangers of globally suspecting 'formal', normative standards of conduct enjoining the treatment of all employees as occupational equals. To do so is both to overestimate managerial antipathy to informality and to underestimate its dangers.

What is the more general lesson of this whole exercise in disaggregating both the formal and informal aspects of 'bureaucratic culture'? It is that if such a concept is to be productive it cannot be organised around the idea of a would-be mutual exclusiveness – concealing dialectical interdependence – of the formal and the informal in the generalised way proposed in the critique of bureaucratic culture. Let us now pursue the implications of this proposition for assessing the scope and limits of the management policies on sexual harassment considered at the outset.

The 'Limits' of EEO Policies

The sexual harassment policy documents make no bones about the circum-scribed character of their approach to the problem. It is consistently and blandly defined as 'improper' conduct. As we have argued in previous chapters, this does not mean that it breaches the norms of conduct expected of a 'gentleman' towards a 'lady'. Rather the standards of conduct which are breached are those 'proper' to a workplace legally committed to treating its members as occupational equals and the positions in its hierarchy as 'careers open to talents'. In effect, then, what is at stake is a problem of occupational manners affecting bodily integrity ('personal space') in a way that denies the victims' entitlement to be treated seriously as an equal in the workplace context.

We know the criticisms to which a stony 'Weberian' emphasis on norms of conduct, the restriction of the complaints process to 'official channels', etc., is exposed. We are told that it is the prisoner of an inadequate liberal conception of equal citizenship which is abstract to women's distinctive needs and wants and of an inadequate sociological theory of sexual roles; and that it restricts regulation of sexual harassment to the public (men's) world of work, and even within that realm to overtly sexual behaviour, thereby legitimating more diffuse heterosexist forms of oppression. But must the fact that management definitions and policies severely circumscribe both the problem to be addressed and the scope for action be a matter for objection?

Part of the reason for confining official attention to the level of conduct lies in the need for procedures to embody a *juridical* element, including both protection of complainants from actions against them as a conse-quence of filing a complaint *and* the protection of respondents from the reputational effects of vexatious, frivolous or otherwise unfounded complaints. But it is also a matter of making the *ethical* issue revolve around the dignity or honour of the parties and the promotion of a kind of 'industrial peace' through informal conciliation or negotiation. So, for example, picking out the norm-of-conduct-breaching element of sexual harassment is more apt to shame the offender into making an apology or other reparation than subsuming 'the whole person' under the category of 'sexual harasser' (FPSB, 1986, p. 27), a term which that document urges should be used with some economy.

Can the charge that focusing on sexual harassment casts a legitimating shadow over other informal 'heterosexist' ways in which men exercise power over women at work be made to stick? Against this view of the arbitrarily limiting consequences of 'official' definitions, it may be observed that in the legal developments, which to some considerable extent underpin management initiatives, sexual harassment is construed as one kind of sex discrimination among others. As *Hill v. NSW Water Resources Commission* (1985, EOC 90–030) dramatically showed, sex-discrimination legislation was powerful enough in this case to get a purchase on the 'sexist harassment' (as it was termed) suffered by the complainant, which was not, as such, of a sexual nature.[20] Moreover, once an effective grid of norms covering sexual harassment in the workplace is put in place, it furnishes a persuasive precedent for drawing attention both to adjacent forms of sexist behaviour and to other failings in personal interactions.

From the fact that sexual harassment policies work within restricted terms of reference and 'take exception' to only one band in the spectrum of possible sexist conducts it does not follow that they 'assume' that the occurrence of manifestations of sexuality is *exceptional*. Not *all* sexual ways of interacting within the modern workplace compromise a woman's dignity as a (working) citizen. Not all sexual banter, for example, has the effect of making a 'joke' out of her work. Thus the policing of sexual harassment involves *a lot less* than a programme for expelling 'sexuality' from the workplace. Pringle's charge that EEO policies do little or nothing to question the 'exceptional' status of non-heterosexual relations is true. But this is only to say that EEO policies 'fail' to associate themselves with a cause of radical sexual revolution for which it is not clear that there is even a popular charter, let alone the practical possibility of persuading governments and 'business' to take it on board.

The main point on which the charge of arbitrary limitation breaks down, however, is simply that sexual harassment policies do not necessarily operate in a vacuum, outside which equally pernicious forms of sexism are invariably free to flourish. Management policies, it will be recalled, embrace not only complaints and disciplinary procedures but staff training, publicity and other preventative measures. The range of such workplace measures is quite broad, extending from trade union sponsored health and safety reforms to proposals aimed at flattening workplace hierarchies. If it is utopian to expect such proposals to be widely adopted tomorrow, it is also worth observing the variety of other grounds on which these changes could be argued for. There is thus scope for linking policies for managing sexual harassment to a broader anti-sexist social policy; a policy which, nevertheless, is not premised on the radical transformation of bureaucratic culture but, on the contrary, *exploits some of its virtues*. Amongst these virtues may be included some of the very qualities of sensitivity and flexibility it is stereotypically thought to lack.

The supposition of an antipathy between bureaucratic culture and the realms of informality and subjectivity sits oddly with the localised inscriptions of informal actions and concern with individuals' feelings at innumerable tactical points in the previously examined trade union and public service sexual harassment policies. Informal action plays a role both inside and outside the formal grievance procedures, whilst the rationale of some of their most formal aspects is precisely the protection of a series of 'sensitivities' to which the 'direct-action' model is apt to be blind. The 'sensitivities' pertain to the dangers of defamation, retaliation, and breaches of natural justice which suggest the need for confidentiality before, during and after the hearing of the complaint. Those who recommend that, in the absence of adequate legal redress for sexual harassment, women should 'take direct action in the workplace' (Tiffin, 1984, p. 7) would themselves do well to be sensitive to the exigency of these natural justice requirements in non-judicial contexts.

Suppose, for example, that a demonstration against a supposed harasser is organised *after* an official complaint has been filed, i.e. whilst procedural processes of investigating, conciliating and/or arbitrating the complaint are taking place. Will the respondent to the complaint not have a legitimate grievance *à propos* his entitlement to natural justice? Both the legal and political-rhetorical consequences of such 'spontaneous' actions can well be imagined: undermining of the procedural case against him; generation of sympathy for him on the part of fellow workers as the complainant loses the proverbial moral high ground; destruction of any possibility (at least sometimes a desideratum) of re-establishing professional work relations between respondent and complainant.

The necessity on such occasions to make hard, undialectical political choices between procedural and direct action cannot be taken as evidence of a general bureaucratic antipathy towards informality. On the contrary, taking personal initiatives is an option in all the policies we considered. Typically, handling sexual harassment informally is regarded as *preferable* if (and only if) prevailing power relations and other circumstances permit. In some cases, detailed and helpful advice regarding personal initiatives is tendered. It may be fitting to conclude this unjaundiced examination of the 'limited' aspects of sexual harassment policies with a discussion of the attitude towards informal counter-action adopted in the text which is probably *least* defensible from a 'radical' point of view: Coeli-Myer *et al.*'s *Sexual Harassment*.

Even if one has no objection to their definition of this conduct as an issue of unprofessional conduct which, the authors say, 'doesn't belong in the office' (Coeli Myer *et al.*, *ibid.*, p. 116) and is not conducive to an effective working relationship, the 'repertoire of statements' (*ibid.*, p. 150) which the authors propose as possible ripostes to sexual harassment will not all be to everyone's liking. Offended by the recommendation in this text of a gentle but firm approach accompanied by a pleasant smile (with its perhaps inordinate preoccupation with restoring harmonious relations), some may want to put up a sharper set of responses, along the lines suggested by Hadjifotiou. Others may note the potentially disastrous consequences of the text's obliviousness to the constraints imposed by different *genres* on what might be sensibly written in the memorandum which they recommend as an alternative to face-to-face confrontations.[21] Yet these reservations cannot detract from the potential effectiveness of the ethico-technical stance implicit in the informal measures recommended by Coeli Myer: namely the importance of seeing one's ethical judgements and responses not as an expression of inmost feelings, but as the exercise of *a set of empowering rhetorical skills*.

Even those who would have no objection to these measures might bridle at the thought that skill in 'squelching' sexual harassment 'without calling in the marines' becomes a promotional proving-ground on which to demonstrate management potential (Coeli Myer *et al.*, *ibid.*, p. 120). This 'virile' proposal seems to echo the old prejudice that sexual harassment is a 'fact of life' which an 'experienced' woman should be able to contend with by herself, a private matter which does not call for managerial action. Yet, despite the competitive 'individualist' tenor of the proposal, it is after all part of a strategy which, as we have seen, offers an array of measures against sexual harassment, including procedural remedies and personal-rhetorical skills. These in turn are linked to affirmative action proposals for flatter authority structures and other preventative measures which are absent from the text's more 'progressive' counterparts. Seen in this context of a broad commitment to restructuring, such a proposal might be seen as a perverse form of emphasis on the need for measures to get more women into managerial positions.

What a contrast there is between the lowly terms of ethical calculation and response manifest in these proposals on informal action and the spontaneous expression of feelings of personal injury commended by the

Alliance document; or the use of sexual harassment policy as an occasion for a political exposé of masculinism commended by Pringle. Yet what is so remiss about the 'mixed motivations' of the EEO management policy outlined by Coeli Myer *et al.*? The range of organisations which may provide institutional possibilities for an imaginative sexual harassment policy to latch onto may be wider than many 'progressively-minded' readers imagine. Not all their values and practices will be found congenial. But if there is an argument for taking managerial approaches to sexual harassment seriously it has little to gain by gilding the lily.

Conclusion: The Place of a Politics of Subjectivity

It would be rash to base too firm a conclusion on the limited array of policies for managing sexual harassment surveyed here. However, their function is merely to provide counter-examples to an unwarranted generalisation. If the general objective of the critique of bureaucratic culture is to undermine confidence in EEO policies of this sort then it is the view of this book that it deserves to fail. If its argument holds water, adverse judgements on particular rafts of policies may be entirely appropriate, but not on that account. Interpreting sexual harassment policies as it does largely from the standpoint of a political romanticism, the critique 'lags behind' the ethico-technical reasoning at work in these policies.

Some of the perceived 'limits' of these policies and forms of reasoning may be read as virtues. A prime example is the focus in procedures, sanctions, etc. on 'unacceptable conduct'. Indifferent as it must be to motivational or social-structural questions, a serious management policy will effectively construe sexual harassment as a problem of inequitable manners. There may be more to it, something more subterranean, than that. Nevertheless this focus on protocols of acceptable conduct is a positive prerequisite for doing something about sexual harassment in a way calculated to secure broad cultural acceptance. Other 'limits' which may well be deemed limitations may be addressed by a range of other EEO reforms linked by a common 'cultural policy' aim of modifying the ethical climate of the workplace in non-sexist directions. These reforms may be quite radical (e.g. involving changes to chains of authority), yet they remain specific.

The claim that sexual harassment procedures pretend that 'sexuality' has no place in a bureaucratically organised environment is therefore inappropriate. Management policies simply and rightly refuse to operate at that level of generality. Nor do they preclude informal action or emotional receptivity – indeed at certain points they expressly depend upon them.

Besides, informality in organisational life may play a part in encouraging sexual harassment. Only by generalising and conflating the meaning and reference of the categories of the informal, the psychical and the sexual, and placing them in a 'dialectical' opposition to equally generalised and conflated categories of the rational or the bureaucratic is it possible to arrive at the conclusion that the management of sexual harassment needs to be opened up to a theory and politics of 'subjectivity'.

Bureaucracies and commercial organisations never will be angels. The question is not whether conscientious attitudes ought to be cultivated towards them but what *sort* of conscience is appropriate to the work of installing (or amending) EEO policies bearing on sexual harassment. An array of non-romantic forms of conscientious action and evaluations in respect to these policies has been reviewed: limited industrial citizenship; democratic manners; calculations of honour and shame; 'casuistical' decision-making and attitude-formation; and other rhetorical-ethical ways of thinking and acting. These materials for forming a conscience do not lack all currency in our contemporary ethical culture.

To argue in this way is not to discount the possible value of all the themes which are subsumed under the rubric of a politics of subjectivity. Is it not possible, for example, to envisage a more restricted contribution from the side of psychoanalysis to a sexual harassment policy? Irrespective of its theoretical (explanatory) value, psychoanalysis might be seen as a more or less complex[22] *art of characterisation* of individuals and their interactions in terms of the unconscious desires and phantasies which are staged in, and read-off from, their overt bodily demeanour, conduct, attitudes, speech, silences, etc. As such, 'psychoanalysis' forms a *rhetorical* aid to the construction of judgements about conducts. It furnishes a conceptual grid of intelligibility, a set of topic-headings with which to locate problematic forms of conduct. It could represent a certain kind of *nous*.

To view psychoanalysis as an ethico-rhetorical art of characterisation places it on the same social-discursive level as the managerial (or legal) definitions by means of which the actionable dimensions of sexual harassment are picked out. In this way there is less temptation to imagine that psychoanalysis yields a more 'profound' knowledge of what is really going on in sexual harassment than do 'official' knowledges. In relation to which conceivable courses of action are the latter inevitably superficial and inadequate? If a psychoanalytical angle on sexual harassment has a role to play, it is unlikely to be of a quasi-legal definitional (forensic) or therapeutic order. The tendency in recent Australian legal decisions has been to shift the emphasis away from intentions, an emphasis which in the past has favoured the perpetrator rather than the victim of sexual harassment (Ronalds, 1987). Still less would a psychoanalytical approach have much to offer by way of therapeutically-oriented counselling. Given that in effect a miscreant would be obliged to undergo it in order to avoid further disciplinary action (counselling, in these circumstances, would itself be an exercise in work-discipline), it would be unlikely to be either acceptable to the workforce or (in the absence of any desire for personal change) to have any preventative efficacy.

Are there other uses of a psychoanalytical approach in an EEO policy on sexual harassment which are not contingent on the ambition to find some general articulation between psychical and socio-political realms? And in which knowledge of the former is not seen as the subversive key to the latter?[23] There *is* a body of psychoanalytically-informed feminist work which has sought to develop far more limited, practical accommodations between psychoanalysis and the calculations of feminist social policy; one which neither avoids the differences between the assumptions about human agency respectively underpinning pyschoanalysis and such policies nor registers this discrepancy as a 'deadlock' to be overcome (Heath, 1986, p. 57). Joan Copjec (1990), for instance, argues that the 'subject-positions' – i.e. the roles, statuses, capacities, dispositions, and socially programmed desires – ascribed to women in the motley of discourses, practices and policies which socially construct them never completely coincide with the habits of mind, desires, etc. of the individuals who occupy those 'subject-positions'.

However, the diverse ways in which the subject-positions or categories of 'woman' and 'women' are socially constructed, excluded, valorised or degraded obey no general logic and have no single negative or positive value. The same has to be said about women's psychical dispositions. There is neither a general global condition of female oppression or subordination nor a privileged locus of female resistance. *Feminist* social norms and ideals can no more be made completely congruent with female desires than can misogynistic ones. This is the case even where the preferred vehicle for this social/psychical reformation is a régime of pleasures and/or rational persuasion, rather than coercion. Copjec is opposed to any general political analysis and strategy predicated on a view of the social reconstruction of sexed subjectivity according to which 'the subject is assumed . . . to come into being by actually wanting what social laws want it to want . . . taking social representations as images of its own ideal being . . . deriving a narcissistic pleasure from these representations' (Copjec, 1989, pp. 228–29).

Psychoanalysis in this feminist perspective cannot be portrayed as providing the key to the citadel of women's subordination. Yet a perspective of this sort does seem to provide a warrant for arguing that *one* determinant of that oppression (and a corresponding provocation or energising motive for the women's movement) is that women the world over enter a cultural order which at some psychical-symbolic level is 'phallocentric'. At the bottom of all the complex arguments behind this proposition is the basic difficulty of *representing* women, no matter how deviantly or deviously, without defining them as, in some assymetrical sense, 'not-men'.[24]

This is not to say that it is only of the world of representations that it ever makes sense to say 'it's a man's world'. And only from within definite ethical-political perspectives need this component of 'lack' in representations of women be experienced as a problem. The implication is rather that the contribution of a feminist-psychoanalytical 'art of characterisation' to a pro-feminist policy on sexual harassment is likely to be restricted to the representation or communication of such a policy, in the light of the psychical reception which may be provoked by it.

One likely point-of-entry for the enactments of phantasies of resistance to such a policy is the requirement that those in managerial authority 'set an example', both in the way they treat subordinates and in the promptness and energy with which they deal with sexual harassment as and when it arises. A managerial 'role-model' may simply function as the bearer of a prudential, mimetic lesson about the social evil of sexual harassment. However, irrespective of whether a certain identification with the persona of the manager, and a corresponding disidentification with those who sexually harass women is encouraged or not, these figures *may* become objects of psychical (dis)identifications. A setting can be conceived in which this possibility becomes a likelihood: viz. to the extent that a sexual harassment policy is linked to affirmative action measures aimed at increasing the number of *women* who enter management at all levels.

Let us suppose, then, that, in Copjec's words, the (self-)representation of the 'model' manager offers itself as the image of the ideal being of subordinates (who may also bear managerial or supervisory responsibilities). Wherever imaginary identifications are in play in political conflicts, it has been argued, there may be reason to ask *which* trait-of-identification is in play: 'The trait on the basis of which we identify with someone is usually hidden – it is by no means necessarily a glamorous feature . . . rightist ideology in particular is very adroit at offering people weakness or guilt as an identifying trait . . . ' (Zizek, 1989, pp. 105–107). Might there not be a lesson here for possible conflicts over sexual harassment policies?

The problem posed by their edifying 'rational' dimensions may be not so much a consequence of complicity between masculinity and rationality and the exclusion of the feminine and the sexual. On the contrary, the danger is that those authorised to enact these policies will become identified in male employees' minds with those previously discussed misogynist images of *maternal* rationality. It is not only women managers who might be tarred by being constructed through this phantasy of the phallic mother; men too might see their responsibilities for implementing such policies as somehow emasculating.

These (dis)identifications may lead only the most flickering existence. In many circumstances, the question of how a policy is communicated will be beside the point. Nevertheless, a concern to preempt precisely this sort of off-putting effect in the way a management policy is communicated could conceivably be important, for instance, for the ways in which the personalities of the 'talking heads' in documentary videos on sexual harassment are constructed. But surely, some will object, the pertinence of psychoanalysis to this issue cannot be limited to the arts of characterisation practised by a documentary scriptwriter. Can't it? I would be satisfied if this essay's attempt to debunk the 'politics-of-subjectivity' school of thought on sexual harassment also worked as a provocation to psychoanalytical theorists to set about more sharply distinguishing what they do from the themes of political romanticism.

Part III
Socialist Politics, Liberal Government

7 The Architecture of Legitimate Inequality

Introduction

Citizenship does not appear at first sight all that promising a vehicle for the great hopes which many social-democratic and socialist writers have pinned on this category.[1] Embarrassing in its churchy connotations – the merely law-abiding citizen of mid-twentieth century school civics courses, whose public spirit is mainly expressed in charitable or patriotic works – the promise of citizenship lies in its seeming capacity to embody elements of the republican tradition whilst cleaving to liberal safeguards. If 'active citizenship' is to become a significant locus of progressive political virtue, the concept of the citizen must also be divested of its Jacobin (insurrectionary) republican associations. To be a citizen on this view is to be more than a passport-holder who may or may not perform good works. But how much more?

Between liberalism and republicanism there lies a fought-over middle ground on the basis of which various syntheses and demarcations are sought. This controversy does not only arise in political theory. The extension of women's citizenship at stake in the sex discrimination regulation examined in Part II time and again provoked these problems about the limits and conflicting priorities of liberalism. Fine judgements are required of EEO practitioners attempting to implement the social justice objectives of the legislation without detriment to the rules of 'natural justice'. An approach to these problems favoured by many radical democratic theorists is to see them as indicative of an originary incoherence in values (liberty v. equality, etc.) which can only be overcome by a *dialectical* political theory. This reconciliation is to be effected by, on the one hand, building on the common 'emancipatory' ground of the liberal and republican traditions; and on the other, detaching both liberal and republican values from their questionable ideological and institutional bases. Liberals, for instance, must be committed to 'autonomy' for *all* citizens, republicans to respecting 'difference' within the popular will.[2]

First impressions are often right. The concept of citizenship may be serviceable for certain purposes, but, as I shall argue, it cannot bear the weight which this dialectical line of liberal-republican thinking wants to place upon it. Above all, in respect to social reform, it is a poor guide to the questions of *which* elements of liberal citizenship need to be safeguarded or expanded, and *how* expansions of citizenship status can be most effectively put in place.

It may be agreed that the libertarian strands of socialist political theory and established liberal-constitutional jurisprudence afford 'critical resources' on the basis of which substantial progressive reforms might be legitimised as consistent with a liberal-pluralist polity (Hirst and Jones, 1987; O'Hagan, 1984). However, as in the case of sexual harassment, aggravated disputes typically arise in policy areas in which even their adjudicative aspects are organised not only by means of established legal categories and liberal principles, but also by the values, objectives and methods of 'social' discipline and policy. Invaluable though these legal-political arguments may be, in order to negotiate the problems of the limits and progressive possibilities of liberalism something more is needed.

The first half of the essay thus argues for initially *discounting* the ostensibly promising points of contact between liberalism, republicanism and radical (post-)Enlightenment values which provide the starting-point for so many attempts to redeem liberalism for the purposes of a progressive politics. My argument will be that progressive political thought can only build on liberalism by initially *cutting back* on what is to count as its core. This is to undermine some of the supposed common ground between republicanism, liberalism and the social movements. Proposed extensions to the current scope of liberal policy in the name of social justice which appear to be at odds with considerations of liberty, for example, can only preserve their liberal pedigree to the extent that they are conformed to an unambiguous liberal bottom-line. This 'fit' is accomplished, I argue, not by dialectical arguments and principles but by *negotiated settlements*. As a politics of negotiation, this conception of advanced liberalism will be illustrated *via* an argument about the value of pluralism, tolerance and discussion.

Only at this point, after having established the need to identify the core of liberalism in this restricted fashion, will the implications of liberalism for the concept of citizenship and its possible extensions be unfolded. T. H. Marshall's (1949) classic essay on the subject is re-examined, with special reference to the way in which it deals with inequality. Both my restatement of the rationale for liberalism and my reassessment of Marshall's conception of citizenship turn initially on relocating liberalism *as a philosophy and technology of government*, as distinct from a general social philosophy, a source of personal ideals, or a purely legal-political doctrine. The ethical constituents of governmental reasoning prove to be the key to casting Marshall's dictum that 'citizenship is the architect of legitimate inequality' in a fresh light. Equally, the governmental 'architecture' of citizenship holds the key to a further path along which *bona fide* liberal extensions of citizenship can take place; a point I will make by means of a brief reference to abortion law.

The Priority of Pluralism

'Liberalism' is usually treated as a combination of certain philosophical ideas concerning 'the individual and society' and an ensemble of characteristic, legally defined political institutions which derive their name and legitimacy from that philosophy and its principles. Thus we distinguish liberal democracy both from the communist one-party political system and from the theories, ideologies, and aims which form the basis of the official social mission espoused by communist parties.

So conceived, liberalism is premised upon the familiar philosophical distinction between public and private realms. The actions of political government are supposed to be subject to a general limit set in accordance with the criterion of the preservation of the liberty of individuals and associations of individuals. The privileged status of liberty tends to rest upon some form of Enlightenment and/or romantic philosophical anthropology. Limitations of liberty through state interventions receive liberal moral-philosophical sanction only if liberty is enhanced and harms prevented. In fact, liberal theories (and critiques of liberalism) differ enormously over the extent of permissible public intervention. Most would agree, however, that the touchstone of legitimate intervention is supposed to be its *neutrality*.

This characteristic of the (ideal) liberal polity is the concomitant of what is taken to be its twin commitment (a) to the value of pluralism and tolerance in the face of conflicting values and lifestyles and (b) to a certain rationalism. This rationalism is expressed in ideals of impartial justice; professional government based on expert yet publicly justifiable and accountable knowledge of the problems confronting it; and political decision-making based on 'open discussion'. Whilst particular attention is given here to the values of tolerance and discussion, it is true of all of these commitments that, whether for the purposes of defence or attack, they tend to be conceived in language which owes more to philosophical forms of reasoning (moral philosophy, epistemology, philosophical psychology and anthropology, etc.) than to the more specialised habits of mind of the 'agents' of a liberal polity themselves (judges, administrators, politicians, diplomats, etc.). Subordination of the language and agency of government to a philosophical ideal-image of the liberal polity will be especially germane to how we regard a final implication of the liberal posture of political neutrality: viz., limits to the powers of a democratic majority.

The fact that liberal philosophical ideals and political systems seem to require limiting democracy sets the terms of our problem about the scope within liberalism for a political programme of extending citizenship. Facilities for legal, safe, early abortions, for instance, arguably represent an extension of women's social autonomy (usually seen as a 'positive' form of liberty). A majority of women in almost all Western countries are in favour of there being such facilities. Is there any ethical or political reason therefore why a government wishing to make such facilities available should hesitate to, or be prevented from, enshrining women's right as citizens to such facilities in legislation? The ensuing attempt to challenge the predominantly philosophical characterisation of the liberal political ethos is directed to the elucidation of this sort of question. How, I want to ask, might one's sense of the limits to extensions of the citizenship status be affected by reframing the rationale for the liberal ethos in the way I have proposed, i.e., as 'a philosophy and technology of government'?

This expression does not portend a shift from the 'softer' idiom of political philosophy to 'hard' political science. Rather, like Miller and Rose (1990) and, indirectly, Weber (1968), it is hypothesised that the centre of gravity of liberalism might be better captured in the language of 'government' than in the language of (state) politics. The latter refers us primarily to the philosophical ideals and legal-political institutional definitions by which liberal government is legitimated; the former refers us to an ensemble of more circumscribed and pragmatic forms of reasoning, to the bureaucratic actions of states, and to a range of non-statist ways of shaping citizens' conduct. Without being devoid of ethical or philosophical dimensions, the language of government lies closer to the grain of liberal practice and to the habits of mind of its practitioners.

To see what it might mean to think about liberalism in this more circumscribed fashion, and why it might be useful to do so, we may begin with an exposition of a recent argument on the ethics of liberalism in Charles Larmore's *Patterns of Moral Complexity* (1987). Consonant with the anti-perfectionist concept of ethical culture developed in the previous essays in this volume, Larmore's argument on liberalism is prefaced by an attack on ethical theories which identify right conduct with conscientious adherence to principles, rules, values, ultimate commitments or some other ideal form. Moral principles are abstract both to the question of whether a given situation imposes an obligation (is this a morally significant occasion for deploying the principle?) and to the determination of how it is to be carried out (is this a fitting response?). Only through the skilled exercise of *judgement* can principles be appropriately adjusted to morally significant situations of action. The problems associated with foundationalist identifications of the ethical with the realm of principles are exacerbated when considerations of irresolvable conflicts *between* principles are introduced. Accordingly, Larmore caps this Aristotelian argument on the centrality of judgement in ethical life with a parallel (although this time anti-Aristotelian) insistence on its irreducible heterogeneity.

It is only in the light of these twin moves that either the originality or the incompleteness of an otherwise traditional argument on liberalism can be appreciated.[3] Larmore questions attempts to found the neutrality and pluralist posture of a liberal state on Enlightenment and/or post-Enlightenment *personal ideals* such as those classically proposed by Kant, J. S. Mill, Rousseau, Habermas or Rawls. All of these attempts fail to provide a justification for the neutrality of the state *which is itself neutral* (Larmore, *op. cit.*, p. 53), in the sense of its not presuming the intrinsic superiority of one conception of the good life over others. 'Liberalism has always urged toleration for the diversity of ideals and forms of life, but almost as often it has sought to justify this position by appealing to some particular and controversial view of human flourishing' (Larmore, p. 51).

Take the problem with the principle of Kantian liberalism (Larmore, *ibid.*, pp. 51–52, 77–83). For Kant, the purpose of state neutrality is to preserve rational individual autonomy. Kant's principle is open to Herder's and Hegel's charge that it neglects human beings' social nature and the extent to which people's sense of self and moral development arises out of attachments to institutions and traditions (Larmore, pp. 94–107). One's family, for example, is in no sense the object of rational choice. Yet few would suggest that one ought therefore to cultivate rational-critical detachment towards it.

If Kant's principle fails Larmore's neutrality test (and so exposes itself to anti-liberal charges of pretending to a bogus objective rationality) this is not solely by virtue of its individualistic and rationalist content. Any (post-)Enlightenment principle of autonomy, from the Kantian to the communitarian, will be a prey to political controversy if it makes the *foundationalist* and *political-romantic* assumption that political aims and practice can only be morally justified to the extent that they *express* positive personal (or theoretical) ideals transcending 'negative' liberty.

As an alternative to this expressivist view of the *scope* of liberal political neutrality and in opposition to all the (post-)Enlightenment versions of *what* that ideal should consist in, Larmore argues that the neutrality in question, together with its concomitant of 'negative' freedom so central to liberalism, is only defensible on certain conditions. Firstly, it must be presented as a purely *political* doctrine: neutrality and negative freedom are 'political ideals' (pp. 45, 47). Secondly, the liberal *raison d'être* for political neutrality must be neither more nor less than to provide a basis for establishing a *modus vivendi* 'between persons whose ultimate ideals do not coincide'.

That is to say, liberalism requires of us that in the name of an accommodating response to conflicts arising out of the diversity of commitments in a pluralistic society, we need to cultivate a mental attitude which Larmore (*ibid.*, p. 59) describes as a 'form of institutionalised myopia' or more positively, following Walzer (1984), as an 'art of separations'. Liberalism requires that in the political realm, citizens to some extent *abstract* from their ultimate commitments. Taking Hegel's point against Kant, it does not require individuals or associations to practise this 'method of abstraction and specialisation in respect to any particular way of life' (Larmore, *op. cit.*, p. xiii) in *all* areas of their life.

Nor does this 'method' of abstraction require that one tempers one's belief in a given ideal with a dose of scepticism (a longstanding argument for liberal neutrality), entailing 'a lack of conviction', 'a loss of substance' (*ibid.*, pp. x, 53). Recalling the ethical premises of his argument on liberalism, Larmore (*ibid.*, p. 39) envisages a liberal pluralism that challenges 'not . . . the objectivity of moral value but its homogeneity . . . the idea that there can be a systematic moral theory that will provide a way of settling all moral disputes without denying some of our deepest moral commitments'. As a condition for successful yet non-violent resolutions of conflict, parties must seek some measure of neutral, i.e. common ground. There is no reason why a measure of their 'personal' commitments should not find expression in this neutral space, but only upon certain conditions. The common demands upon them, *qua* citizens, are thus distinguished from the demands placed upon them by their 'private' attachments (which may of course be individually or collectively articulated) to some particular way of life, pursuit or values. Only for a limited set of public, political purposes can citizens place the former above the latter. With an eye to criticisms of liberalism as a pretender to the throne of objective rational rule, Larmore insists that the neutral posture of a liberally-minded government

> . . . is not meant to be one of outcome, but rather one of procedure. That is, political neutrality consists in a constraint on what factors can be invoked to justify a political decision. Such a decision can only count as neutral if it can be justified without appealing to the presumed intrinsic

superiority of any particular conception of the good life. (Larmore, *ibid.*, p. 44)

In short, the intellectual core of liberalism is cut right back to an unnegotiable belief in the political virtues of *tolerance and pluralism*, interpreted as a *modus vivendi*. And, by implication, it is also pushed back into history:

> The fundamental liberal insight is the inescapable controversiality of ideals of the good life and thus the need to find political principles that abstract from them. For this reason the toleration theories of Bodin, Locke and Bayle offer a surer model of what political liberalism ought to be like than many of their eighteenth or nineteenth century successors. (Larmore, *ibid.*, p. 130)

The question of what, if any, place *ought* therefore to be found within liberalism so understood for the values of these 'successors' – in essence, the status of its (post-)Enlightenment inheritance – is hardly addressed by Larmore. And to judge from the 'mirage'-like quality (Macedo 1990, pp. 260–63) which his conception of liberal neutrality seems to acquire in the course of a succession of qualifications (such as the one cited above) on its meaning and scope, his chances of arriving at a satisfactory answer may appear slight.

Nevertheless, Larmore's argument comes very close to what I take to be an appropriately minimalist view of liberalism. On this view, liberalism has to figure as a touchline within which attempts to formulate and implement what we suppose are more 'advanced' liberal, social, democratic or socialist policies must confine themselves. One cannot move the line further out so as to favour one's own political side. Yet there are at least three hitches in Larmore's argument. First, insufficient attention is paid to the ethical significance of the *modus vivendi* rationale. The second hitch in the argument concerns the way liberal differentiations between the political and the personal are conceived, and points to the need for a broader conception of liberalism than Larmore's 'political ideal' provides for. The third pertains to the epistemological dimension of the rationale for a *modus vivendi* and points to a case for seeing liberalism as an art of negotiatory government.

The Ethical and (A-)Political Content of Liberal Pluralism

The first and third of the hitches in Larmore's argument surface in his disarming statement that political neutrality is 'simply a means of accommodation' (Larmore, *op. cit.*, pp. 74, 53). This locution encourages us to think of the *modus vivendi* rationale for liberal neutrality as merely a commonsense prerequisite for peaceful coexistence, a pragmatic arrangement which *ipso facto* is devoid of ethical significance. This implication puts Larmore back on the very terrain of political romanticism and foundationalism which the *modus vivendi* rationale for liberal neutrality is intended to counter. Evidence for this proposition can be gathered from two critiques of modern liberalism: the classic Marxist-communitarian critique of Robert Wolff (1969) and the neo-Aristotelian-communitarian critique of Alisdair MacIntyre (1981).

In Wolff's view, the need for 'a new philosophy of community beyond pluralism and beyond tolerance' (*ibid.*, p. 61) which will transcend the limitations of modern US liberal-democracy stems from its irredeemable lack of a moral core.[4] Liberal pluralism and tolerance, he argues, are at best *a*moral. Did not early-modern arguments for tolerance emerge prior to and independently of the Protestant-sectarian belief in the freedom of the individual conscience? Were they not merely based on the desire to overcome incessant religious and civil warfare? Wolff characterises this early-modern institutionalisation of religious tolerance as no more than the 'grudging acceptance' by religious authorities of *de facto* heterodoxy. Seen as merely 'a necessary evil' (*ibid.*, p. 23), 'such tolerance', he argues, 'is not a virtue – a strength of the body politic – but a desperate remedy for a sickness that threatens to be fatal' (*ibid.*, p. 28). No matter if they are more humane and accommodating, modern liberal politics are also denied ethical significance. Modern tolerance, he maintains, is essentially an 'economic' concept, rooted in industrial capitalism and its ideology of the individual as basically self-interested and of society as a competitive battlefield.

This political-romantic derogation of *modus vivendi* arguments is a staple ingredient of communitarian critiques of liberalism, including those which owe little to Marxism. A typical example is Alisdair MacIntyre's cavalier attack on the US Supreme Court's stance towards moral conflicts, as exemplified in its decision in the *Baake* racial discrimination case, where 'as . . . in other cases . . . [it] played the role of a peacemaking or truce-keeping body by negotiating its way through an impasse of conflict, not by invoking our shared moral first principles. For our society as a whole has none' (MacIntyre, 1981, First Edition, p. 236). Both from MacIntyre's ivory tower and from Wolff's *engagé* campus-eye-view of politics, the existence of negotiated settlements confirms the spectacle of a moral wasteland relieved only by marginal prefigurations of a more communitarian way of life. Larmore both helps us and fails to help us to see why this should be so.

On the one hand, we can see how logically this jaundiced estimation of negotiation follows from a conception of morality as (i) essentially homogeneous (in Wolff's case determined by the mode of production, in MacIntyre's, by the existence of a culturally embodied set of common purposes); and (ii) as necessarily and exclusively manifest in some idealised form. For Wolff all social action is grounded either in principles, and hence moral value, or in base material interests. If conscientious adherence to principle was one of the principle *causes* of internecine religious warfare, then on Wolff's foundationalist view of social action, the political settlement of these religious differences can only be read as having been driven by self-interest. MacIntyre's is a Canutean attempt to philosophically legislate contemporary ethical discourse out of existence. Either ethical value ('properly speaking') shall be enshrined in a (narratively) coherent set of common principles . . . or it shall not exist!

Larmore attacks the political-romantic tendency to morally look down upon *modus vivendi* arguments; however, he too endows them with a merely pragmatic significance. Worse, he seems content to leave the work of conceptualising his alternative view of the ethical rationale for liberalism to the literary-romantic imagination (Larmore, *ibid.*, p. 19–21). It remains unclear how *literary* romanticism (in the form of D. H. Lawrence's celebration of individual creativity) would avoid the errors of ethical-political judgement for which Larmore so effectively castigates the *political* romantic tradition.

To develop Larmore's (Aristotelian) point that the practice of virtues 'requires the use of judgement if we are to know when and how we should exercise these virtues' (p. 151), we must look not to the art of D. H. Lawrence, but to the more overtly technical, historical arts of ethical and political judgement: rhetoric and its diverse offshoots, such as manuals of conduct and speechmaking, casuistry, diplomacy and other techniques of negotiation. It is only by reference to contemporary equivalents of these arts of judgement (or 'arts of living') that Larmore's 'method of abstraction' from personal and political commitments derives any ethical intelligibility. We are, unhelpfully, disposed to regard this 'method' not as an ethical skill but as indicative of an inability to be true to one's convictions. This propensity only confirms how far our ethical and political culture has come to repose upon a dissociation of ethics and rhetoric; as if in politics, ethically speaking, there was no alternative to being either an altruistic keeper of the party's conscience or a self-interested trimmer. These arts of judgement and self-fashioning are in fact concomitants of the history of governmental rationality and practice. It is in definite governmental forms of reasoning and in the rhetorical dimension of political conflict over government policies that the ethical character of liberal neutrality might be sought.

A history of ethics which gave due recognition to training in rhetorical capacities and their relations to the realms of government would make it harder to continue to regard the early-modern institutionalisation of religious toleration as a purely pragmatic self-interested concession to circumstance. We might want to see it as a remarkable political achievement which is partly predicated on (and subsequently productive of) a transformation in ethical culture. And we might then learn to reconsider how we classify forms of 'negotiation' in both the French and the English senses of the word . . .

Early-Modern Humanist Liberalism

Larmore's restatement of liberalism as a 'core' political ideal entails as much an historical shift in its centre of gravity as it does a conceptual one. To capture the intellectual complexity and 'ethical substance' of the *modus vivendi* posture and to question the universal commonsense character attributed to it by Larmore, let us follow his example and consider a further pre-Enlightenment figure, Erasmus of Rotterdam. Erasmus stands at the forefront of Reformation arguments against internecine warfare over doctrinal differences. He is also one of the most influential exponents of a rhetorical approach to ethical problems, an intriguing product of which was the concept and practice of *adiaphorism*.

A vital component, we might say, of a practising Christian's art of judgement as to when and how doctrine is applicable, this concept permits the categorisation of certain matters as 'morally indifferent', as 'neither good, nor commanded'; and as 'neither evil, nor forbidden' (Verkampf, 1977). Erasmus deploys adiaphoristic reasoning in appraising traditional Catholic religious ceremony and ceremonial legislation. At some points in the English Reformation too, adiaphoristic thought was used as a *via media* – to argue that the increasingly burdensome traditional ceremonies were neither as indispensable as the Roman church had believed nor as detestable as the puritanical iconoclasts and 'biblical reductionists' maintained (Verkampf, *ibid.*, p. 159). A basis was thus established on which men of religion and reason might set aside profound doctrinal differences for the sake of peace.

This use of adiaphorism to signify an 'indifferent mean' was neither inevitable nor necessarily persuasive. By playing on its negative connotations ('neither good nor commanded'), it could be a polemical stick with which to attack and reduce the amount of ecclesiastical ceremony

(Verkampf, *ibid.*, pp. 36f). On the other hand, in the hands of Erasmus and others, who drew on its *stoic* philosophical/ethical ancestry,[5] it became associated with sceptical arguments against making too much of doctrinal differences. Luther's retort to one of Erasmus's interventions – 'The Holy Spirit is no sceptic!' (Rabil, 1988, p. 253) – epitomises the point that the plausibility and rationality of a *modus vivendi* doctrine are more contingent than Larmore's rationale provides for. They are contingent upon the availability of a style of reasoning suited to the theologically-minded times and to the specific peacemaking purpose.[6]

Of all the many other early-modern intellectual contributions to the emergence of what I am calling the core of political liberalism, perhaps the most unlikely, yet also the most illuminating is that of Thomas Hobbes. Between liberalism and *Leviathan* there are two connections from which any attempt to 'extend' liberalism has something to learn. The first has to do with the ethical significance of commercial pursuits (*négociation* being the French for trade as well as peacemaking), the second, with the political-governmental conditions for pluralism.

The first point is well made in Hirschmann's (1977) archaeology of 'arguments for capitalism before its triumph'. 'All men naturally strive for honour and preferment; but chiefly they who are least troubled with caring for necessary things', wrote Hobbes (cited Hirschmann, *ibid.*, p. 125). If early-modern attempts to harness the moderating effects of enlightened self-interest against the destructive consequences of mobilising passion in the service of a religious cause hold any lesson for us today, it is to remind us of the *ethical* content of liberal arguments for pluralism and tolerance insofar as these appeal to the 'interests' of conflicting social groups. When we think of the ravages of capitalist development, from the slave trade to the destruction of the world's forests, we are apt to be staggered by seventeenth and eighteenth century philosophers' endorsements of the innocence of commercial pursuits.[7] But they might in turn wonder at their critics' forgetfulness of the possibly even more horrendous consequences of a time when social and political existence was dominated by rival religious zealotries.

It is precisely an ethical intent of this order which underlies the *prescriptive* aims of Hobbes 'egoistic' model of human nature in *Leviathan*. Far from assuming that men really were essentially rational egoists, the purpose of Hobbes' philosophical anthropology was rather to promote a 'cultural transformation' in their ethical make-up (Johnston, 1986). Only when men's lives were invested less in irrational religious imaginings and more in 'caring for necessary things' would they possess those characteristics required of political subjects in the Leviathan state (especially constancy and a fear of death and insecurity) which Hobbes thought necessary to procure civil peace (Johnstone, *ibid.*, pp. 120–21).

On Hobbes' own argument, the condition for establishing social peace is not only the imposition of authoritative government but also an associated 'work on the self by the self'. If the core of liberalism is the establishment of a *modus vivendi*, and if this entails an appeal to 'interests', then this appeal is by no means to the lowest, amoral or most destructive of human impulses. The self-interest which Hobbes enjoins men to cultivate bespeaks a stoic desire to fortify the self against worldly perturbation. (In this sense he is much more of a *Renaissance* thinker than many English-speaking political philosophers give him credit for.) Self-interest of this stoic order is not only useful for commercial life, as Wolff supposes, although the problem of how to govern the labouring poor was a major concern of early-modern political authorities (Tully, 1988, pp. 13–14). The possibility of giving priority to economic concerns also depends in part upon a cultural transformation, at both governmental and ethical levels, aimed at rendering ineradicable differences in religious conviction politically inconsequential. The displacement of the promotion of religious faith as the overriding objective of government entails that governments and individuals ethically adjust the comparative weight accorded to religious imperatives and enthusiasms and, on the other hand, to the preservation and enhancement of orderly and prosperous life. From a governmental point of view this could never be a simple choice between God or Mammon.

The nature of this ethical-cultural change and its *liberal* character and implications come through in Reinhart Koselleck's (1988) interpretation of Hobbes, the father of the doctrine of unlimited state sovereignty, as something of a pluralist.[8] Hobbes' strategy, argues Koselleck, was to marginalise religion by according it the status of a *private opinion* and by envisaging a form of political rule in which 'private mentalities' – above all the religious 'conscience' – have a reduced political effect. Hobbes sought to discredit a 'sense of self' and a supporting political culture, according to which religious foes were licensed to imagine that the public interest lay within 'the jurisdiction of conscience' (Koselleck, *op. cit.*, pp. 30, 31). The implication of the maxim *Auctoritas non veritas facit legem* was to make religious differences matters of private morality, the interiority of believers being of no concern to the sovereign who decided the laws. As long as unorthodox religious 'opinions' are not publicly promulgated, political subjects are free to believe what they will.

The usefulness of Koselleck's reconstruction of Hobbes' 'pluralist' solution to the problem of religious and civil warfare can best be appreciated by showing how it flows into a broader argument on the origins of Enlightenment utopianism. The overcoming of religious civil warfare in the era of Absolutist monarchies has to be seen as a major cultural achievement. But the unanticipated consequence of attaining and maintaining social peace in this fashion was the creation of intellectual enclaves such as the masonic lodges and philosophical societies (the spiritual ancestors of the Jacobins . . . and modern philosophies of history). Denied any share in the exercise of political power and hence any experience of its practical constraints, their representatives invested their apolitical ethical concerns with an independent and rival moral-messianic authority. Institutionalised as the privileged vocation of this enclave culture, *criticism*, 'the tenth muse', as Voltaire called it, arrogated to itself the right to submit all domains, practices, authority to its judgement, including and in particular those of the *ancien régime* (Koselleck, *ibid.*, pp. 114–15).

Unable or, later, unwilling to assume responsibility for their character as a political factor,[9] these enclaves of Enlightenment utopian reasoning helped engineer a revolutionary crisis which could only end in terror and confusion. Neither in 1789 nor in 1848 does the radical French republican opposition display a capacity to assume the responsibilities of exercising political power (von Stein, 1850, 1964; Donzelot, 1983). The communitarian critique of liberalism (exemplified by MacIntyre and Wolff) is heir to this anti-Absolutist utopian-enclave tradition.

Koselleck's arguments lend support to Larmore's move to define the core of liberalism around pluralism and tolerance, rather than around the autonomous person. Koselleck also helps to clarify the contingent relation of democracy to liberalism. A rationale for pluralism and tolerance, and hence for a type of liberal government, may be conceived inside an Absolutist political framework, in other words prior to and independently of the age of democracy. Liberalism and authoritarianism are not always mutually exclusive. A liberal doctrine of *raison d'état* need not limit the use of State power to emergencies stipulated in law. In the cause of 'social peace', dictatorships may be found straying onto the terrain of a 'liberal' policy.[10] Yet if democracy is not the inevitable concomitant of liberal pluralism and tolerance, neither is the vista of a nightwatchman state. In tracing the core of liberalism to the pre-history of liberal democracy, one is constrained to loosen the connection between liberalism and discourse on liberty in general, including therefore doctrines of *laissez-faire*. *Laissez-faire* is itself a form of governmental intervention, requiring enabling legislation, policing, fine-tuning, etc. In its most doctrinaire forms, it is no more liberal by Larmore's criteria than the *libertinage* of the Marquis de Sade.

Even if there are powerful reasons to go along with the minimalist definition of liberalism outlined here, to judge from Larmore and Koselleck, this
way of seeing liberalism may still appear to exact an unacceptable price.
It seems to identify 'government' with a juristic-institutional definition of
the political system. Amending their arguments in such a way as to avoid
this implication generates the final ingredient in this attempt to restate
a rationale for liberalism by resorting to early-modern humanists and
political developments: namely the need to see it not just as a political
doctrine and ideal but as a form of 'governmentality' in Foucault's
sense.

Koselleck tends to subsume the exercise of power under Absolutism
under the Machiaevellian conception of *raison d'état*. In so doing, he
risks conceding far too much to the (post-)Enlightenment views that
the *modus operandi* of 'the Absolutist state' is essentially governed by
the amoral criteria of *realpolitik* and bureaucratic instrumentalism and
that consequently the Enlightenment anti-statist representatives of civil
society held a monopoly on morality. Perhaps Koselleck's perspective
on Absolutism is overly dependent on Hobbes.[11] *Leviathan* may be
a brilliant hardheaded rationale for the establishment and exercise of
sovereignty as a condition of civil peace. But as Hobbes' insistence on
cultural transformation has suggested, the task of an Absolutist monarch
is not merely to preserve his sovereignty (to keep the peace, administer
justice, secure national frontiers, etc.). Foucault's (1979, 1981) work on the
political rationality of early modern 'governmentality' links it to a diverse
and perpetual work of 'policing' populations. As conceived in the originally *anti*-Machievellian doctrines of *raison d'état* in the related literature
on *police*, argues Foucault, the work of governing populations could not
be purely repressive. The German cameralists' desire to strengthen the
state required attention to the *ethical* reconstitution and 'happiness' of
a population who may have been politically excluded, but who are also
seen as in need of help and a framework of regulation precisely in order
to enable them to pursue peaceful civil activities, especially trade, under
their own steam.

Larmore does not consistently view the work of government as ethically
vacuous. Max Weber's notion of the politician's 'ethics of responsibility'
for the way the world goes as a result of political action or inaction
is endorsed; likewise, the ethical value of bureaucracy as a factor of
predictability in social life (without it, the pursuit of an independent life
of one's own choosing would be impossible). However, like Koselleck,
he continues the tradition of identifying liberalism as a type of political
system (along the lines of legal-constitutional definitions of a *Rechtsstaat*).

It is for this reason that Larmore is forced into equating the private realm with (inter-)personal commitments and pursuits.

This equation may be questioned without subscribing to radical critiques of liberalism on the grounds of its alleged commitment to 'the' private–public distinction. Rather, it was *Absolutist* theories and programmes of government, with their commitment to preserving the political sovereignty of the monarchical public power, which first attempted to institute a singular dichotomy between private and public. Far from depending upon it, modern liberal government *cannibalises* this dichotomy, chewing it up into bits and pieces in ways that both liberal political philosophy and the critics of that philosophy persistently fail to acknowledge. Larmore's point about the need to make the definition of liberalism independent of contentious personal-political philosophies or ideologies is well taken. But its corollary is the necessity to reduce liberalism not to a purely political doctrine, which is heir to a unitary public–private distinction, but to a philosophy of 'social' governance. From this perspective, the realm of 'public' concerns by no means invariably coincides with the constitutionally defined province of the political. But equally, the *depoliticising* purposes of liberal-governmental actions – their commitment to circumventing the effects of irreconcilable ideological-political differences – can now be evaluated on a case-by-case basis.

In general, then, if the arts and purposes of liberal government amount to less than a philosophical vision of man and society, they are not for all that entirely pragmatic, in the sense of lacking an ethical dimension altogether. However, picking out the ethical valences of the liberal prioritisation of tolerance and pluralism makes it even harder to see what relation these priorities might have to the (post-)Enlightenment inheritance of liberalism. To take an example which lies at the heart of the whole question of how a collectivity handles political and ethical differences, what are the implications of cutting back the core content of liberalism in this way for the preeminent value placed by liberals on *open discussion*? Is a revaluation of the value of discussion on the cards?

The Ethics of Liberal Discussion: Dialogue or Arts of Negotiation?

For many, even to suggest the need for such a revaluation as the price of readmitting this value back into the liberal fold will seem odd. How could commitment to the liberal value of open discussion *not* be an absolute precondition of social peace, whether or not this is accorded priority over other liberal concerns? To begin to see why a problem about the compatibility between the value of discussion and the *modus vivendi* rationale for liberalism arises at all, we might recall our original allusion to discussion in Chapter 1. There it was singled out as an example of the propensity to identify the ethical value of something with its idealised forms of expression. The price of an exclusive focus on the principle of free and open discussion is a lack of attention to the personal dispositions and competences which are prerequisite to the successful conduct of discussion. Attention to these underestimated ethical qualities will serve to clarify why, paradoxically, there is indeed a question about how the value of discussion is to be accommodated to the prioritisation of social peace in liberal theory, and consequently, a need for a revaluation of that value. The ethical competence attaching to the conduct of political discussion may also hold the key to how this revaluation can be effected: namely, by reorienting it towards the 'value' of negotiation.

Discussion is idealised in three main ways in liberal political philosophy: first, by making the ultimate purpose of a free and open exchange of views the attainment of truth and justice, through a process of rational persuasion; second (the paradigmatically political-romantic option) by idealising political discourse itself as an 'endless conversation', a never-finalised process of problematisation and dialogical mutuality; and third, by indexing it to the virtue of democracy as the ideal way of running society.

The inclusion of the second of these rationales within the liberal tradition might well be contested by 'critiques' of liberalism whose ambitions to transcend its limitations 'dialectically' through a politics of difference provided the initial foil against which the present argument has been constructed. If our general argument that liberalism cannot be advanced by dialectics is to be sustained, then it would be as well to begin by underlining the (post-)Enlightenment liberal credentials of the open-conversational ideal. This preliminary step is all the more important in the light of the frequency with which the term 'negotiation' is itself associated with idealisations of politics as a perpetual conversation.

In this usage, extremely common in 'post-structuralist' and/or communitarian critiques of liberalism, 'negotiation' refers to an idealised practice of politics governed by the imperative to always seek to involve 'the other' in reciprocal, dialogical relations (without, however, ever seeking to assimilate them to 'indifferent' norms). This imperative stems from the ambition to transcend what appears as a limited concern with keeping the peace, including the pacification of the subordinate social groups whose formal equality is proclaimed in liberal law and ideology. Real equality of condition is held at bay by abstracting from these groups' distinctive identities and subjecting them to 'monological' norms and decisions. In so doing, those who differ from these abstract norms are constructed *as* 'other' (their true, multiple identities going unrecognised). Acceptance of cultural difference as the rule entails a commitment to replace fixed norms by fluid processes of consultation and adjustments to the specific and changing desires of these hitherto excluded categories (Yeatman, 1992).[12]

A very different account of liberal discussion as an art of negotiation is developed in the following pages. This account is based upon a more radical series of objections to post-Enlightenment liberal idealisations of discussion. Here, we will concentrate on the stumbling-blocks to using them as standards for evaluating parliamentary discussion.

In his brilliant and notorious polemic on liberal parliamentarism, Carl Schmitt (1926, 1988) outlined a series of damaging comparisons between political-romantic ideals of open, rational, unending discussion[13] and the real world of electoral and parliamentary procedures – whether in relatively settled circumstances, or in emergencies when holding to democratic arrangements would exacerbate dangerous social divisions. Schmitt was neither the first nor the last to drive a wedge between liberalism and parliamentary democracy in this way. How would his critique fare, were the value of discussion to be redefined in terms of a general ethico-rhetorical notion of 'negotiation',[14] premised upon our redefinition of liberalism as a governmental doctrine of *modus vivendi*?

The *OED* defines 'negotiation' at its most general and ethically neutral as any action which is aimed at getting over or around some obstacle in a skilful fashion. This opens up a spectrum of possibilities as to how the content of that 'skill' might be filled out. The definition neither excludes a forum of discussion from seeking to reason its way to truth or justice nor allots a privileged place to these categories. Accentuating the rhetorical aspects of discussion does not license a sceptical attitude or relativistic indifference to truth claims; merely circumspection about the ethical meaning and value of pursuing the 'game' of truth-seeking and its products in all political debates with equal singlemindedness. To require that parliamentary politics should be conformed to the ideal of a university seminar would be absurd. Yet does not Schmitt's attack on parliamentary democracy as a supposedly liberal institution rest upon precisely this premise?[15]

A more important advantage of conceiving all political discussion as a general species of negotiation is to bring out the disingenuousness of rationalist and romantic ways of idealising *truth-oriented* discussion itself. In this regard, Benjamin Constant's disquisition on discussion in his *Principles of Politics* (1815, 1988, pp. 221–25) offers a shrewd if partly unwitting guide. Applauding a recent ruling banning written speeches in the national assembly, Constant eulogises the benefits of true discussion in which men listen to others' views and permit what has just been said to modify views already held by them. The problem with prepared written speeches is not only that they preclude discussion in this sense (a prepared speech is only related to its successor by chance); it is also that they are driven by 'the need to impress' (p. 223): 'I have seen representatives looking for subjects on which to speak, so that their names should not remain unknown' (Constant, *ibid.*).

The histrionic tendencies of French Revolutionary political culture are well-known. Nothing said so far stands in the way of our reading Constant's eulogy to discussion as though it were entirely organised around a standard commonsense contrast between a 'modern' liberal-rationalist, democratic ideal of discussion as a disinterested meeting of minds and the realities of discussion as occasions for self-display. Such a reading, however, is arrested when we discover what Constant takes to be the essential precondition for the realisation of rational discussion. What we get is a rhetorical flight of fantasy on the true life of enlightened political discussion, a fantasy from which 'the need to impress' has by no means been banished:

> By banishing written speeches, we shall create in our assem-
> blies . . . that silent majority which, disciplined, so to speak, by
> the superiority of the men of talent, is reduced to listening to them,
> in default of being able to talk in their place, and becomes more
> enlightened because it is compelled to be modest, and more reasonable
> by being silent. (Constant, 1988, pp. 223–24)

Disclosed in Constant's fantasy is the extent to which Enlighten-ment moral and epistemological ideals were in their eighteenth and early nineteenth-century heyday inseparable from a certain practice of self-enhancement. Koselleck (1988) has drawn attention to the masonic origins of Enlightenment utopianism. Is it unduly speculative to suggest that in Constant's eyes to be a true discussant is to be an Illuminatus? Constant beautifully confirms Schmitt's point about the tensions between liberal *ideals* of discussion and democracy. For this French republican, the point of turning the National Assembly into a forum of discussion is to 'deprive mediocrity of the opportunity to produce any effect whatsoever' (Constant, *ibid.*, p. 223). It does so by limiting the opportunity for (virtuous) self-display to the Enlightened few possessed of the requisite intellectual *and* oratorical talent.

The point of debunking the epistemological and political idealisation of liberal discussion by pointing to its 'elitist' shadow is neither to promote a general scepticism about the value of truth and argument in politics nor to create the impression of a complete dissociation between discussion and democracy. Quite the reverse. The point is to establish the contingency and variable value of the nexuses between them. Thus, listening to others and modifying a previously prepared speech as a result may be as much a recipe for establishing a reputation as a supreme parliamentary performer – witness Paul Keating in the Australian Federal Parliament – as it is for advancing the cause of truth and justice. In regard to the nexus of discussion and democracy, there is something to be learned from the US Congress ruling which permits a written speech to be entered into the record of Congressional proceedings without ever having been verbally presented.[16] Here the value of discussion *is* linked, contingently, and for Constant, abominably,with democracy. Free discussion of issues, we now assume, is predicated on the public availability of views and supporting information.

   To be consistent with the promotion of a *modus vivendi*, the value of discussion in general has therefore to be identified with a range of ethical-rhetorical aptitudes for 'negotiating' differences. Conceiving discussion as a general class of negotiation predicated on the exercise of definite ethical competences no longer allows us as a matter of course to privilege truth-seeking over truce-seeking. For the purposes of governance, the ethical-rhetorical norm of liberal discussion becomes the steering of a pathway to a decision that preserves the common ground shared by conflicting parties. The condition of inclusion is that, whether oriented to truth or to agreement, discussion must culminate in a decision. The ethical norm of liberal political discussion can thus no longer be identified with the political-romantic dialogical ideal. Unending conversation and binding decisions do not go well together. Once that ideal is dropped, variability in the forms, purposes and extent of political discussion do not have to be construed as 'limits'. To weight valorisations of discussion in favour of some single higher epistemological purpose is to make liberal laws and policies vulnerable to charges of pretending to represent a spurious 'balance'. But this is a topic best discussed in the light of an exploration of how, suitably adjusted, citizenship may be readmitted to the liberal fold.

Marshall's 'Governmental' Concept of the Citizen-Status

As with discussion, so too with citizenship, it is a question of building its limits into its definition. Like Walzer (1983), my argument on the significance of this status for 'progressive' politics involves seeing it simultaneously as a badge of equality *and* as a way of demarcating acceptable social inequality. To arrive at this perspective on the limits of liberal citizenship, the first step is to elucidate the meaning of citizenship from the point of view of a liberal style of government.

T. H. Marshall's (1949) essay on citizenship has furnished a regular point of departure for recent attempts to refurbish socialist (or social democratic) theory and aspirations. Yet how little of this *locus classicus* of modern thought on citizenship seems to have been read. Critical commentary has concentrated on Marshall's historical typology of citizen statuses. The evolution of citizenship begins with the removal of civil disabilities and protections of individual liberty, such as the writ of *habeas corpus*, the right to work in a calling of one's own choosing, contractual rights, freedom of religious belief and political opinion, jury service, etc. Most of these civil liberties are associated with common law decisions rather than with the legislation of a democratically elected government. In a second phase, citizenship is duly extended to the political sphere in struggles over the franchise. This democratic moment then provides the impetus for expansions of the citizenship status into the social and industrial spheres. Here are located the 'rights' to health, education and other concomitants of the welfare state.

Secondly, critical attention has been focused on Marshall's *ideal* of citizenship. His dictum that citizenship is 'the architect of legitimate inequality' (*ibid.*, p. 77) offers a point-of-entry for anti-reformist criticism that the rights of citizenship place an ideological cloak over the structural inequalities of capitalism and other sources of oppression (Turner, 1986, Barbelet, 1988). Much debate over Marshall turns upon whether or not this 'ideological' function of citizenship overrides its benefits (especially where these are the fruits of political struggle) or undermines the autonomy of the citizenship status *vis-à-vis* the calculations of 'class' organisations. A tendency to endow citizenship with too homogeneous a significance has also been frequently documented (e.g. Hindess, 1987).

Critical revisions of the Marshallian typology and ideal have centred on dimensions of citizenship and its historical vicissitudes which he is alleged to have neglected.[17] By contrast, my starting point is the literature's neglect of Marshall's more 'governmentally-minded' arguments. Such neglect may be traced to a parallel failure to attend to the governmental-intellectual milieu in which Marshall's thought was arguably shaped. The 'milieu' consists in the habits of mind fostered by that brand of British sociology, the institutional formation of which seems to have been closely bound up with the tertiary educational study and the practice of social administration (Bulmer, 1985, pp. 21–22; Abrams, 1985, pp. 188–89).

The impact of those habits of mind on Marshall's conception of citizenship and equality is nicely illustrated in his views on 'industrial citizenship'.[18] Supplementing the system of political citizenship, this 'secondary system' (Marshall, 1949, pp. 103–104) is viewed as a vehicle for extending civil and social rights into the economic sphere. On the question of what form any equalisations flowing out of collective bargaining would have to take, Marshall makes the following clipped observation:

As in mass schooling, so in mass-employment, questions of rights, standards, opportunities, and so forth can be intelligibly discussed and handled only in terms of a limited set of categories and by cutting up a continuous chain of differences into a series of classes whose names instantly ring bells in the mind of the busy official. As the area of (wage) negotiation spreads, the assimilation of groups necessarily follows on the assimilation of individuals, until the stratification of the whole population is as far as possible standardised. *Only then can general principles of social justice be formulated.* There must be uniformity within each grade and differences between grades. (Marshall, *ibid.*, pp. 124–25, my emphasis)

It is instructive to set this passage beside Marshall's more familiar idealisation of citizenship:

Citizenship is a status bestowed on those who are full members of a community . . . . Societies in which citizenship is a developing institution create an image of an ideal citizenship against which achievements can be measured and towards which aspiration can be directed. The urge forward along the path thus plotted is an urge towards a fuller measure of equality, an enrichment of the stuff of which the status is made and an increase in the number of those on whom the status is endowed. (Marshall, *ibid.*, p. 92)

The two passages present a true study in contrasts. To begin with, there is a gaping discrepancy over the status of the *principles* of citizenship. In the second quotation, citizenship is a coherent and transcendent ideal, the essence of which is more or less 'richly' embodied (or further developed) in specific citizen statuses and provides the measure of their worth. This is the classic romantic-republican ideal of a self-governing community of citizens, sustaining themselves from a common pool of social resources and participating in a common political and cultural heritage.

By contrast, in the first quotation, the ideal of equality and citizenship entailed in 'principles of social justice' are *immanent* to a complex set of social-administrative calculations and practices (Hunter, 1992). In this case, the very possibility of talking about citizenship at a more or less abstract level of generality, or even of creating an ideal political image out of it, is predicated upon a set of practical, social-administrative 'generalisations' of institutional space. 'Popular' education thus meant education for the entire populace. The jurisdiction of 'common' law extended throughout the kingdom. And so on. These governmental developments require the equipment of national populations with a roughly homogeneous set of normative attributes by virtue of which they may be compared; discrepancies in respect to these standards (in some circumstances) can then be registered as a problem. In short, generalisations about citizenship may be seen as not so much the ultimate goal or transcendent standard of governmental practices as their practical outcome and internal horizon.

This line of argument is of a piece with Marshall's typological observation that medieval life organised into 'orders' lacked the institutional and conceptual bases with which to even think of positing equalisations of status cutting across the several estates. Here, Marshall undercuts his incipiently teleological history of citizenship statuses, according to which pre-capitalist collectivities such as Elizabethan England provide forerunners of social citizenship (*ibid.*, p. 81). We are asked to consider the institutional and discursive conditions under which it becomes intelligible to talk about *generalising* this or that aspect of the citizen status to 'the whole of society' in the sense of an adult national population. Marshall's point is that a pre-capitalist collectivity such as Elizabethan England can only retrospectively be described as a 'society' (in which gross 'social' inequalities were officially sanctioned in law, ideology, etc.).

Returning to our contrast between his remarks on industrial citizenship and his classic formulations on the citizenship ideal, let us examine Marshall's point that, if differences in pay and conditions are to be registered as 'differentials' and subjected to policy-oriented judgements in terms of equity, such (in)equities 'can be intelligibly discussed and handled only in terms of a limited set of categories and by cutting up a continuous chain of differences into a series of (officially recognised) classes'. This emphasis on the localised categorisations entailed in the institutionalisation of a given citizen status chimes in with those aspects of Marshall's historical argument which fail to fit the 'big picture' of an ultimately coherent, evolutionary pattern of development – even critics of Marshall's evolutionism seem impelled to continue this tendency (Turner, 1986, pp. xii, 103–104, 133, 135).[19] Yet this is where Marshall disaggregates citizenship into a plurality of differentiated statuses bearing no necessary relationship to one another.

Once equality is conceived in terms of limited categorisations and practices of equalisations, it is not clear what it means to speak of people acquiring, for example, a 'capacity for full participation in public life' *tout court*, as distinct from the mixes of capacities and dispositions associated with access to specific social arenas. This is not to say that one citizen-status cannot lead to another. It is simply that the significance of a given citizenship status cannot be assessed, as Marshall contradictorily assumes in the more familiar stretches of his argument, solely in terms of its being either a cumulative contribution to the attainment of an ideal of 'full' citizenship or else a retrograde step. The possibility of formulating 'general principles of social justice' rests upon a 'chain' of institutions and categorisations within and between which the ideal of full equality makes no sense.

Education furnishes Marshall with an example of the impossibility of aggregating the equalisations associated with citizenship status into a single developmental series, and furnishes his readers with a further reason to question the republican citizenship ideal. In order to see the equalisations associated with education systems as fragments of 'full citizenship', it would be necessary to assume that all inequalities of whatever sort have a single ethical or political significance. Marshall's egalitarianism turns on the rights to equal participation and access, not on a general equality of economic outcomes (Hindess, 1991a). Nevertheless, to the extent that he also defines the equal citizenship ideal in terms of a general contrast with the inequalities of social class associated with capitalism, Marshall implicitly links all social inequality to an origin in capitalist society and hence to an underlying economic inequality (Held, 1989, pp. 200–203). However, as the expert in social administration, Marshall points out that the simple concern for uniform national educational standards generates an unequal distribution of capacities, qualifications and associated social standing in the population. It is difficult to envisage how this form of inequality could be either reduced to an effect of capitalism[20] or sensibly form the target of an attempt to extend citizenship.

Marshall's concept of citizenship presents a rare attempt in English social and political theory to think through a form of socio-political betterment which is neither provided by the state alone nor purports to transcend the practical constraints of worldly milieus such as those of social administration and the common law. Albeit not consistently, Marshall forces us to confront the multifariousness of the governmental 'element' in which citizens swim and the plurality of ethical commitments associated with promoting citizenship statuses. To the extent that he diverges from the romantic-republican script prescribed by the ideal of citizenship which formally overarches his argument, Marshall depicts the citizen not as Rousseauean 'citizen of the world' but rather as denizen of a highly organised and differentiated, *urbanised* community. The 'community' to which citizenship statuses are supposed to give equal access is a plurality of more or less localised legally or administratively established 'social' units: streets, schools, neighbourhoods, the catchment areas of municipal amenities and social services, legal jurisdictions, economic enterprises (insofar as they are subject to incomes policies, or public inspection and accountability for the welfare of employees). The citizen thus appears in a mosaic of cameo parts rather than as one who struts the stage as a world-historical hero.

The Governmental Architecture of Liberal Citizenship

How do Marshall's disaggregation of the 'stuff' of citizenship and his appreciation of its social-administrative 'scaffolding' and 'buttressing' bear upon agendas for extending citizenship within the framework of a liberal-constitutional polity? To answer this question requires us to look at the 'progressive' implications of seeing liberalism as a governmental doctrine committed to negotiating differences. It will mean taking this 'other' (governmental) Marshall seriously. But then can we continue to suppose that 'extending citizenship' possesses some single visionary significance ('full' citizenship) by virtue of which it could perform the role of socialism's (or social democracy's) 'big idea'?

In attempting to dampen down expectations that extending citizenship could function as a general formula for socialist or social democratic reform, I am not impervious to the advantages of constructing the political subjects of a liberal democracy as citizens rather than as workers, capitalists and 'others'. Nor would I deny the advantages of exploiting the common currency of the citizenship idiom in order to capture demands for the provision of social resources and political access without which certain liberties and entitlements remain merely notional. To draw attention to the governmental 'architecture' of citizen statuses can only aid in identifying the nature of those preconditions for exercising the prerogatives of citizenship, such as the availability of resources, abilities, institutional encouragement of interest, etc.

What then are the drawbacks to utilising it as a general formula for a progressive liberal and/or socialist politics, especially where citizenship is identified with *democratic* rights? One problem is that the ostensible 'demonstration effects' (De Palma, 1990) of old or newly successful implantations of citizenship statuses may lead to a somewhat leaden uniformity in approaches to disadvantaged groups – EEO measures in Australia have recently come in for criticism on precisely this count (Pointer and Wills, 1991).

Another problem arises in connection with all those equalised statuses of citizens which (as Marshall shows us) are linked to their being, so to speak, inhabitants of a city – i.e., the products of a social-administrative 'gelding' of individuals (Gellner, 1983) through the institution of national education systems. Yet it is by these means that individuals become equipped with certain expected civic and cultural competences. Health may become the subject of rights-claims but the establishment of public health norms was hardly the result of the influence of Enlightenment ideals of citizenship and popular struggles. Furthermore, even where citizenship entails mutually responsible relations with fellow-citizens, these links are more likely to be of an impersonal, administrative character, as in redistributive schemes (fiscal policies, social insurance, etc.) than of the shoulder-to-shoulder variety suggested in the republican vision of a community of self-governing citizens.[21] In Ignatieff's (1984, p. 141) words: 'the moral relations that exist between my income and the needs of strangers pass through the arteries of the state'. Marshall's emphasis on the administrative logics of the citizen status compels us to question the necessity of regarding the terms citizenship, democracy, community as coterminous.

But of all the problems associated with the programmatic extension of citizenship, the one which is most pertinent concerns its compatibility with liberalism, especially in the reduced sense of the term developed in these pages. Of course, there are extensions and extensions. The liberal credentials of radical romantic-republican programmes for extending citizenship, which set out to overcome the limits of liberalism dialectically by taking advantage of its most progressive aspects, are wide open to objection. David Held's liberal socialism, for instance, calls for a 'double democratisation' of both state and civil society entailing a massive extension of citizens' rights on the basis of a 'principle of autonomy':

The principle can be stated as follows: individuals should be free and equal in the determination of the rules by which they live: that is they should enjoy equal rights (and accordingly, equal obligations) in the specification of the framework which generates and limits the opportunities available to them throughout their lives. (Held, 1989, p. 165)

In this principle, the recurrently conflicting values of liberty and equality, freedom and social responsibility have been dialectically reconciled. The virtuous liberal concern to limit the power of the state over citizens is preserved, but only upon the condition that these limits are not prejudicial to the autonomy of oppressed groups. In turn, the socialist demand for equality must be opened up to the diverse directions of change implied by the demands for autonomy emanating from the social movements. Held's debts to the Kantian concept of autonomy are no less apparent than his debts to Marxism, feminism and civic republicanism. Not surprisingly therefore, his version of the principle of autonomy falls foul of the test devised by Larmore, viz. that liberal public policy shall not impose any single controversial ideology of the good life. As a general citizens' charter it would appear inhospitable to an energetic commercial and industrial culture. And how would religious communities fare, for whom the multiplication of self-realising choices would be incompatible with beliefs in serving their respective gods or prophets and with communal definitions of personal identity which preclude challenging certain sorts of hierarchy and dependency? Held's principle of autonomy is vulnerable to being interpreted as a charter for a pseudo-pluralist socialist polity, the moral tone of which is mainly determined by left-republicans and the radical edges of the social movements. As such, it is incompatible with the constitutional-liberal *Rechtsstaat* framework to which Held formally (and forcefully) adheres.[22]

By contrast, the lesson of Marshall is that there can be no single *principled* charter to extend liberalism. We must therefore learn to live with the fact that liberal philosophy is *not* open to the dialectical *Aufhebung* desired by radical critics. Fishkin (1987) is right: we must learn to cease conceiving the task of pro-liberal political theory as one of generating a coherent set of ideals to which, we hope, policies will one day approximate asymptotically. Logical or dialectical demonstrations of compatibility between the principles of equality and liberty cannot conjure away the diverse circumstances in which respect for one may clash with respect for the other. The diverse adjustments and compromises required by these circumstances in order to evade or cope with potential clashes cannot be deduced from some prototypical synthetic formula for harmonising competing lines of action (or non-action) at the level of general principles.

However, pessimism regarding the repertoire of (post-)Enlightenment principles of expanding citizenship does not have to lead to the conservative conclusion that pruning liberalism back in this way makes the idea of an advanced liberal social-democratic polity a contradiction in terms. This would seem to be the implication of Stephen Macedo's (1990, pp. 260–63) criticism of Larmore. No *red* republican for sure, Macedo nevertheless constructs an ideal liberal-constitutional republican community of interested (if not 'active') citizens who are at least committed to reflecting on the decisions that affect their life and demanding that they be subject to public, rational forums of debate and/or accountability. Liberal states, Macedo argues, should and to some extent actually do seek to inculcate these civic virtues in their citizenry. A virtue such as the capacity for critical reflection goes beyond the minimalist core of liberalism outlined by Larmore. Above all, Macedo claims, it breaches the rule of neutrality with regard to conceptions of the good life which a liberal state, according to Larmore, is bound by its paramount concern to sustain a *modus vivendi* to respect. And so it must, if, along with the liberal civic virtues in general, this commitment to critical reflection is to perform its assigned task of rebutting communitarian critiques of liberalism as inevitably committed to bourgeois individualism and as indifferent to socially-minded community values. It is with this aim in mind that Macedo targets Larmore's rule of neutrality, seizing on the latter's series of qualifications concerning the character and scope of that neutrality as evidence of its being a 'mirage'. Not an apostle of a nightwatchman state, Larmore wants to limit the scope of the neutrality of the liberal state to procedures rather than requiring absolutely neutral outcomes; and to conceptions of the good life and policies which would be common ground to 'reasonable people' (as distinct from Nazis).

Macedo has a point. But as an argument against identifying liberalism with a moral-ideological neutrality on the part of government it holds good only on certain conditions. The first condition is that the common ground to which government is required to stick is defined in terms of a moral-epistemological concept of rational dialogue. The second is that government be identified with 'the' government – i.e. with state or central (including local) government policy in the narrow constitutional sense. Thirdly, the substantive ethical value of a policy must be reducible to some identifiable ideal of the good life which it favours.

The conception of the core of liberalism and the means by which a more 'advanced' liberal polity may be built up which I have sketched in this essay 'fail' to meet any of these conditions. The ethical value of pursuing a *modus vivendi* in governmental matters was linked not to a principle but to practical arts of living (including an art of judgement). Notable amongst these intellectual/conscience-forming technologies was that neostoic reworking of the classical sceptical ethos through which to build an attitude of indifference (adiaphorism) towards overly contentious matters of theological doctrine. Similarly, the value of discussion was pegged to the conditions for attaining a *modus vivendi* sensitive to the virtues of consensus as such.

Finally, it was suggested that whilst the purposes for which liberal neutrality required us to bracket off personal-political commitments were limited ones, it might be a mistake to draw those limits between personal and political life in too narrow a fashion. Larmore is right to argue that the neutrality associated with liberalism is not a derivative of a social philosophy of personal liberty. I sought to suggest, however, that this more narrowly focused liberal doctrine need not be identified with a constitutional-political doctrine of limits to state action. For this would mean espousing an excessively homogeneous, not to say fictional, way of distinguishing between private and public spheres. Instead I linked the posture of neutrality in liberalism to the broader history of 'governmentality' understood as a patchwork of organised forms of reasoning and practical interventions. These interventions certainly affect aspects of citizens' personal lives, but they do not only limit liberty; even in some of the more coercive governmental actions the aim is to foster it. Under liberal government liberty is not indivisible in the sense prescribed by a right-wing liberal ideology. Nor do liberal government rationalities yield a clear way of demarcating 'socially' desirable from undesirable liberties as left-wing proponents of general post-liberal doctrines of positive freedom would like to see. Between a sometimes overlapping, sometimes conflicting multiplicity of public authorities and private arenas a kind of circuitry or 'exchange' is established. Private arenas are neither entirely free from nor entirely encompassed by the 'powers' of government.

Taken together, these moves suggest two broad, overlapping ways in which it makes sense to speak of reincorporating elements of the post-Enlightenment inheritance of liberal citizenship which were bracketed off in order to arrive at a non-negotiable core of liberalism; two roads to a more advanced liberal democracy which do not breach the liberal doctrine of governmental neutrality prerequisite to sustaining a *modus vivendi*. The first of these roads follows the path of negotiation; the second goes through governmental channels and *depoliticised* governmental norms and values.

'Liberal government' may be as coercive as its cameralist ancestors. It certainly does not always depend upon negotiation. Nevertheless it makes available institutional channels, regulative techniques and norms and values which may be tendered as bargaining chips in the transactions between the parties to negotiation over the direction and pace of social and economic 'development' (Donzelot, 1983, ch. 4). The parties to these transactions include state agencies (who need not see eye to eye), private 'public-interest' or 'issue' organisations, prominent social stakeholders such as the business sector, professional associations and organs of public opinion. Personal desires and demands are not absent from the agendas. But their presence will by necessity be refracted through the organisational bodies that take it upon themselves to 'reflect' what they take to be the feelings of 'their' constituencies. Inevitably these popular or sectional 'feelings' will be represented at the negotiating table in highly formulaic ways (Miller and Rose, 1990). In the face of this diversity in the parties, we must ask if the question of whether liberal polities and societies can sustain 'progressive' developments which respect the test of liberal neutrality can be adequately posed, as Larmore would have it, in terms of whether 'state' policy avoids being captured by any single set of 'personal' commitments whilst nevertheless in some way advantaging them.

Progressing Liberalism: an Example

Abortion legislation is by any reckoning a paradigm case of a 'progressive' liberal policy which advances the 'life-chances' of one section of the population more than others, namely women who want to discontinue their pregnancy. Some feminists may be dissatisfied with the law as it stands, but not nearly as dissatisfied as members of anti-abortion organisations. The reasons for dissatisfaction on the feminist side of the argument vary, but one of the most persistent of these objections is precisely that the legislation fails to sufficiently promote women's 'autonomy'. Not the doctors, not the state, let women alone decide their fate, runs the slogan. Yet to accede to such demands would put reforming governments unambiguously on one side of a moral-ideological divide. There is a sound political rationale, therefore, for the fact that in legislation and case law, the abortion issue is constructed as a medical–administrative problem and public policy issue arising in the context of a pluralist society in which people with conflicting values must arrive at a *modus vivendi*. This construction issues in a liberal law which is much harder to repeal than a more ideologically loaded one. Moreover, it is *not* left to some abstraction called 'the authority of the state' but to the professional discretion of medically qualified personnel to 'adjudicate' on the legality of requests for abortion. Whether they work in the private or public sectors, these practitioners enjoy considerable autonomy *vis-à-vis* the government of the day in the conduct of their affairs.

Earlier, I suggested the need to construe the neutrality of liberal policy-making in a non-epistemological fashion. In the case of abortion law, it could be said that abortion legislation and practice is only neutral in that it avoids giving expression to any single identifiable moral-ideological viewpoint. However, it is not ethically vacuous. In a way which overlaps with the more governmentally-oriented sides of the pro-choice argument, this legislation and practice comes down on the side of promoting women's health and discouraging the forces that threaten it (in the shape of the illegal or medically unsupervised abortion to which women will certainly resort if they have to).

This rationale concerning the avoidance of dangers to women's health scarcely meets a philosophical touchstone of neutrality in the sense of 'rational' impartiality. It is no more (or less) rational than the diverse forms of organised reflection and categorisation out of which it is built up. One of these, rarely commended for its logical consistency or 'rationalism', is the precedent system of the English common law. It is for example in this very peculiar form of organised reasoning that the concept of 'danger to health' has, since *King v Bourne* (KB, 1939), come to be firmly entrenched in law as a category which cannot be unambiguously distinguished from 'danger to life' (*K v T*, 1983, Qld R.396). The *Bourne* decision was a precursor of even more elastic social-psychological extensions of the category of danger to health (in case law and legislation) to include the mental as well as physical strain of coping with a newborn child in poor social conditions, at a certain age, etc.[23] From a logical point of view, the concept of health outlined in *Bourne*'s case and further developed in the 'social' clause of the United Kingdom Abortion Act (1967) may be reckoned rubbery in the extreme (Skegg, 1984, pp. 4–19).[24] Nevertheless this concept could be described as a crystalline expression of the diverse meanings the term health has historically acquired (in the discourses and minds of doctors, parents, patients, lawyers and administrators) in the sphere of governmental policies aimed at the welfare of national populations.

A similar point about the non-epistemological and unprincipled yet not unethical or unreasonable bases of the neutral posture required of 'progressive' liberal social legislation has been made in the accompanying essays on sex discrimination law. There too governmental logics cannot be represented as a purely negative constraint upon the expansion of women's citizenship statuses. On the other hand, these statuses cannot be represented as way-stations on a path to 'full' equality.

Limits of Liberalism: the Architecture of Legitimate Inequality

Perhaps we can now see a way in which citizenship statuses may be extended in the direction of ethical-political objectives which apparently lie beyond the pale of ideological consensus, yet which continue to respect what we have taken to be the pluralist core of liberalism. A question remains, however. What attitude should those committed to such extensions of citizenship take, according to this argument, in regard to the constraints upon the fulfilment of such expectations which inevitably accompany these liberal-governmental and negotiatory paths to reform? Answering this question involves rereading the Marshallian dictum which gives this essay its title in such a way as to decline its seeming invitation to a general critique of citizenship. Not all the prerequisites for this reading are to be found in Marshall himself, who has little to say with regard to the 'subjectivity' of citizenship, or the ethical skills and forms of self-fashioning prerequisite to conducting oneself as a citizen. It may be that attention to these 'moral experiences' of citizenship and the governmental and non-governmental statuses that support them will help us through to a realistic yet ethically justifiable attitude of 'adiaphoristic' indifference to inequality in general and to (some) particular inequalities in one's concrete surroundings.

The discussion of the citizen status so far has already furnished reasons not to pose inequality as a general problem (and, as such, a source of conscientious anxiety) to be addressed through a general theory and politics of citizenship. To the extent that the bureaucratic cultural milieus in which equalisations or expectations of treatment as an equal arise are hierarchical (education and health systems, employment, law, etc.), 'modern' statuses of equality are no less at home in a context of taken-for-granted inequality and subordination than in a society dominated by an aristocratic culture. The question must surely arise as to whether there exist ways of 'relating oneself' to inequality with which one can 'live', ethically speaking; ways of thinking and living in which inequality (and by association, subordination and hierarchy) do not, as such, necessarily constitute a problem.

Here it is appropriate both to draw on and take a certain distance from Michael Walzer's (1983) influential critique of undifferentiated ideals of equality. Walzer regards the problem of distributive justice in terms of an 'art of differentiation' rather than a science of total coordination (Walzer, *ibid.*, p. xv). The diverse social meanings invested in social goods which are created within specific 'spheres' are seen as relevant reasons for determining the (in)appropriateness of equal distributions within or across spheres. Walzer elaborates what it means to practise equality in somewhat the same way as Foucault (1987) bids us attend to the particular statuses, constraints, techniques and ethical attributes and experiences associated with 'practising' liberty. Central to the practice of equality is the attribute of self-respect. The self-respect appropriate to democratic citizenship pertains to a sense of oneself and others seen, however, not as universal persons but as a more particularised bearer of a dignitary status: 'a person effective in such-and-such a setting' (Walzer, *op. cit.*, p. 277). (For instance, discrimination against a colleague in a promotion round might be 'ethically' experienced as a waste of a particular set of talents and personable qualities.)

So far so good. But if so, to what extent does treating someone as an equal at the level of conduct and practical attitude have to do with their 'general standing in the community' (Walzer, *ibid.*)? *Which* community? one wants to ask. If it's the workplace then what does it mean to insist on seeing citizenship as a status 'radically disconnected from any kind of hierarchy' (Walzer, *ibid.*)? Walzer's argument swerves at this point because his discussion of democratic society and its citizenship is framed on the dubious assumption of a discontinuity between democratic and aristocratic society considered as historico-social totalities. This assumption cannot be squared with the historical emergence of social administration and bureaucracy within Absolutist regimes. (Fore-)shadowed as it has always been by administrative apparatuses, the democratic revolution does not reconceptualise self-respect, as Walzer contends, so much as redistribute it. At the level of conduct, the business of conducting oneself and 'conducting' the conduct of others brings both universal *and* particularistic norms into play. These norms include ways of behaving ourselves in respect to others' 'personal space'. As we saw in respect to sexual harassment, the *manners* appropriate to respecting another's industrial citizenship do not differ in every way from those associated with pre-liberal aristocratic society. If hierarchies and inequalities in general are not alien to the equalisations of status involved in industrial citizenship, then at the level of 'moral experience' we can begin to discern an unproblematic sense in which equalities 'legitimate' inequalities.

Once more, Walzer (*ibid.*, p. 321) offers a promising starting-point which needs to be taken further: ' . . . the autonomy of spheres will spread the satisfaction of ruling more widely . . . and establish what is always in question today – the compatibility of being ruled and of respecting oneself'. Clearly, a democratic culture is incompatible with domination of certain kinds. But why link the compatibility of being ruled and self-respect to 'rule without domination' *tout court* (*ibid.*)? Members of more aristocratically ordered societies in early modern times had to come to terms with complex hierarchical organisations; citizens in liberal democracies also have to acquire the '*skill*' *of subordinating themselves to forms of domination in such a way as to preserve or enhance their self-respect*. In this perspective, equalisations of citizen status indeed, in Marshall's phrase, 'legitimate' surrounding inequalities; but not in the sense of furnishing a *liberal-ideological* ground for (inherently bad forms of) subordination, as so many Marxist and feminist sociologies assume.

Rather, equalisations of status provide conditions and components of ethical-governmental practices of self-restraint. We have fewer practical models, but no less need than our forebears for these casuistical arts of self-subordination. These require us to learn how to survive and flourish in complex hierarchical organisations, which inevitably require people, *qua* subordinates, at certain times and for certain purposes, to subordinate all manner of desires, partialities, political aims, etc. to organisational norms and the orders of superiors. Democratically organised organisations, in which 'altruism' is at a premium, may require not less but *more* willing and active self-subordination of this order. Participation only increases the numbers of individuals for whom equal statuses are a prerequisite ethical and political condition for managing an honourable and dignified 'subordination'. Citizenship statuses are the price exacted by citizens for not regarding their subordinate statuses in other respects as a problem. Without this capacity to willingly (or unreflectively) subordinate oneself, including one's most deeply cherished principles and values in some circumstances, there can be no security or civil peace, no public good, no democracy, no opportunity, therefore, for individuals, and organisations to pursue their preferred projects; including, of course, 'progressive' ones.

8 The Participatory Imperative

Too Much of a Good Thing . . . ?

Socialist thought in the Western democracies currently presents a virtually unbroken prospect of agreement concerning the pre-eminence of democracy in its various redefinitions and visions of the 'good society'. It is also widely assumed that the best forms of democracy involve the active participation of citizens. How *much* participatory democracy is feasible is of course a matter of debate.[1] In this chapter I suggest that to over-identify the socialist idea with 'democratisation' is to miss something of both the value and limits of active participation and hence to overstate its significance for socialist reform programmes.

In debate on this topic, talk about the ethical-political value of participatory democracy almost invariably makes reference to its *ideal* forms of expression (principles, ends, values, prefigurative models). The result: endless stand-offs and unstable compromises between champions of the participatory ideal and 'realists', to say nothing of a sometimes overpowering element of *Schwärmerei*. It is in the interests of evading some of these intellectual and sentimental *cul-de-sacs* (and, maybe, injecting a touch of zest into the debate) that this essay sets off by arguing a case for provisionally *bracketing off* consideration of democratic idealisations altogether.

This is not to cast aspersions upon all such idealisations, merely to let every dog have his day. Setting aside democratic idealisations allows some familiar, yet less frequently analysed aspects of democratic organisation to step into the limelight: namely the personal aptitudes, attitudes and demands which are entailed in the *procedures* of democratic participation. Less edifying than their ideal counterparts though they may be, these personal dispositions do not lack ethical significance. Two sets of practical-ethical concomitants of democratic-participatory organisation are singled out: a self-disciplinary or *ascetic* dimension and a pragmatic or *negotiatory* dimension.

This is not a proposal to stop looking at theories and busy ourselves with the real world. Procedures are discursive artefacts which are neither more nor less 'real' than democratic idealisations and may be just as unrealistic. To target the routines of participation is rather a tactical way of challenging those species of democratic idealisations which aspire to transcend the limits of formal democratic procedure, especially what I call *romantic republicanism*.[2] And *what* will be challenged under this rubric is itself not only an ideal but also a practical ethos. Romantic-republican democrats, too, must perforce practise forms of *ascesis* and negotiation. Some of these are *sui generis*,[3] others duplicating the more standard ethical concomitants of democratic procedures which are the subject of this essay.

The fact that these democratic virtues are located in the quotidian world of organisational procedures raises questions about the appropriateness of conducting the debate on the limits of participatory democracy in terms of how far an ideal can be realistically achieved. Not all the limits to the extension of participatory democracy take the form of either obstacles to be overcome or necessary evils with which a realistically-minded democratic socialist must come to terms. On the contrary, if my argument holds water, many of the limits to 'democratisation' are inseparable from what is ethically valuable about it. That is to say, they are both of an ethical nature and internal to the practical conduct of democratic organisation.

A series of challenging implications for the socialist 'prospect' of a radical extension of democratic participation ensue. These implications do not so much tell in favour of less democracy or less participation. Rather they suggest a need to disaggregate 'the participatory imperative' in such a way as to challenge the supposition that participatory practices are necessarily bound up in a general process of democratising society. Inevitably, the value from a socialist point of view of certain non-participatory practices must also be reconsidered.

An Alternative Ethical Strategy?

In order to identify the disadvantages of organising arguments about participatory democracy around its idealisation and for the purposes of subsequent contrast, let us recall some of the contours of the 'participatory imperative' as expressed in post-1960s radical political theories.

With the credibility of the economic and social programmes associated with class politics and state socialism in tatters, it is not surprising to find many thinking socialists from the 1960s onwards huddled around a kind of 'alternative ethical strategy' according to which socialism becomes virtually 'synonymous' with *active democratic citizenship* understood in its most radical liberal sense (Habermas, 1970, p. 49; Keane, 1988, p. 3). This commitment to making the 'progressive' facets of liberal-democratic rhetoric come true entails a programme of 'deepening' and 'broadening' the purchase of democratic arrangements, norms and values throughout the social body, thereby overcoming the (alleged) one-sidedness and moral and political contradictions of mainstream liberal democracy.

The process of broadening and deepening democracy may be variously conceived. It may involve (either singly or in combination) the extension of citizenship; the autonomisation of civil society; or giving a softer complexion to (state) economic planning. Democratisation may be conceived as primarily driven by the social and (or) labour movements. Or else a more catholic range of civil associations and corporatist forms of social participation may be invoked.[4]

The traditional republican community is a self-governing body of 'sovereign' active citizens. These are possessed of the will and capacity (the proverbial 'civic virtues') to run the affairs of the community (including its non-citizens) in accordance with a shared conception of the common good (Hindess, 1991b). Romantic republicanism seeks to expand the ranks of active citizens, drawing especially on subaltern social strata in order to make the nominal popular sovereignty proclaimed in liberal-democratic constitutions more of a reality. What counts as the common good has to be dehomogenised. Participatory democracy is the medium through which the diverse needs of citizens and collectivities are recognised and mutually adjusted to one another.

The dialectical logic and transcending aims of this model *vis-à-vis* liberal constitutionalism is well illustrated in Carole Pateman's (1970) well-known reconstruction of the participatory-democratic tradition. According to Pateman (*ibid.*, p. 22), true democracy means far more than the intermittent opportunity for voters to vote out their rulers; the vote being merely 'a protective adjunct'. Democracy is a self-governing community of citizens in name only unless people are both institutionally and subjectively engaged. The experience of participation psychologically transforms participants; it constitutes an *ethico-political education* in the virtues and benefits of taking others' interests into account. It represents an avenue for the *free yet socially responsible self-development of individuals* who thereby acquire a real degree of control over their lives and environment.

Participatory democracy is also a dialectical *vehicle of social and subjective integration*. It generates common feelings of belongingness, willingness to work together for the public good, and a preparedness to accept decisions one dislikes by virtue of the way in which they were arrived at. As such, it *transcends both the 'formal' equality of citizens required for representative democratic arrangements and the formalism of the arrangements themselves*: 'the only policy that will be acceptable to all is the one where any benefits and burdens are equally shared' (Pateman, *ibid.*, p. 23). Finally, it is by virtue of these supposedly transformative effects upon political subjects that the generalisation of participatory democracy is proposed as the best way of overcoming the notorious 'limits' to participation, which liberal constitutionalism reinforces.[5] Only systematic generalisation can overcome these ostensible limits. 'The participatory system . . . becomes self-sustaining because the very qualities that are required of citizens if the system is to work successfully are those that the participatory system itself develops . . . ' (Pateman, *ibid.*, p. 25). Other representatives of romantic-republicanism (e.g. Mouffe, 1988, 1989) accentuate both the differences and the constructed character of the subjects whose capacities for self-determination are to be promoted somewhat more than Pateman does. Nevertheless, *Participation and Democratic Theory* captures what is essential to the tradition: the principle that ideally there should be no pockets of unaccountability in the social body. In Roberto Unger's phrase everything must be 'cracked open to politics'. This imperative is also nicely caught in Claude Lefort's (1988) conception of democracy as an emancipatory cultural epoch characterised by its opening up the *status quo* to perpetual critical reflection, creative exchanges of views and innovative reformations. Procedural norms and decisions figure as obstructions to a vision of democratic politics as an endlessly provisional 'process'.[6] Hierarchies are similarly a perpetual source of worry to the romantic republican,[7] not because they stand in the way of a 'mechanical' equality of outcomes, but because they represent a bar to the autonomous self-realisation of individuals and social groups.

Has not such political romanticism been left behind in recent convergences between socialist-participationist views, such as Pateman's, and realist-elitist conceptions of liberal democracy?[8] One recent example is David Held's (1987, 1989) amalgamation of 'progressive' liberal, feminist and Marxist perspectives. In the resulting case for a 'double democratisation' of 'the state' and 'civil society' the prospect of overcoming all distinctions between state and civil society is rejected. The need for protection of individual and associational freedoms is affirmed. So is the need for self-limiting rules and, moreover, predictable (and necessarily hierarchically organised) centralised administration where this is necessary for purposes of regulating, co-ordinating and ensuring the distribution of social resources to the activities of the civil society.

Nevertheless, albeit inconsistently, Held's 'liberal-socialist' theory continues to run with the romantic-republican baton. Socialism is nominally subsumed under the banner of a general democratisation. At least where 'civil society' is concerned, this is equated to an assertion of popular republican sovereignty (or as Held calls it, 'autonomy'):[9] active citizens either directly or indirectly participating in determining the more localised decisions and the broader regulatory framework which generate and limit their life-chances (Held, 1989, pp. 165, 247 *et passim*). As in Pateman, generalisation of participation is invoked as a solution to popular lack of interest in it (Held and Pollitt, eds, 1986).

If romantic-republican idealisations of democracy are the butt of my argument, why is it necessary to bracket off idealisations of democracy *per se*? The answer is that the influence of political romanticism upon democratic theory today cannot be estimated on the strength of its political-romantic programmatic *content* alone. Even programmes of democratisation such as those organised around corporatist arrangements, which are uncongenial to the romantic-republican ethos, are not immune to its influence.

By definition, no matter how mindful it purports to be about the problems of getting from here to there, any radical reform programme locating itself under the rubric of democratisation is bound to posit an ideal of 'full' democratisation as an asymptotic 'direction of movement' (Connell, 1987, pp. 287– 88). The point of overlap between even the most 'sensible' of such socialist programmes and romantic-republicanism lies in the formers' tendency to locate themselves by reference to this horizon of a general social and subjective emancipation. Even if not all ideals of political emancipation necessarily commit one to romantic republicanism, is there not a *studied incoherence* in any concept of a democratic *society* as an ideal way of life?

This incoherence in socialist programmes of democratisation is most blatant at those points at which administrative reforms are envisaged which do not depend upon democratic arrangements (e.g. Laclau and Mouffe, 1988, pp. 188– 89; Mathews, 1988, pp. 33– 38). What is the connection, for example, between democracy and, say, the provision of retraining for the unemployed? A break with the forfeiture of rights associated with some liberal welfare policies? Opportunities to participate in a core socio-economic activity or to have access to key social and political resources? To secure support for the displacement of labour by new technology? Such answers merely establish a connection to two possible concomitants of democratic arrangements, viz., participation and legitimation. In the absence of any necessary conceptual connection to specified democratic arrangements it can only be assumed that the reference to democracy is to 'Democracy' as in Lefort's larger and largely metaphorical sense of a 'free' society.

Could it be that the identification of socialist agendas with the democratic ideal is largely the result of a play on words? Only by virtue of a *pun* on 'election', 'choice', 'participation' can the capacity to 'elect' improve one's work-skills; to 'participate' in 'public' life or to make sexual choices appear to be part of the same overarching democratic way of life as being part of an electoral and decision-making mechanism. All too frequently, scenarios of democratisation resemble romantic-nationalist novels, in which the final uniting of the couple mirrors the achievement of national unity and independence.

The identification of socialism with democratisation also disingenuously exploits the popular association of 'democracy' with a non-republican appreciation of freedom in which the desire not to be pushed around (or worse) by an overbearing state unites with the desire to have access to a choice of basic consumer-items.[10] No wonder if in established 'democracies' the catch-cry of 'democratisation' persistently falls on deaf ears (Hirst, 1989d, pp. 66–67). For better or worse, 'democracy' in this genuinely popular sense equates to the very liberal-constitutional model which socialist romantic-republican idealisations suggest must be transcended. Democracy is also only one condition of the 'freedoms' with which it is associated.[11]

Compounding this reliance on an incoherent concept of a democratic culture, a further problem with idealisations of democracy is that, irrespective of their pedigree, they tend to be forced into the orbit of romantic-republicanism simply by virtue of the way in which the *distinction* between the 'ideal' and 'reality' of democracy is conceived. With unfailing regularity, participatory democracy is identified with idealisations which, when enacted, transcend the limits of actually existing democratic institutions. Conversely, democratic actualities are identified with 'formal' procedures bearing little or no ethical import. The virtues of participatory democracy listed by Pateman (1970, p. 22), for example, are not all the exclusive property of romantic-republicanism. What casts them in that mould is the way they are made to function as vehicles for dialectically transcending the 'formal' limits of parliamentary democracy. This dislocation between a perfectly self-governing community and an (almost) ethically vacuous set of 'actual' institutional arrangements is virtually endemic to the field of debate on the forms and limits of democracy.

On the side of the the participationists, the romantic pedigree of the contrast is canonically mirrored in J. S. Mill's (1838, 1969, pp. 99–100) comparison between the 'onesided' Benthamite-utilitarian view of democracy as 'the means of organising and regulating the merely *business* part of human affairs' and his own vision of democratic government as a vehicle for the spiritual development of the individual and the national character. A more recent echo of the same political-romantic imperative can be heard in Claus Offe's contrast between the 'dialogical' collective action of rank-and-file unionists and the 'monological', hierarchical *modus operandi* of trade union bureaucracy. In the latter, workers are treated merely as an aggregate of individual interests, according to the formalistic 'rules of the game' prevalent in collective bargaining and corporatist bodies (Offe 1985, ch. 7, esp. p. 208).[12] Similarly, in Claude Lefort's (1988) anti-positivist objections to political science models of democracy, democracy as a way of life signifies an ever-present ethical possibility of negating 'given' institutionalised realities.[13]

It is a testimony to the cultural ascendency of the romantic ethos that attempts to evade romantic-republican conceptions of democracy in favour of addressing the institutional realities of democratic organisation only confirm its ethical pre-eminence. It is as if a bargain had to be struck. Romantic-republicanism having secured a monopoly over the 'higher' ethical basis of democracy, *anti*-romantic analyses have to pay the price of evacuating their conception of democracy of intrinsic ethical import. Schumpeter's (1943, p. 242) well-known definition of democracy as a 'political method . . . (an) institutional arrangement for arriving at political-legislative and administrative decisions' is a classic instance. Interestingly, the cost of bracketing off the ethical side of democracy in this way is that *aspects of democratic government which are by no means reducible to their ethical dimensions fall out of sight as well.*

For example, few in the political science literature have contributed as much to a 'realistic' understanding of democratic politics as Robert Dahl.[14] Nevertheless, the consequence of his attending to the procedural – especially the decisional – aspects of democratic organisation largely at the expense of its ethical aspects is, paradoxically, to detract from the 'realism' of his argument. For all its 'hard-headed' characteristics, Dahl's representation of democracy is cast in the mould of a legalistic utopia. If any association, political or otherwise, is to achieve its purposes, argues Dahl, it

> . . . needs to adopt policies with which members will be obliged to act consistently. Ordinarily their obligation . . . is expressed in a rule or law that includes penalties for non-compliance. Because members are obliged to obey the rules or law the decisions may be said to be *binding*. Taken collectively, the decisionmakers who make binding decisions constitute the *government* of the association. (Dahl, 1989, p. 107)

Here we have what Foucault (1976) called a 'juridico-discursive' view of government. To govern is to lay down the law (i.e. make 'binding decisions') governing the behaviour of the members of the associations. For all his alertness to ways of exercising governmental capacities which do not conform to this model, these always somehow remain marginal to what Dahl takes to be the fundamentals of democratic government. Rejection of romantic-republicanism along these lines makes for a perpetual and largely barren debate between 'idealists' and 'realists' who (like Dahl) are frequently as utopian as their idealistic opponents (Hindess, 1991b). The value of maximising citizen participation becomes either everything or nothing (saving its role in the mechanism of furnishing or replacing a government). Time and again, 'arguments for participation are grounded in the nature of decisionmaking, of communities in general and of the state in particular, and sometimes in an ideal of men being autonomous agents . . . . Arguments against tend to be less fundamental, but not necessarily less weighty, considerations of practicality' (Lucas, 1976, p. 139).

Is this bifurcation of democratic thought into the ideal and the procedural (together with its assumption that the former is the privileged repository of the core ethical value of democratic organisation) inevitable? Is it simply an instantiation of the no doubt perennial dilemma faced by any reforming political party: 'how to maintain a realism that doesn't kill expectation whilst maintaining an idealism that doesn't become self-delusion' (Hitching, 1983, p. 140)? I think not. The point is not to kill socialists' expectations but rather to question the advisability of placing all of them in the single basket of democratic idealisations.

With a view to further clarifying the dimensions of ethical *and* governmental reality which is obscured by locating the ethical solely under the sign of the ideal it will prove instructive to follow a few of the twists and turns taken in Paul Hirst's and Barry Hindess's initially parallel, subsequently divergent,[15] attempts to negotiate the bifurcation between the ideal and the procedural in their contributions to socialist and democratic theory. This discussion will serve both to clarify how much my approach to the ethics of participatory democracy owes to their work and to expose the *lacunae* in their arguments which necessitates this attempt to develop its ethical implications.

Democracy Limited

Hirst's and Hindess's common point of departure is a relentless opposition to utopian and philosophical views of socialism and democracy which are abstract to institutional frameworks and indifferent to the currently intractable problems which any party of government must address. Political theory must accordingly be placed in the service of developing a doctrine, strategy and style of responsible governance which has a recognisably social-democratic profile, yet does not have the effect of frightening off the unconverted.

Nor surprisingly, in the light of the current state of intellectual relations between the ethical and the procedural aspects of democracy, Hindess's and Hirst's first move is to take a leaf out of the book of political science. In a manner reminiscent of Schumpeter and Dahl, democracy is disaggregated into a varied repertoire of organisational instruments for providing decision-making personnel and procedures, and for attempting to circumscribe the objects and outcomes of decision-making, usually within rather broad limits (Hindess, 1983, pp. 48–54; Hirst, 1986, p. 39). From this perspective, both the tendency to identify socialism with the extension of democracy and the romantic-republican bias towards participatory democracy appear extremely questionable. If democracy is a general concept for a class of 'decision-procedures' (Hirst, 1990a, p. 148), then how can it be associated with any single 'ideological' set of allegiances or substantive policy decisions? Radical opinion holds no monopoly on the value of active citizen participation in government. Right-wing republican thinkers such as Benjamin Constant (1988), who favoured constitutional monarchy and limitation of suffrage to landed property owners, bear witness to *that* point. Considered, therefore, merely as one set of formal procedures among others, 'participatory democracy' cannot furnish a universal paradigm of democratic purity by which alternative social arrangements can be ranked as exhibiting greater or lesser degrees of democracy (Hindess, 1991b). On this view, democratisation in the romantic-republican sense cannot on its own provide either a coherent or a distinctive basis for a socialist politics.

So far, in this critical side of their work on democracy, Hindess and Hirst are at one both with one another and with the 'realists' in the North American political science tradition in refusing to organise their account of democracy around democratic ideals. However, contrary to some critics' assumptions (e.g. Jessop, 1980), neither their refusal to accord these ideals a foundational place nor their focus on its procedural dimension necessarily signify a reduction of democracy to merely a 'means'. Why should not democratic ideals be seen as one consideration among others? Hindess (1991a) has recently displayed interest in analysing more precisely what *sort* of demands are embodied in the deployment of political principles such as equality in particular circumstances; and how such appeals to principles might function in relation to other kinds of political calculation.

For his part, Paul Hirst has gone on to develop a substantive doctrine of socialist governance, associationalist socialism (see Chapter 9). For the purposes of this argument, a particularly crucial characteristic of Hirst's doctrine is its emphasis on the *negotiatory* governing style which is required of a socialist (or social-democratic) government, both as a litmus test of its pluralist/libertarian commitments; and as a prerequisite for securing widespread agreement for urgently needed socio-economic and political reforms. Is there a problem here? It is surely an essential part of the rationale for 'summitry', for example, that even reluctant participants at least have to present an appearance of taking the public interest into account (Di Palma, 1990). At first sight then, the substantive civically-minded outcomes implied in Hirst's proposal for a negotiatory social pact seem incompatible with the formal characteristics attributed by Hirst to democratic organisation in general.

If there is a contradiction, it may be a result of Hirst's having, like Hindess, omitted to take note of the ethical complexion of democratic procedures. Hindess certainly sets out to analyse democratic ideals. In contrast, Hirst seems to assume that once the ethical has been dislodged from its pretensions to *found* a politics, it can simply be left to look after itself, to find its own various levels of importance in determining outcomes, along with other considerations. Generally speaking, there is justification for a political analyst to treat ethical values as a 'given' in this way. If they do not necessarily lie at the *root* of all political life and its conditions of existence, then why should they be the object of perpetual (self-) reflection? However, to the extent that ethical reflection on democratic politics tends to be expressed in the form of idealisations, the ethical value of social-democratic governments' cultivating a negotiatory style of political rule is not at all self-evident. On the contrary, as we saw in the previous chapter, it is likely to be perceived as a formula for, at best, a politics of enlightened self-interest.

So we have not one problem but two: how does a 'formal' decision-procedure tend to promote a socially beneficial outcome and what is 'good' about it, ethically? If Hirst's (and Hindess's) arguments on democracy do not supply the means to resolve those questions, this is not, as we have seen, the result of failure to take its ethical dimensions into account, *per se*. The gap in their arguments arises from their identification of the ethics of democracy with its principled components and, consequently, in their legal-formalist characterisation of democratic procedure. 'Substantive' ethical outcomes of democratic government-by-negotiation only appear paradoxical in the absence of attention to what is involved, once again, ethically speaking, in *carrying out* democratic procedures – i.e. how negotiators 'conduct themselves'.

Hindess (1990, p. 19) is no doubt correct in his intuition that the opposition between 'principled' and 'pragmatic' approaches to politics, between altruistic and self-interested political motivations is an incorrigible feature of 'the language of Western politics' – an anthropological fact – rather than a reflection of a universal reality. The ethical benefits of a negotiatory style of governance point to at least some aspects of democratic political practice which seem to cross-cut such oppositions. Even so, if there is a 'third way' of looking at democratic participation, we should resist the temptation to suppose that it will take the form of a dialectical reconciliation between democratic ideals and gritty procedural realities. If an alternative to political romantic (and, more generally, foundationalist) approaches to the relations between ethical-political ideals and political practice is to be had, it might be more advisable, *pro tem*, to write out as far as possible consideration of the *ideals* of democratic participation and the 'spirit' of democracy in general. This leaves us free to concentrate on the ethical characteristics of democratic procedures themselves.

The Ascetics of Participation

Central to the recovery of these familiar yet insufficiently examined ethical characteristics of democratic organisation is the hypothesis that they are not of a *purely* ethical nature. As Dahl's work illustrates, the problem with the ways in which debate on participatory democracy tends to be organised lies *both* in its reduction of the ethics of democracy to its idealisations *and* in its excessively rule-oriented conception of the organisational pole of this opposition.

A useful framework from which to consider these blindspots of democratic idealisation can be supplied by bringing together Michel Foucault's (1979, 1981) work on the history of 'governmentality' in the modern West and his concurrent attempts to distill a way of looking at ethical practice today out of the history of ancient sexual ethics (Foucault, 1984a, 1984b, 1987).

As we have seen, by contrast with those forms of monarchical rule characterised by concern to enhance the power of the ruler, or with the spiritual salvation of the populace, the realm of political rationality and organising practices picked out by the term 'governmentality' is characterised by a continuing and comprehensive concern with improving the living standards and quality of life (health, wealth, security, moral welfare) of populations. It is partly because these populations and the problems they pose are never simply pre-given but rather, by a well-known circular process, always *(re-)constructed* by these investigative practices, interventions and policies, that the element of *ethical rehabilitation* of individuals and relationships belonging to 'target' populations (including the classes responsible for 'administering' them) becomes so crucial to the success (or failure) of governmental strategies and techniques. We have also had repeated cause to comment on the fact that 'liberalisation' of the field of government did not entail its diminution but, on the contrary, saw the invention of new and more institutionally specific forms of regulation such as social insurance (Defert, 1991). As such, liberalisation of government only accentuated a vital ingredient of even the most *étatiste* of early modern strategies for governing populations: namely, the emphasis on *self-government*:

> When we are governed . . . . we do not become the passive objects of a physical determination. To govern individuals is to get them to act and to align their particular wills with ends imposed on them through constraining *and facilitating* models of possible actions. (Burchell, 1991, p. 119, emphasis in original)

Important though legal frameworks may be to the operation of liberal government (in defining the conditions, forms and limits of discretionary action of social actors), only within circumscribed limits can governmental objectives and arrangements be practically monitored by legal agencies or conformed to the ethical-political principles or legal codes in the name of which they are carried out. Making a code or principle one's own is not simply a matter of giving expression to them in word and deed. As we saw in Chapter 6, even something as ostensibly passive as a public servant's learning to obey orders without question may involve a whole technical and ethically positive 'work on the self by the self'.

This labour of 'ethical problematisation' has a material density of its own. Living in accordance with an ethical imperative requires 'application', as our teachers used to say: the disciplined application to oneself of regimens of exercises, *ascetic* 'arts of living', both mental and practical. These may include casuistical techniques for determining when and to what extent a given state of affairs contravenes some code or principle; and/or whether something must be done about such contraventions. Foucault's emphasis on the material cultural dimensions of ethical experience does not entail reducing it to the dimension of action. Moral problematisations entail *intellectual actions*, in particular the specification of the 'ethical substance' – the realms of oneself, one's conduct and milieu which are open to ethical scrutiny. Equally, they typically involve reference to 'ideal' elements: the 'mode of subjection' or the particular set of 'reasons for action' by which one is led to recognise one's subjection to a principle or code; and the *telos*, the ideal type of ethical personage to which one desires to approximate through this work of self-fashioning (Foucault, 1984a, pp. 33–35). However, important though these reasons for action and images of personal-ethical perfection may be, the point is that they can never play a role of *founding* the practices on/of the self involved in living out an ethic (Minson, 1986). A familiar example would be the way in which the ascetic practices of the self associated with the Protestant Ethic evaded the desperate consequences of the Calvinist doctrine of predestination, giving the flock means of detecting signs of 'election' about which these 'principles' of Protestantism forbade its adherents to seek assurances (Weber, 1920, 1965).

It is on the strength of this anti-foundationalist postulate of a radical contingency in the relations between the ideal and practical aspects of an ethic that the following examination of the ethical/governmental dimensions of democratic participation stands. In bringing together Foucault's perspectives on the ethical and governmental fields, the task is to redescribe what is involved, ethically, in the procedures of democratic participation, keeping in mind the irreducibility of this realm both to ethical idealisations *and* to formal (legalistic) codes or rules of practice. What is involved, to put it another way, in seeing participatory democratic practices as comprising an ethical/governmental habitus?

Provisionally and provocatively, participatory democracy now appears as a form of government of the self by the self. The democratisation of an institution is bound up with the institution of an ascetic régime of conduct. Such a regime comprises a range of minor ethical *practices and techniques of the self* applied to the diverse self-disciplinary demands placed upon participants. Participation in a democratic organisation thus requires the cultivation of a definite *ethical competence*[16] *and style* through which, at the same time, organisations conduct their business and persons conduct themselves within these organisations.

Pace 'political science', democracy is not simply a set of mechanisms for *furnishing* the personnel of decision-making apparatuses, agenda setting, authorising the decisions made and subsequently holding those who exercise power to account. Democratic procedure may also function as a technique for ethically *forming* that personnel. Many of the most formal-procedural dimensions of democratic organisation are precisely more or less efficient devices for getting its participants to 'behave themselves' democratically. These ethical-technique-bearing formalities include: decision-making quorums imposing the discipline of minimum attendance levels; house-rules for attempting to make factional 'caucusing' work for rather than against the effective and harmonious functioning of a political party; or, to take an example more congenial to radical democrats, rules governing how long and how often people may speak and other affirmative action techniques aimed at bringing in oppressed groups to the democratic process. Paradoxically, radical democratic organisations dedicated to maximising members' involvements may require *more* such normalising bureaucratic formalities than do more hierarchical, conservative organisations (Lühmann, 1989, p. 223).

The inventory of constraints on conduct which are inseparable from the practical functioning of democratic organisations might be extended to include a huge range of ethical-political competences, such as the art of chairing meetings. This may include forcing people to circulate written materials which require time and thought in advance; ensuring people are heard out without interruption; keeping discussion to the point; and imposing a guillotine on discussion in order to produce decisions. Further, for all participants, the meetings and committee work inseparable from participatory democracy presuppose myriad forms of small-scale disciplinary work on the self: the cultivation of the capacity to 'manage' one's time[17] required for regular attendance at meetings, reading up on and mastering the issues, etc. Or again, think of all that is involved in the ability to work with others or to cope with tedium. What does it take to cultivate the composure, patience and 'interest' of one who has to curb their tendencies to dominate discussion? Or to listen attentively to others no matter how stupid, long-winded, incoherent, or self-aggrandising? All this requires a definite work on the body, at very least the moulding of facial and corporeal demeanour.

If the ascetic, self-governing dimension of participatory democracy supplies the lack discerned in anti-romantic, procedurally oriented views of democracy, it cuts the ground even more radically from under the feet of the political romance of participation. Pateman and others are right to associate it with a psychological or ethical transformation of participants. But it should be apparent that the 'processual' dialectical form of this transformation envisaged in her perspective is a poor guide to the more demanding self-administered modifications to individuals' 'ethical substance' entailed in democratic participation. A dialectical harmonisation of self-and-other is particularly hard to square with one sub-set of the self-constraints associated with committee work, which deserves to be treated as a separate category of ethically significant concomitants of democratic procedure in its own right: namely the cultivation of *negotiatory* aptitudes.

The Pragmatics of Democratic Negotiation

A lack of fit between political-romantic idealisations and a practical negotiatory style is particularly apparent in romantic-republican worries about the corrosive effects of corporatist arrangements on the standards of public discussion. Here, for instance, is what the socialist philosopher David Miller has to say about Lijphart's (1980) model of 'consociational democracy', which, it is alleged:

> . . . depends on bargaining between a small number of decision makers, each holding an informal power of veto in case a decision appears to him to damage seriously the interests of the group he represents . . . The consociational model conflicts with the ideal . . . of a society in which each person plays an active role in deciding its future shape . . . it is essential that people should participate politically not as advocates for this or that sectional group but as citizens whose main concerns are fairness . . . and the pursuit of common ends. This is not to say that everyone has to agree at the outset on a common set of principles; on the contrary, . . . political debate . . . has to be dialogue in which each tries to persuade his fellows that the reasons for his views are good ones, not a process of bargaining [between] sectional interests . . . which at best amounts to horsetrading . . . (Miller, 1988, pp. 247–48)

Programmes of democratisation based on such negotiatory forums can only represent a continuation of the worst sort of liberal 'interest-group' model of democracy in which every group seeks to advance their own narrow goals at others' expense. Whence Miller's defiant conclusion: a socialist democracy which is as distinct from its liberal counterpart as the socialist-republican commitment to ideals of 'common citizenship' requires it to be must ban all political parties which merely represent sectional interests. Political competition in Miller's ideal socialist republic will only be permitted if the competing parties are 'held together' on the basis of (competing) *principles* concerning the common good (Miller, *ibid.*, p. 248).

Other-worldly though this conclusion may be, it does not lack a certain logic. Above all, Miller's argument against corporatism is organised around an opposition between discussion as 'dialogue' and discussion as 'bargaining' which faithfully mirrors standard political philosophical and political science classifications of political life into the politics of altruism (or conscience, or principle) and the politics of (self-) interest (e.g. Macedo, 1990, p. 112; Heineman *et al.*, 1990, pp. 69ff). Like the opposition between the participatory ideal and procedural realities of democracy with which we began, this opposition between true dialogue and its particularistic and selfish counterpart even finds its way into arguments which recognize the progressive possibilities of corporatist arrangements. Marquand (1988), for example, constructs the negotiations between organised interests envisaged in his ideal 'developmental state' [18] in terms which could have been drawn directly from Miller or Pateman. As distinct from the 'battlefields' or 'auction rooms' or 'bazaars' of contemporary political life, Marquand (1988, p. 232) holds up the prospect of a way of negotiating differences and making decisions based upon a classically political-romantic ideal of 'mutual education'. 'The political arena becomes a forum for the expression, not of self-interest but of empathy and altruism where 'whole human beings with their loves and hates, hopes and fears, traditions and histories, engage with each other as living persons.'

Not the least unworldly facet of David Miller's very similar argument is its presupposition that 'the politics of principle' and an associated regard for the common good are necessarily conducive to the actual *achievement* of the common good through open discussion. To test this assumption, consider the implications of introducing political organisations identified with the 'politics of principle' into the discussion of how substantive 'public good' outcomes can sometimes be reasonably expected from negotiatory forums. Political scientists interested in this topic tend to confine themselves to forums made up of interest-groups who are identified by means of the standard political-philosophical categories of 'self-interest', 'particularism', etc. For example, Goodin (1986) conceives the constraints on conduct imposed by participation in such forums in terms of a 'laundering of preferences', whereby representatives tailor their contributions so as not to appear to be seeking to impose their own egotistic preferences. Here is one way in which democratic arrangements *may* entail ethically 'substantive' outcomes, but is it the only way?

Suppose forums are driven by an ethos like that commended in Hirst's associationalist doctrine. Negotiated outcomes are sought, which respect national economic goals and interests and allow genuine power-sharing. Then, not being seen to 'push your own barrow' applies with equal force to interest groups associated with altruistic preferences, such as concern for the welfare of the people or the planet. Which form of intransigence is more destructive for the effective functioning of democratic organisation: that based on possessing the biggest battalions or protecting profit-margins, or that based on the possession of the highest principles? An environmental organisation such as the Australian Conservation Foundation may on occasions portray itself as standing for ecological principles which brook no compromise. But on the one hand, for a government to concentrate solely on the environmental impacts of economic development to the detriment of concern with the economic impacts of environmental policies would be irresponsible and a 'betrayal' of its legitimate objectives and responsibilities to its respective constituencies and to the national population generally. On the other, the ACF is itself an interest group with a calculable quantum of electoral 'clout'. It does not possess a monopoly of political virtue.

In general, therefore, the romantic-republican framework in which altruism, universalism, and dialogue are privileged over self-interest, particularism and wheeler-dealing fails to supply the means to appreciate the ethical qualities required of a good committee member, or chairperson, or anyone faced with the inevitable task in democratic organisations and political orders of negotiating differences. Not the least of these qualities is an appreciation of the limits of negotiation itself. Romantic-republican idealisations of discussion as dialogue ignore the presence of an element of 'friend-enemy relations' in all political society. The romantic-republican cult of democratic openness also ignores the impossibility, pointlessless or oppressiveness, in many circumstances, of seeking to implicate 'others' in dialogical relations aimed at their emancipation.

Implications

It is not that participatory democracy can never be festive, personally involving, exhilarating and rewarding. But then the same has been said of fasting – not all the exhilarating aspects of the experience of participation assume the general form of a release. Behind such idealisations of the democratic virtues lies an incapacity to acknowledge that 'freedom' is a set of practices (Foucault, 1987), the 'practice' of which is inseparable from forms of ascetic constraint and (self-) discipline and a related set of negotiatory aptitudes and attitudes. On the whole, neither romantic nor anti-romantic political analysis has shown many signs of recognising the ethical dimension of those qualities.

It will not do then to write out these mundane, all-too-familiar dimensions of active democratic participation. If my argument holds water, they deserve to be treated as more than just the small change of most people's experience of democracy, to be remarked upon in passing *after* the political meeting or the seminar on democratic theory. These material, ethical-cultural dimensions of democracy are not accidental or degenerate by-products but indispensable constituents. Political activism *is* a kind of asceticism, with all the personal demands that implies. It follows that limits to peoples' interest and preparedness to take responsibility should not therefore automatically be seen as obstacles to the ideal of a totally politicised or actively involved community. The ascetic and negotiatory, 'character-forming' prerequisites of participatory democracy mean that independently of political obstacles to the generalisation of participatory democracy there are also practical *ethical* obstacles to consider.

Seeing democratic participation as not only a decision-making procedure but also as a way of 'making' decision-makers impacts on the questions of the place of 'the participatory imperative' in democratic arrangements and the place of democratisation in a socialist politics in a number of unsettling ways. Romantic-republican idealisations of democracy, it will be remembered, carry with them various implications concerning the *direction, goals, extent* and *form* of 'progressive' socialist or advanced liberal social-democratic change. The direction of democratisation is thought to run from parliamentary and electoral politics to the wider sphere of civil society; and from passive to active citizenship. The main goal is autonomy for all, with all the 'socially' minded constraints on autonomy implied by both the 'for' and the 'all'. The implicit form of democratisation exposed by the ensuing argument was that of attempting to realise an asymptotic ideal as far as possible. As such, and having regard to its egalitarian implications, democratisation is a principle of permanent and ubiquitous problematisation of hierarchies and expertise. Let us now proceed to indicate how these assumptions might need to be reassessed, beginning with the *direction* of democratisation.

The Dispersion of Democracy

To assume an ideally indefinite spread of participatory-democratic decision-making from an originally narrow liberal-constitutional base is to forget about the social distribution of the *pedagogy* of participation. If democracy presumes active interest, competence and involvement in decision-making, the reverse is not always the case. As a pedagogical technique of personal formation and government, participation leads a widely dispersed and task-specific existence in a variety of institutions, in which consultation, discussion, voting etc. may not be the norm either ideally or in fact: in the family, the workplace, the school, the therapeutic community and in team-work of all sorts. Confirming our earlier criticisms of the idealisation of democracy as a type of society, this view of participation as a technology of (self-) government suggests that it might bear a contingent relation to democracy. What are the implications of disaggregating participation and democracy for the way we see the trajectory of the participatory imperative?

For one thing, it might prove necessary to question the usual historical accounts of the rage for participation (amongst everyone from students to town planners)[19] of the 1960s and 1970s. The rediscovery of radical philosophical traditions and the greening of popular consciousness usually invoked in such accounts might be seen as themselves effects (albeit in some cases of an irruptive and unforeseen kind) of the rise of participatory-pedagogical techniques inside 'civil society' itself, as much as in state institutions. Thus, developments in school classroom-management parallel, presuppose, and build on interventions in child-rearing aimed at responsibilising children precisely by making them more autonomous. It is the child who at home has been made to discuss how they want to spend the day, to 'elect' when their bedtime should be, the child who has to strike a balance between desires and responsibilities, who is most likely to respond to the 'contract' method of school discipline, the setting up of classroom or school-student committees, etc. (Smith, 1989). We might further speculate that it is to this network of technologies of child and adolescent government, rather than simply to a breakdown or conscious rejection of authority, that we might look to furnish the conditions for the emergence of the 1960s student movement.

Similarly, demands for industrial democracy cannot be understood independently of the emergence of participatory-democratic pedagogical styles of *personnel management* (Rose, 1989). David Marquand's (1988) model of democratisation is envisaged as a process of 'mutual education', deriving from organisation theory (the managerial technique of 'double-loop learning' (Marquand, *ibid.*, pp. 230–31); and from religious and secular teaching techniques (e.g. political leadership being remodelled on the order of 'pastorship' (*ibid.*). In this case, democratisation entails a reabsorption of participatory-pedagogies located inside a scatter of civil institutions back into core political ones.

The force of these speculations is thus to question the assumption of a progressive and (in principle) unlimited 'spread' of the ideal of participatory democracy *via* the struggles of the social movements from a narrow base in political government and constitutional and civil law to the wider civil society (see, for example, Turner, 1986, pp. xii, 133, ch. 4 *passim*). If 'participation' names one set of governmental technologies among others, then democratic participation need not be taken *either* as the general model for all public policy on education and everything else besides (Hadley and Hatch, 1981, pp. 134–37); *or* as some kind of general threat to the stable authority patterns on which civilised life depends (Eckstein, 1966, cited in Pateman 1970, pp. 12–13).

Rather, the issue of participation in schools is much more like a question of whether to add on a localised set of pedagogical techniques to other, more compulsory forms of educational discipline, such as standard assessment procedures. These participatory techniques do not prefigure a general problematisation of all non-democratic and hierarchical aspects of school government. The development of independently minded and cooperative, rather than authoritarian, types of personality in children is entirely dependent on their exposure to an expertly organised, disciplinary educational habitus (see Appendix 1).

In this section, I have sought to bring out some of the critical implications of the ethical-governmental aspects of participation for the usual assumption made by champions of democratisation about the direction of democratic change. In so doing, criticism fastened onto the further assumption that, in principle, the participatory imperative entails the possibility of putting all non-democratic hierarchies 'on notice'. Attention to the pedagogy of participation worked to drive a wedge between participatory techniques and democracy as such. In the following section participation and democracy are once again conjoined as criticism now turns to the implications of their ethical-governmental dimensions for participation in a social-democratic political party.

Party-Political Activism in the Shadows of Hierarchy

In so doing, the target of criticism shifts from the direction to the *goals* of romantic-republican democratisation strategies: a participatory social system which, whilst offering 'autonomy' to all, works to the rhythm of common purposes.

Is participation in the life of a political party to be seen only as a vehicle for augmenting participants' civically-minded 'autonomy'? Are no other ethical rationales conceivable? The more one reflects upon the ascetic and negotiatory demands of party-political activity, the less convinced one is likely to be by the romantic-republican assumption that lack of interest in participation can only be related to a structurally determined lack of opportunity to participate in such a way that their voice counts for something.[20] The obverse of this view is of course that interest in democratic participation can only be sustained by the power it gives one over the regulation and resources around which one's life is organised.

One problem with this argument arises in connection with the perennial debate over how much say activists should have in determining social-democratic parties' electoral manifesto and policies in government. Where, on the whole, the activists are more radically minded than the passive membership, MPs, and the electorate at large, the price of making a social democratic party's manifesto 'express' the convictions of its activists would be to render the party unelectable. Nevertheless, the problem remains: if not in this expressive mode, how *are* members of such a party to relate themselves to it? What does party-political involvement mean as an ethical experience in an electoral climate uncongenial to radical 'emancipatory' objectives? And where the party itself comprises a coalition of ideologically diverse factions, none of which can be allowed to prevail at the total expense of the others? Somehow, a social-democratic party must be, for its members, both more than a philanthropic society-cum-social club and yet less than a vehicle for dramatically transforming the world. How it deals with this ethical conundrum may affect its capacity to recruit and keep its members. Without presuming to resolve this question here, I simply venture a couple of related observations which have to do with what Foucault called the 'ethical substance', the 'mode of subjection' and the *telos* involved in ethically shaping oneself and one's relations to the world.

Party-political involvement might be viewed not only as a vehicle for expressing autonomy but also as offering an antidote to a widely sponsored disaffection with big government, economic policies and the political system, a disaffection which goes well beyond the degree of cynicism warranted by their more mundane shortcomings. Economic illiteracy, mistrust of statistics, governmental expertise and institutionalised forms of politics in general are not solely the result of ignorance or exclusion, but frequently a positive mark of ethical and political superiority. In this circumstance, it might be desirable to increase the quantity and quality of participation in political parties not only in order to put one's commitments into practice but also as a form of *ballast* with respect to them. Democratic participation so understood is about inculcating a sense of political responsibility and *nous* (Weber, 1947). It would be intriguing to chart the changes to party organisation which would have to be rung were the production of that sort of political 'experience' to become an official party-political aim.

The second observation concerns one of the motivations behind party activists' push for more power to determine party policy: namely the desire that the time and energy expended in party work and the knowledge of public issues acquired in the process be politically recognised in the form of a greater political influence and power. It may be unreasonable to expect that either the physical extent or the *intensity* of those commitments – as gauged by the lengths to which one goes, as a party activist, to further them – could be expressed in this way (Dahl, 1956, ch. 4; Hirschmann, 1982, ch. 7). What is not unreasonable, however, is the demand for some kind of reward. To distinguish it from its more careerist counterparts, let's call it *ethical reward*.[21] This idea is not without precedent in the socialist tradition – it looms large in Bellamy's celebrated (1888) utopian text, *Looking Backwards*. It is the idea of seeing democratic involvement as a way in which individuals might ethically distinguish themselves. Is it too heretical to suggest that we need to think of participation as a form of government not only 'of' and 'by' but also *for* the self?

The ethical cachet attaching to participation in turn arouses suspicion about the tendency to view democracy and (aristocratic) hierarchy as opposing principles of social organisation (Offe, 1985, pp. 170–72).[22] Generalised conscientious unease in respect to hierarchy implicit in romantic republicanism now appears in something of a hypocritical light; for it seems to entail turning a blind eye to its own exclusivism.

The exclusivist implications of the republican participatory ideal are nicely caught in Lucas's (1976, p. 230) terse observation that 'any system that caters for more than minimal participation will favour the active over the passive'. The accession to power in city councils of leftist Labour parties in Britain during the 1970s and 1980s offered many examples. 'The community' whose advice (or even instructions) was sought out (in preference to that of experienced officials) by 'the town hall left' was all too often its own creature: a congeries of radical minority voices (Corrigan *et al.*, 1988, p. 13), which merely echoed the voice of their own political-romantic conscience. Traditionally, of course, the ethical hierarchy implicit in republicanism was grounded in the supposed *incapacity* of the majority of the populace to exercise the responsibilities of rule; only those with the breeding and financial means, hence the freedom from material concerns, were qualified to do so. By contrast, the ethical and political hierarchy implicit in modern Enlightenment and romantic republicanism is rather rooted in the distinction between those who *interested* enough in politics to get involved and those who are not (Weber, 1968, II, p. 1457).[23] This ethical hierarchy is made explicit in an exemplary way in Hannah Arendt's (1963, ch. 6.) proposal to resurrect the republican tradition of revolutionary soviets or councils, the non-jacobin *sociétés populaires* and Jefferson's embryonic ward system. These constitute open, self-selecting democratic republican elites – only those who exclude themselves are disenfranchised. The democratic hierarchical pyramid is said to be formed, not on the basis of unpolitical careerist qualifications (as is so often the case in parliamentary politics) but on the basis of peer assessment.

The aristocratic tone of Arendt's republicanism is not unusual in the republican tradition (Loraux, 1986). Yet, as we have noted, the ethical-political exclusivism involved in democratic participation just as frequently finds expression in more demotic Labor Party circles. It would be self-contradictory to make this hierarchical element in active participation an occasion for *general* criticism. The point is rather to bring out the self-defeating character of the vision of a participatory society in which, as Max Weber might have put it, *the distinction between those who are interested in politics and those who are not no longer applies.* Paradoxically, the more the participatory democratic style proliferates throughout the political culture, and the more such participation is culturally valorised (the less 'thankless' it becomes), the greater the possibility of an ethical-hierarchical distance opening up between the involved and the uninvolved.

The implication of this paradox is thus to highlight the *ethically desirable* aspects of the fact that any programme of democratisation, however broadly conceived, will inevitably entail a disestablishment of the 'political class' rather than its dissolution. The fact that these ethical limits to the pursuit of global democratisation derive from the hierarchical constituents of participatory democratic practices themselves points to a need on the part of democrats to cultivate a more discriminating range of practical ethical-political attitudes to hierarchies. It is with this need in mind that the ethical hierarchy implicit in characterisations of the progress of democratisation as a passage from *passive* to *active* citizenship will now be examined.

'Passive' Citizenship: Too Much or Too Little?

The distinction between active and passive citizenship is nothing if not unstable. Considering all the conflicting ideological investments in democracy, and the impossibility of subsuming it within any single theoretical or classificatory framework, it could hardly be otherwise. The sorts of public-minded activities and organisations for 'good citizens' listed in 1950s secondary school 'civics' textbooks – becoming a lay magistrate, helping out on school sports days or serving on the Board of Governors, joining the local Rotary club, etc. – might not impress some left-activists as exceptions to the general 'rule' of passive citizenship – they are 'apolitical', reinforce class relations, etc. Nevertheless, there is, on the left, a well-established distinction between active and passive citizenship which often results in an indiscriminate deprecation of ways of being a citizen that do not require active involvement in public realms.

Claus Offe's contrast between rank-and-workers' solidaristic struggles and the 'bureaucratic' forms of union representation and action was previously taken to illustrate the tendency to bifurcate democracy into its formal-procedural and politically substantive dimensions. In so doing, it also made active participation the *sine qua non* of 'true' democracy. Offe's contrast turns on the distinction between the mere 'willingness to pay' required of passive union members in a hierarchically run union in which representation of unionists' interests is entirely divorced from 'struggle', and the 'willingness to act' involved in 'conscious and coordinated active participation' (Offe, 1985, p. 185). This deprecation of what we might call 'chequebook citizenship' effectively conflates primarily financial contributions to organisations responsible for 'collective welfare' with indifference to anything but personal-pecuniary gain.

Yet in the last few years of British politics, for example, it is difficult to conceive of a more insidious threat to 'social' citizenship than the erstwhile Thatcher government's 'community charge'. The 'street-politics' to which its imposition gave rise should not blind us to the fact that the form of citizenship deliberately rejected by the Conservatives in their 'user pays' and 'no representation without taxation' rationales for the charge involves no more, but no less, than a 'willingness to pay' on the part of the better-off. The 'cheque-book citizenship' at stake is based of course on preparedness to cross-subsidise the more extensive infrastructures of social and health services needed in poorer administrative areas (MacGregor, 1988, pp. 12–22).

Other examples of 'passive' or 'cheque-book citizenship' worthy of socialists' attention and emulation include high levels of public support for the NHS;[24] concern for the environmental and architectural quality of cities; possibilities of 'democratising capital' such as the establishment of collective employee investment funds or trade union superannuation schemes; the fledgling 'ethical investment' trend. All that these actual or potential examples of citizenship involve is a minimum level of interest in something other than solely private income, welfare, and consumption. None entail a challenge to hierarchical structures as such. All may be *linked* to more 'pro-active' forms of participation but they are not reducible to them and may have the effect of making some look irrational. Passive citizenship sometimes deserves better than the derogatory status handed out to it by democratic theorists. The next step in the argument is to hint at how these forms of 'cheque-book citizenship' might be connected to broader historical developments in 'social' government.

Passive Citizenship and Social Solidarity

Illustrating the Austrian trade union movement's successful experience of involvement in corporatist institutions of economic management, a union official interviewed by members of the ACTU European 'Mission' recounted how the last time his union went on strike it was necessary to seek out the services of an elderly former member who still remembered how to organise one (ACTU/TDC, 1987, p. 174)! The lesson of such anecdotes is that even the most 'inclusive' corporatist arrangements are likely to have a 'demobilising' effect on precisely those forms of solidaristic action celebrated by Offe; and, accordingly, are likely to be denounced. However, once the assumption of the superiority of 'active' over 'passive' citizenship is challenged, it becomes possible not only to re-evaluate forms of passive citizenship on a case-by-case basis, but also to investigate the alternative *patterns* of public interest and involvement which some of them embody; alternatives, that is, to the model of 'mass' or 'direct action'. One tradition of socialist and social-liberal thought on which such an investigation might begin is the theories and related programmes which were developed during the life of the Third Republic in France and which went under the rubric of 'social solidarity'.[25]

Undoubtedly, like its modern 'open corporatist' democratic descendants, the early-twentieth-century governmental philosophers of social solidarity construct citizens as consumers, desirous of improving their living standards and the quality of their private lives. As such their committment to the *res publica* is likely to be limited. However, contrary to the dim view of consumer culture traditionally taken by socialists, the social solidarists argued that these limits are not inevitably pre-set at zero. Consumer culture should not be opposed *in toto*, therefore, but rather socially refined (Williams, 1982, ch. 5). Moreover, governmental régimes of 'social solidarity' bring socio-economic protagonists to what Donzelot (1984) sardonically calls 'the great and permanent negotiating table'. Behind this 'model of negotiation' (*ibid.* pp. 249–51) stands a desire for an alternative way of addressing forms of social oppression, exclusion, insecurity and immiseration. Hitherto, in the absence of any channels of redress other than hopelessly biased, pro-capitalist legal ones, dreadful social and industrial conditions had provoked violent conflicts between workers and employers. The social solidarists sought to transform such conflicts into semi-technical disputes about socially just relativities, opportunities, remedies, levels of risk, etc. The political-governmental logic of nineteenth-century 'social insurance' schemes in respect to industrial accidents (Donzelot, *ibid.*, pp. 129–32), for instance, is to seek 'social' progress and greater autonomy for all through the institution of governmental techniques located not only at state level but dispersed through the social body. The masses are now to be involved in *both* individualistic *and* public-minded ways in a complex network of social-technical interdependencies, responsibilities, benefits and 'life-chances'.

No doubt many of these 'social' governmental techniques deliberately sought to marginalise solidaristic forms of action based on eighteenth- and nineteenth-century radical republicanism. However, even the least socialist of them opposed the despotic powers and appalling social conditions from which radical action drew its rationale. Moreover, radical republican forms of political action were seen by the social solidarists, not without reason, as potentially imperilling not only capitalist economic order but also the possibility of a *liberal* polity. The universalistic tenor of the republican rights discourse could not prevent it from fracturing into two radically incommensurable conceptions of citizenship, one around the right to work, the other around the right to security of private property (Donzelot, 1983, pp. 33–49). Nineteenth-century radical republicanism posed this threat because (as even Donzelot's not unsympathetic account makes clear) lacking a governmental philosophy capable of negotiating this fracture in the social body, it offered only the uninviting prospects of Jacobin statist authoritarianism or political chaos. Whilst not all social solidarist policies will be acceptable to socialists, they cannot all be written off as inherently conservative. On the contrary, it is the traditional forms of 'pre-social' solidaristic action which, often, today, appear backward-looking and exclusivist.

If a case is to be made for reevaluating the sorts of 'passive citizenship' constructed through schemes of social administration governed by a logic of social solidarity, it is crucial to break the mental habit of assuming that only by instituting participatory mechanisms of representation can the remoteness to people's needs and the self-serving attitudes supposedly characteristic of social administrative bureaucracies be combated.

This assumption is forcefully challenged in Ann Summers's (1986) response to some feminist criticisms of Women's Affairs units in the Australian Federal bureaucracy established under the Hawke Labor government. She takes as an example the setting up of an annually published 'Women's Budget Programme'.

In this case, 'pressure' from above on departments by an undoubtedly male-dominated 'Task Force', made up of the public service 'mandarins' who headed up these departments, produced a previously unavailable 'big picture' of women's degree of equitable access to, and take-up of, external government programmes. In its comprehensiveness, differentiated detail and political potential this sort of knowledge of the impact of government on the female population compares quite favourably with the other, more 'missionary'-oriented ('client-driven') approach discussed by Summers: the often fraught relations between the Federal government women's units and special advisory bodies drawn from 'women's and community groups'. In the case of the Women's Budget Programme one could speak of the establishment of an apparatus of knowledge, power and influence which includes the organised opinion of 'client groups'. This *dispositif,* as Foucault would have called it, produces results into which political discourse, either emanating from or directed at women can profitably tap. In other words, this apparatus is not an instrument of social control bearing down on women from without, but rather a kind of circuitry, implicating not only highly-placed bureaucrats, departmental form-filling and statistics but (partly through electoral pressures) the preferences of the female Australian electorate. To that extent it is an apparatus of social solidarity. Whilst this governmental technology may not work through participatory-democratic mechanisms it is nevertheless committed to fostering higher rates of 'participation' in 'social' resources such as health, education and welfare.

Conclusions

In this essay I have sought to ask some awkward questions about the ethical limits and mundane ethical realities of democratic participation. The value of such practices gain nothing from being inflated to the level of a general paradigm of socialist progressiveness. In the previous section emphasis has been placed upon the virtues of non-participative governmental techniques for engendering social solidarity, even where their tendency is to make traditional forms of active political involvement appear redundant. The primary concern of this essay of course has been to draw attention to the much underrated ascetic and rhetorical-negotiative dispositions required for participation itself.

This revaluation of the ethical aspects of democratic participation was predicated on bracketing off both the *telos* and the rationalisation of democratic involvements. But suppose we *are* interested in finding some more general rationale for giving up all those evenings. There are no end of reasons for deciding to join a 'progressive' political organisation – the world is full of intolerable injustices and not entirely devoid of opportunities for making life better. Yet it has been a constant theme of these essays that reasons for action never suffice to align the will of individuals to act in conformity with the ends to which they subject themselves. If political participation entails not only government of and by the self but also an element of government *for* the self, then for people who devote a significant portion of their lives to it, the question may arise: what sort of an ethical personage do I imagine I want to *become* through my expenditure of time and energy in the service of a given cause?

The historical anthropologist Marcel Détienne (1989) has written eloquently of 'the surprising power of annexation' exercised by Christianity on the programmes and programmers of the ostensibly secular, early twentieth-century French socialists such as Durkheim. Renewal of solidarity between members of society was represented in terms of a 'lofty', Christian conception of sacrifice (Détienne *et al.*, *ibid.*, pp. 19–20). In the name of socialism the state schools of tomorrow[26] were to be charged with this 'mission to raise us above ourselves'. Any ascetic practice entails some element of self-denial. Still, to be reminded of the Christian-sacrificial element in these socialists' sense of purpose is to appreciate the paucity, today, of credible personal 'life-models' to which the ascetic/altruistic practices of the self entailed in democratic participation can readily be attached.

It would be contrary to the spirit of the argument to read it as merely sceptical and conservative with regard to the place of participation in the life of government. Attention has been drawn to ethical aptitudes which often go insufficiently appreciated. These do not represent an argument against joining political parties but a challenge to think about ways of making them more congenial and ethically rewarding places to be. The point of the exercise is not only to criticise 'the participatory imperative' but also to make room within the socialist imagination for a more varied, less romantic yet not unworthy repertoire of ethical-political objectives, policies and policy-instruments, sentiments and attachments. The 'mechanical' character of technologies of social solidarity was no bar to seeing them in a positive light and as potential objects of popular *interest* in the public good. (Besides, thinking of our 'involvements' in international affairs, is there any necessary correlation between intensity of interest in the news of those affairs and opportunity for hands-on experience? Could it not be the other way around?)

The crux of the argument is the need to disaggregate arguments for participation from romantic republican dreams. We may therefore sympathise with Niklaus Lühmann's (1989) wish to issue the participatory-democratic vision of the 1960s and 1970s once and for all with its 'death certificate' without buying into an overgeneralised disdain for participation. The moral governmental technologies we call participation and democracy are good for some jobs but not all (and not all the *same* jobs). In which case, recent attempts to place the socialist project behind the flagship of republican democratisation have little going for them.

Appendix 1. Utopian idealisations of the democratic ethos: two examples

(1) The celebrated educational psychologist Jean Piaget furnishes a particularly telling example of the cost of idealising democracy: denigration of the mundane conditions of acquiring ethical attributes. The conceptual basis of Piaget's (1965) analysis of children's moral development is a combination of Kantian moral philosophy and contemporary liberal political philosophy. The virtues of the modern democratic citizen, such as the dispositions to cooperate with others and respect them as equals, are assumed to be instantiations of the Kantian good will – forming moral judgements through the application of universal rational principles (treat others as ends not means, etc.). Piaget wishes to ground this Kantian view of the liberal-democratic virtues in a 'normal' trajectory of every child's psychological maturation, together with a corresponding 'democratic' model of good parenting. The *a priorism* of Piaget's 'empirical study' of what it means to grow up in ethical terms is particularly apparent in his treatment of the practicalities of moral training. For Piaget, the parental models through which the child learns to practice reciprocity in relations with others are paradoxical. On the one hand, they are empirically necessary to the acquisition of a sense of justice; on the other, parental examples and precepts actually *weaken* it (since justice presupposes the undetermined Kantian will). Justice and reciprocity cannot be prescribed by parental authority – as if the pedagogy of reciprocity worked only by commands and rigid norms. Piaget's (*ibid.*, p. 319) discomfiture in respect to the ethico-technical concomitants of participatory moral pedagogy (with its implication that 'autonomy' is an effect of a kind of subjection to authority) thus leads him into a flagrant self-contradiction. See his unpersuasive polemic against Durkheim's view that the difference between constraint and cooperation in respect to morality is basically one of degree rather than kind (Piaget, *ibid.*, p. 346).

(2) Considered as intellectual technologies of government, it will not be expected that either management-based or education-based theories and policies of participation will be necessarily less utopian than philosophical ones. We have seen the power of philosophical modes of thought at work in Piaget's mythopoeic 'operationalisation' of Kantian philosophy in the sphere of education. Idealisations of democracy are after all themselves one of the material forms in which the democratic ethos is disseminated in contemporary society. Who could ignore the affinities between programmatic utopian thought and the standard ways in which contemporary English-speaking students of philosophy and sociology are

taught to think about politics: between Robert Owen, for example, tirelessly preaching his environmentalist view of human character and seeking to reconstruct the whole of society on this one intellectual-ethical foundation (whilst the 'New Harmony' community went to wrack and ruin), and the student of philosophy trained to reflect on the consequences of running 'society' on the basis of the principle of utility? A utopian programmatism may be assumed by social democrats or political philosphers who would not dream of calling themselves utopians: *de te fabula narratur*. One might also think of the way in which conceptions of 'full' equality and freedom are built into sociology curriculae which divide up the field of social relations into the standard trinity of social inequalities.

9 The Associations of Socialism

Introduction

Paul Hirst has long argued that the English pluralist tradition contains important lessons for both socialist theory and the British Labour Party.[1] With the publication of *The Pluralist Theory of the State*, an elegant and scholarly edition of writings drawn from three of the leading participants in this tradition – Cole, Figgis, Laski – Hirst has placed a capstone on this increasingly influential line of argument. The appearance of these hitherto out-of-print texts presents a suitable occasion on which to venture a preliminary assessment of what this tradition might have to offer.

The social ideal of these theorists is a plurality of semi-independent, self-governing associations. As in Durkheim's related social programme, associations provide intermediate institutional sources of citizens' interests, values, involvements, and self-development. In Hirst's eyes, the associationalists exemplify a vision of socialism which unwaveringly champions pluralism as a perpetual challenge and *valuable* limit to the sway of any public power, however progressive, rather than something to be transcended in a harmonious future socialist society 'beyond tolerance' (Wolff, 1969). If pluralism presents obstacles to socialist objectives,[2] it is also rich in progressive human and organisational opportunities which go unappreciated in other socialist traditions. So conceived, the associationalist socialist tradition constitutes a valuable antidote to the bad 'associations' of socialism with 'actually (or 'recently'?) 'existing' authoritarian–socialist regimes in Eastern Europe as well as with 'statist' populist-workers'–state conceptions of socialism (Hirst, 1989a, p. 37).

More explicitly, associationalism also offers a telling early-twentieth-century critique of the elective despotism inherent in the Westminster system (Marquand, 1988, pp. 175–208). To argue against parliamentary governments – of whatever political colour – forcing through changes, Thatcher style, on the basis of a nominal electoral majority is not to be committed to Cole's utopian scheme for reducing central government to a constitutional 'court of appeal' for resolving differences between associations (Hirst, *op. cit.*, p. 103).[3] On the contrary, argues Hirst, following Figgis (*ibid.*, p. 125), an associational society which is not

220

riven by a fatal 'antagonistic pluralism' is inconceivable in the absence of a *Rechtsstaat* equipped with the sovereign authority and means necessary to construct and coordinate the interrelations of associations and regulate their scope of action. Support for such a *Rechtsstaat* is not inconsistent with criticism of the British model of representative democracy as little more than a plebiscitarian legitimation of large-scale and largely unaccountable government by a legally omnicompetent sovereign state and, by implication, of equally unaccountable private corporate empires.

Having pinpointed the impossible assumptions underlying the model of democracy as the 'representation' of geographically located constituencies and individual wills, Cole and Laski suggest a model of democracy based on a functional principle of social/democratic division. In Laski's words, 'the railways are as real as Lancashire' (Hirst, *ibid.*, p. 145). Functional democracy is both a legitimation *and* a practice of rule, based on the idea of members of the citizenry's participation in running those functionally specific types of institution or activity in which citizens take a personal interest, and about which they possess practical know-how.

Whilst Laski saw industrial life as perhaps the single most important locus of democratic (self-) government, he was far from advocating a worker's state: churches no less than unions must be free to determine their own institutional and spiritual development (Hirst, *ibid.*, pp. 155, 175, 189).[4] By the same federalist, devolutionist logic, associationalism undermines both the traditional parliamentarist and the radical participationist critiques of *corporatist* strategies which for Hirst offer the best hope of extending democracy within the upper echelons of political decision-making. If both the idea of an omnicompetent sovereign (whether elected or otherwise) and generalised participation in governance are equally unsustainable, then a reasonably 'open corporatism' cannot be seen as necessarily subverting the authority of either parliament or the general will. (Hirst, *ibid.*, p. 38). Under the conditions of representative democracy and big government, political activism is inevitably a minority pursuit (Hirst, 1989, pp. 69–71).

Suitably qualified, the pluralist and functional-democratic premises of associational socialism thus form the basis of Hirst's recommendation that the British Labour Party reconstruct itself in the image of a 'social leader', an orchestrator rather than master of society and its organised interests. Public policy should emerge as the product of coordination, bargaining and agreement between a plurality of relatively autonomous associations in open corporatist forums. The radical changes to both economic organisation, political structures and cultural attitudes required to reverse Britain's industrial decline, argues Hirst, require enlisting the support of a far broader coalition of interests and forces than could be ever expected to vote for the Labour Party (Hirst, *ibid.*, pp. 73–74, ch. 7 *passim*).

Rather than attempting a direct assessment of Hirst's reprise on associationalism, I am more interested in seeing what these associationalists might have to offer over and above the value which Hirst himself explicitly derives from them. What are the implications of the romantic side of the associationalist *ethos*? What is its relationship to the associationalists' arguments on the *legal* powers of associations and to their view of *administration*?

There is Romanticism and Romanticism

For Hirst (1989a, p. 1), it is not the least of the English pluralists' virtues that, by contrast with the 'relentless forms of abstraction' from the 'consideration of specific constitutional and political issues of demo-cratic government' characteristic of both Marxist and liberal-individualist political theory, Cole, Laski and Figgis offer an informed critique of specific state institutions and policies, focusing on the legal and pol-itical constitutionalist doctrines of unlimited state sovereignty by which they are justified. True, but what is striking about their writings is the mixture of both the practical and the visionary, the focus on both the ethical and the more technical–legal bases of democracy and liberty. No doubt, associationalism is suffused with romantic notions of 'life' and its human possibilities. But are these notions all of a piece?

Throughout this book evidence has been presented about the extent to which contemporary progressive political culture is pervaded by a dialectical form of political romanticism. The romantic dialectic man-ages both to evade the complexities and compromises of institutional (re-)organisation, by reducing them to a 'one-sided' expression or failure to express essential human desires or chosen political ideals; whilst simultaneously eschewing the *simplification* of institutional life achieved by norms, procedures and binding decisions, seen as limiting human developmental possibilities.

This kind of political romanticism is calculated to breed suspicion of associationalism's commitments to a pluralist political culture as well as to its engagement in legal and political institutional reform. The former necessitates forms of consensus-building and compromise, the latter, giving workable procedures and binding decisions priority over the endless 'pro-cess' of dialectical self-shaping. Cole's argument for the functional basis of democracy undercuts a romantic-expressivist conception of democratic representation as an expression of the will of the elector-subject. Functional democracy views representation as 'merely a means of providing the personnel of certain bodies' for a limited range of decision-making purposes (Hirst, 1986, p. 33); suffrage being limited only by the number of associations for which the individual has the time, energy and abilities. Yet one of the (Rousseauian) philosophical premises for functional democracy is indeed what Hirst (1989a, p. 31) calls an 'exalted' conception of individuals as a universal set of potentialities. How could the multifarious 'wills' of such a creature be truly represented by another? Cole is led by this romantic explanation for the impossibility of representation to deny any 'function' for parliamentary representation. Accordingly, the 'functional' principle of democracy does not only focus attention on the specific purposes and 'political mechanisms' entailed in democracy *qua* organisational method. It also reverberates with organicist connotations. Associations are conceived as vehicles for forms of individual self-fulfilment and social integration unattainable by isolated individuals – or in 'mechanical' (community-less) social organisation. In *The Social Theory* Cole's vision of a virtually stateless society rests on faith in human beings' essentially sociable nature (Hirst 1986, p. 64 n. 4) and on a preordained harmony between associational functions:

> strictly speaking, no anti-social purpose can be part of the function of an association. But . . . the production of commodities for use and the preservation of order . . . may be pursued in anti-social ways which give rise to opposition and perversion of function. (Cole, in Hirst, *op. cit.*, p. 65)

These forms of political romanticism may be readily sloughed off. However, associational pluralism cannot be quite so easily dissociated from the rather different outgrowth of political–romantic thought which marks Cole's social theoretical starting-point: the concept of the plurality of communities which constitutes the core of social and individual life. 'Essentially a subjective term', argues Cole, community is whatever constitutes a relatively self-contained locus of a conscious sense of belonging and purposes which could not be pursued or even entertained by single individuals. Community is distinguished from both associations formed solely for the furtherance of a particular interest and from the 'social' field in general (Hirst, *ibid.*, pp. 51–53). 'Society' is 'a resultant of the interaction . . . of the various functional associations'; it is concerned solely with the organised cooperation of human beings and . . . not directly in the feeling of community among individuals' (*ibid.*, p. 54). This sense of 'fellowship' is indeed for Cole the ultimate condition of association (Hirst, 1986, p. 64 n. 4).

These concepts are unquestionably permeated with a romantic-dialectical ethos of cultural perfection. A trade union, for example, offers a means of social connection. Yet, Cole maintains, 'it is not a self-contained group of complete human beings' and hence a source of true 'belongingness'. 'Community' is defined as antithetical to organisation (p. 55). However, this also taken up by Cole in a way which is logically independent of the romantic dialectical ethos.

No doubt it will be to Tönnies' concept of *Gemeinschaft* that most sociologists would first turn for the classical romantic concept of community.[5] But an earlier *locus classicus* of this concept of community may be found in Hegel's argument that the heart of the ethical resided in *sittlichkeit*. Building on a key theme in Herder (and in opposition to Kant), Hegel developed the idea of relatively closed sets of customs and institutional milieus (e.g. the family, religions) as not merely vehicles for the expression of values but as the positive conditions and constituents of 'an habitual practice of ethical living' (Hegel, 1952, p. 108). *Sittlichkeit* is the means by which a person is tied into an identificatory 'ethical order' said to be constitutive of their pre-ideational 'ethical substance'.

Whilst this *sittliche* ethics figures as but one 'moment' in Hegel's dialectical history of social and individual development, in some respects *Sittlichkeit* is out of place in this scheme of things. First, by comparison with the romantic (or Kantian) ethical accent on achieving conscious agency and choice, principled reasons and obligations, the transcendence of conventional limits, taking charge of one's destiny, *Sittlichkeit* links the ethical to the unreflective, the passive, the derivative and the compulsive dimensions of human comportment. Ethical attributes bred by communal ties are 'creatures of habit', artefacts of social training; involving 'prestigious imitation' (Mauss) of norms articulated through 'in-group' idiolects, rituals, ceremony, symbolic arrangements.

Second, and by implication, *sittliche* ethics stands in contrast to the dialectical romantic investiture of human beings with an inherent 'negativity' or reflexivity. In Herder's arguments on the sociality of the self, customary ethics 'prescribed a normative constraint on the extent to which we should develop a critical distance towards the social forms that have shaped us' (Larmore, 1988, p. 95). Is it a sign of incomplete (undialectical) development if in some departments of their existence people feel at ease where their ways of conducting themselves in relation to others and relating to themselves are shaped within the circumference of a relatively self-contained and self-containing cultural world?[6] Collective self-containment may be taken to destructive lengths in nationalist movements, cults, police culture, etc. However, does the solution to the extremist implications of nationalism lie in encouraging nationalists to cultivate a more 'universalist' cosmopolitan outlook? More likely it is a question of their being brought to a rueful acceptance that for the sake of peace a way of coexisting with the hated enemy will have to be found. You do not thereby become a more 'rounded' individual, rather you cultivate 'enlightened self-interest'; that is, learn to compromise with a vital part of your *persona*.

Third, a *sittliche* ethics based in habitual training and practice undercuts the assumption of an inherent tension between community and social–administrative organisation. A *sittliche* ethos may therefore be an instrumental component or effect of complex, technical forms of social–administrative or economic organisation. 'Community values' understood in this way may thus be factored into social policies directed at the family.[7] Or into inner-city cultural policies, e.g. assistance in the establishment of a 'Chinatown' or heritage precincts which in Cole's language help to turn what was hitherto 'merely an administrative area' into a revitalised hub of sociable activity with 'a life and feeling of its own', a 'real and inclusive centre of social life' (Hirst, 1989a, p. 52).[8] Ethnically oriented policies of this order, moreover, affect the quality of life of not only the ethnic group concerned but also that of more cosmopolitan inhabitants.[9]

To acknowledge the importance of *Sittlichkeit* in the ethical formation of citizens is not to imply that it is either the only way in which this formation can be effected, or that it is invariably beneficial in a 'social' sense. Despite its frequently troublesome implications, from a social-democratic or socialist point of view, however, there is much to be said in favour of binding individuals, up to a point, into a plurality of relatively self-enclosed 'life-orders' or cultural enclaves. Apart from the usual liberal grounds, one reason for socialists and social democratics to take pluralism in respect to belief-systems seriously has to do with a problem which Hirst himself posed in an earlier work:

> For all the benefits of freedom of conduct . . . which stem from a decline in religious practice, subjects are no longer interpellated as obligated to duty and charity. We face problems of motivating people to behave in altruistic, dignified and considerate ways without transcendent goals. This is not a matter of 'ideals' or 'morals' but of a daily practical mechanism of conduct keyed into practices and institutions. No civilisation can provide its members with means of conducting themselves that depend entirely for compliance on utilities, pleasures,

satisfactions and reasons . . . Social democrats and libertarians alike predicate the future of social organisation on an unproblematic world of satisfactions . . . We beg to doubt this. Without a new model of a pattern of conduct and disciplines to accompany it, we can expect increasing problems in the management of behaviour . . . Our problem is that . . . we lack the ideational means to order and justify social actions often possessed by 'poorer' or more 'ignorant' peoples. (Hirst and Woolley, 1982, p. 138)

Here, arguing from a 'material-cultural' view of the ethical, Hirst in effect reinvents the 'idealist' insights of Herder and Hegel into the centrality of *Sittlichkeit* to ethical life. Glimpsed in this passage is something of the reasons why, at the ethical level, associationalism came as the answer to a thinking socialist's prayers. Bearing in mind socialism's romantic stripe, it is perhaps not so much for the lack of 'ideational means' or 'transcendent goals' that socialist ethics has always seemed so thin. It is more that a 'wish-list' of hopes, ideals, rights, etc. is no substitute for the dense and detailed complexion of a *sittliche* 'pattern of conduct . . . keyed-in to practices' by accompanying 'disciplines'. Today, who really believes that a *socialist state* could supply this lack? Attempts to construct a 'new model' socialist republican ethical community inevitably fall prey to a phantasy of totalitarian control or a simplistic rationalism of maximising choices; the assumption being that once oppression and ignorance have been eliminated, people's choices will be conformable to a 'social(ist)' conscience (Hindess, 1991b).

The ethical-political force of associational pluralism thus rests in part on its capacity to accommodate itself to the impossibility of institutionalising a general socialist ethos in the sense of a complex 'model' of conduct and motivation. Conversely, associational group life, with all its particularistic limitations and ethical costs, offers indispensible institutional *loci* of identification and hence fellow-feeling on which the cultivation of unselfish attitudes or other socially desirable attributes compatible with liberal/socialist standards of 'civic virtue' and the national interest partly depends. Even if associational life is not impervious to 'outside' normative governmental influences it has to be recognised that more 'universalistic' prescriptions of socialist or social democratic political ethics can only ever function at most as one component of associational life.

The social and cultural implications of pursuing a 'flexible specialisation' industrial policy illustrate the sorts of hard choices by which socialists who embrace associational pluralism are likely to be faced. One of the main economic adjuncts of Paul Hirst's associationalism (Hirst and

Zeitlin, eds, 1988), flexible specialisation, entails, firstly, a proliferation of semi-customised goods produced by firms of varying sizes; and secondly, the creation of industrial districts comprising a mixture of cooperative as well as competitive relations between interdependent enterprises and their sub-contractors. In the most celebrated and successful exemplars – Sakaki, Emilia-Romania, Baden-Würtemberg – these socio-economic arrangements frequently go hand-in-hand with extremely traditional, conservative relations of kinship and personal acquaintance.[10] One would not expect these enterprises, many of them small family firms, to shine on the fair wages and conditions and equal opportunity fronts – and 'the Italian model' has already attracted criticism on this score.[11] It has to be asked, though, whether the national economic benefits of flexible specialisation are completely outweighed by these considerations of social justice. Leaving aside the technical and ideological obstacles to policing the group-life of family firms, it would be most unworldly of socialists not to acknowledge that the *sittliche* facets of such firms compensate to some extent for the problems of (self-)exploitation of men, women and children often associated with them.

Incorporating associational pluralism into socialist theory means abandoning the aspiration to achieve an integral socialist *society*. One way of possibly making this implication more palatable might be to suggest that its *sittliche* ethos offers not only a way of 'associating' socialism once again with the cause of liberty but also opportunities for the exercise of politically acceptable liberal-socialist forms of social control. It is to this end that the associationalist emphasis on *legal politics* will now be brought in for discussion.

Associationalism and Company Law

In their preparedness to grapple with both the technical complexities and the politics of legal systems rather than viewing them as ideological reflexes of capitalism, the English pluralists invite comparison with Eeuropean socialist theorists such as Kirchheimer and Neumann. However, these writers were perforce steeped in European 'civilian' or 'Roman' law. What is exemplary about the English associationalists is their interest in the problems of instituting radical socio-economic and political changes within the context of a *common-law* legal culture. This interest is well illustrated by their interventions with respect to company law; so too is the practical purchase of associationalism's *sittliche* ethos.

For Figgis, Cole and Laski, one of the main lines of attack on British constitutional theory's vesting of unlimited sovereignty in parliament is at the level of its implications for the legal standing of both corporations and unincorporated bodies. Following Gierke and Maitland, they attack the 'concessionalist' or legal-positivist view of corporate personality as merely creatures of an omnicompetent state law and hence as incapable of acting other than in legally prescribed ways.

The insufficiency of this view of incorporation (which Hirst [1986, pp. 54–55] himself, in the context of a polemic against essentialist conceptions of rights, had once endorsed) was exposed by drawing attention to a series of problematic early-twentieth-century legal decisions concerning clubs, unions, churches and business corporations. The law lords' decision in the Free Church of Scotland case is a case in point. A merger with the Presbyterian Church had been agreed upon by an overwhelming majority of the Free Church's members. Yet the resentful minority was able successfully to claim the title to the church's property at law, on the grounds that the democratically reached decision was *ultra vires* the legally established, contractually binding founding constitution of the church. The decision placed the law lords in the invidious position of arbitrating on issues of Calvinist theology and ecclesiastical governance; and, ultimately, on what believers ought to believe.

In such judgements the concessionalist view of corporate personality was yoked to a logically distinct 'fiction' theory, according to which 'corporate personality' is only a convenient shorthand for an aggregation of individuals around a property or capital for the purposes of reaping personal benefits. (For a classical articulation of the two theories see Hohfeld, 1909.) As against these legal-positivist views of legal personality, the associationalists took up Maitland's appropriation of Otto von Gierke's 'realist' theory of the corporation as an integral 'personality', a 'real body' with a capacity for purposive action and autonomous development. As such, it is irreducible to its status as a legal personality and hence to the rights and duties prescribed in its original articles of association. Accordingly, Figgis and others emphasised that, contrary to the assumption behind the fiction, bodies such as unions and churches were not aggregations of individuals linked together solely for the sake of private benefits. On the contrary, these bodies were dependent upon the commitment and loyalty of at least some of their members.

Hirst's qualified endorsement of this conception of the 'real' personality of corporations is largely premised on the possibility of separating out the pluralists' claims about how a corporate body should be constructed and recognised at law from the romantic-metaphysical arguments about the nature of 'group life' by which these claims were justified. The Maitlandian realist theory need not deny the concessionalist point that, like all persons at law, corporations must be 'artificially' delineated in respect to some of the institutional forms and lines of action open to them. But which ones? Only those originally constructed in law? There are many things in life which are neither prescribed nor forbidden by law. Strict concessionalism places narrow and needlessly authoritarian constraints on the range of corporate capacities it is prepared to recognise. These constraints inhibit corporate bodies' capacity for internal self-development. Law appears as an imperious sovereign unreceptive to developing social needs.

Yet Hirst's argument is itself predicated on an assertion about the nature of group life. 'The group is a necessary relation', argues Hirst, and 'it will not help group life to insist on the primacy and reality only of the elements related' (Hirst, 1989a, p. 21). There are functions, activities, forms of decision-making, etc. which cannot be carried out by individuals or even aggregates of individuals. In some cases, it might be added, not only the corporate body, but the social milieus affected by it might benefit, were that body to function in a more integral fashion than it currently does. The possibility of conceptualising the integral qualities of group life – seeing groups as social or moral persons if you like – without invoking metaphysical hypostatisations such as a 'group-mind' is nicely elaborated in French's (1979) concept of a 'corporate internal decision structure'. This has two components: a general corporate strategy (as recorded in its articles of incorporation, mission statements, annual reports, etc.); and an organisational chart which maps the interdependent and dependent staff relationships involved in corporate decision-making. This 'chart' is the discursive expression of what might be called an internal, 'administrative incorporation' of the acts and intentions, plans, recommendations, reports associated with human individuals and sub-groups.

Interestingly, the point of this exercise in the reconceptualisation of corporate personality is to 'license the predication of corporate intentionality' and hence moral responsibility for corporate actions. Granted, not all or even most of the actual *sittliche* 'bonding' of individuals which may be part of corporate life would necessarily be prefigured in the formal chart of organisational responsibilities and interdependencies. Nevertheless, for all its formalism, the concept of a CID structure provides a warrant to treat corporations as members of a 'moral community' of equal standing with the traditionally acknowledged human residents (French, *ibid.*, p. 208). French's argument thus returns us to the romantic insight into the moral value of institutions as training grounds and foci of identification for responsible individuals. Not all the 'constitutive ties' which bind individuals into the activities of a corporation will be of this *sittliche* quality; especially when 'the corporation' is a holding company with possibly hundreds of subsidiaries dispersed throughout the world. Nevertheless, the lesson of French's instantiation of Hirst's argument on the claims of group life is that there may be both political and theoretical reasons to pause before throwing out all the romantic furniture in the associationalists' arguments.

With its relentless polemic against the doctrine of unlimited state sovereignty, associational pluralism lends itself to being interpreted as a libertarian argument obsessed with freeing of associational life from the shackles of big government. Whilst not altogether unwarranted, this interpretation of associationalism ignores the extent to which the associationalists' vision of a self-governing society of associations is inflected by their engagement with British legal and political institutions. For example, Laski's inventory of the absurd and unjust consequences of unlimited state sovereignty in the field of company law includes not only unreasonable constraints on the freedom of associations; the difficulties of constraining them is also noticed. In 'the personality of associations', Laski dwells on the impossibility of indicting corporations on counts which require proof of *mens rea* (Hirst, 1989a, p. 172). At common law, the influence of the aggregate theory thus clearly stood in the way of that 'predication of corporate intentionality', in French's words, without which a corporation as such cannot be prosecuted for criminal behaviour.

Let us therefore not be too quick to criticise associational romanticism. The more corporations are legally and normatively categorised as a *sittliche* order of relations, as akin to a *Gemeinschaft* as opposed to a *Gesellschaft*, even if only notionally, the more their legal categorisation as an integral entity is capable of functioning as a means of not only according them greater autonomy but also of subjecting them to a measure of social control and accountability. The idea of *Sittlichkeit*, moreover, legitimates moves to prevent individual malfeasance from escaping legal sanctions behind the veil of corporate personality. If the whole is to be responsibilised for the behaviour of the parts, then, *mutatis mutandis*, following the example of European legal systems such as those of France and Germany, there may also be a case for limiting the right to limited liability for directors and major shareholders (Le Gall, 1974, pp. 249–50; E. J. Cohn, 1968, pp. 69ff). This is to make limitation of liability a privilege rather than the right of every corporate body and hence to drive a wedge between limited liability and corporate personality.[12] In any attempt to make corporations and their members behave more responsibly by means of such a stratagem, the legitimising potential of the romantic concept of community ties constitutive of individuals' 'ethical substance', and hence capable of requiring their loyalty and commitment, should not be underestimated.

Attitudes to Administration

The seeming irony of romantic communitarianism's being summoned to serve as an instrument of liberal-bureaucratic social control underscores the importance of distinguishing it from the dialectical romantic model of social and subjective development. For if there is widespread disaffection with centralised state government, law, and bureaucratic rules, this is almost certainly due as much to the influence of this latter brand of romanticism in shaping popular ethico-political sensibility as to any empirical track-record of governmental inefficiency, heavy-handedness, unresponsiveness, etc. This differentiation between forms of political romanticism is thus central to the question of the whether associationalism's animus against big government borders on the utopian.

The question takes on added urgency in the light of the fact that the associationalists' engagement with legal politics, exemplary though it may be, seems to have come at the cost of giving short shrift to the *administrative* sinews of government. True, part of the associationalists' case against the doctrine of unlimited state sovereignty turns on the fact that decision-making powers are necessarily dispersed more broadly than the doctrine provides for; *vide* Cole's discussion of the difficulty of maintaining a clear distinction between law-making and law-administering (Hirst, 1989a, p. 95). Yet the business of government (where it is not conducted by a self-governing association) never escapes the shadow of the law. Cole's examples of administration invariably concern cases where discretionary authority has been legally delegated (e.g., in the case of 'special orders'). There is little appreciation of the symbiotic relays through which associations and administrative systems are intermeshed with one another.

In general, 'classical' associationalism is marred by an excessive dependence on a singular distinction between state and civil society which owes more to political philosophy and constitutional law than it does to administrative knowledges. As the example of the social control of corporations illustrates, any associational pluralist strategy with even the most modest socialist ambitions must strive to hybridise the 'government' of social life. This means on the one hand (as Hirst insists) involving associations in consultative relations with central government (in return for ensuring that their members carry out the policies which result from these consultations). But equally, the condition for a viable associationalism is not only a legal *Rechtstaat* framework but in addition a complex of administrative and management apparatuses of government. These must be capable of regulating associations both from without and, indirectly, from within (*via* the incorporation of public norms into their internal functioning, incentive schemes, etc.). Social control in this self-regulatory sense presupposes rather than precludes an important role for central government in ensuring a roughly equitable provision of social and economic infrastructure, cultural facilities, apparatuses of security, etc. Irrespective of whether these services are actually *provided* by state apparatuses, or (as the associationalists would prefer) merely *regulated* by them, an associational state needs a strong *administrative* order.[13]

To what extent therefore is associationalism driven by a generalised *a priori* negativity towards state-run administration? Even where, as in Figgis's case, its necessity is acknowledged, is it not conceived as at best a necessary evil and as something only to be conceived in terms of its legal-regulatory remit and limits? The important question is not so much what the associationalists actually thought but whether their doctrines are adjustable to take into account the symbiotic relations between civil associations, state bureaucracies and the techniques of (self-) government which are common to both. A focus on the ethical dimension of associationalism may be one way of approaching these questions. Insofar as associationalism is inflected by dialectical and holistic concepts of social life, it will be blind to these symbioses of private and public government. For example, to distinguish between community and social administrative organisation after the fashion of Cole is not only (as we have seen) to make the former appear necessarily recalcitrant to social administrative reform; it is also to assume that the value of 'fellow-feeling' cannot be truly cultivated beyond the warm confines of associational life.

This is of course fully in line with the standard political-romantic imputation that social administrative reasoning is essentially driven by amoral 'instrumentalist' motivations. As a counter-example, consider the nineteenth-century administrative theorist Lorenz von Stein's elevating social programme for binding members of the population into an equitable *administrative* form of 'association':

> At the horizon of our human collective consciousness the knowledge arises that the prime condition of all earthly happiness and individual fulfilment is *the happiness and fulfilment of the other* . . . While we as individuals are hesitant and uncertain when faced with this knowledge its truth develops quietly and powerfully. It builds schools . . . establishes hospitals, it finances associations . . . and creates assistance, it cares for the wealth of the lower class, lights its houses, lays out gardens . . . , gives water, gives bread, . . . It seeks to involve all members of the possessing class in novel, cultural and uplifting

pursuits, it makes the one class responsible for the peaceful yet certain development of the other, and the Christian duty . . . of love for one another is raised *with or without conscious formulation* (my emphasis) at first in terms of *interest* (emphasis in original) into the obligation of societal order. And the great organ through which this obligation is fulfilled, untiringly active in all its parts, is *administration*. (Cited in Kästner, 1981, pp. 16–17)

Stein's bountiful administrative programme is administered by the state.[14] But its supreme aim is to enhance the free-standing capacities of individuals. And many of its equivalents in the social solidarist tradition, such as insurantial techniques, need not necessarily be run by the state. In a way the quotation could be said to dramatise both the insufficiency and the necessity of associationalism to a modern socialist governmental philosophy. It offers a precedent – and a lesson to the English associationalists – in the possibility of investing 'high administration' with a positive ethical mission (and an example of how the down-to-earth practical work of administration is already saturated in ethical norms); and hence of seeing it as something more than a necessary evil always-already overstepping its proper limits.

If the higher vocation which Stein accords to administration is implausible to most thinking socialists today, this is not merely on account of its Christian-altruistic tenor. These days we would be more likely to lay emphasis upon the more down-to-earth, ethical-political objectives and attractions of administration, such as the socialisation of the problem of insecurity (Donzelot 1983; Goodin and Le Grand, 1987). Only from a dialectical-romantic standpoint, it seems to me, can one refuse to grant that such 'insurantial' technologies represent a *bona fide* administrative registration and relay of fellow-feeling. The depressing impact of obsessively market-driven 'corporatisation' strategies in the public service sector on the principle of cross-subsidisation, for example, brings this 'human', social-solidaristic potential of 'big government' into stark relief. Yet this cannot detract from the implausibility of a general social(ist) ethical administration of 'the whole of society'. Whence the importance to socialism of ethical (*sittliche*) communities which can never be entirely the creatures of social reform programmes and the indispensability of associationalism to socialist theory. Learning to respect the importance of civil associations is a condition for socialists (at last) learning 'to trust the people'; or, as Hirst (1989b, p. 181) puts it, 'to recognise themselves as members of society and not masters of it . . . to speak to others who do not identify with it . . . (to collaborate) with non-socialists in common political and economic enterprises'. This means accepting the prospect that, beyond the enforcement of this 'liberal minimum' of security, liberty, equality, environmental responsibility and the like, and indirect inputs into associational life by state government and the administrative systems, power to bring about the kinds of social participation, sociability, social justice and social control envisaged in the socialist tradition, *or not to do so,* does not primarily lie with state administrations but with civil associations.

Yet at the end of the day associationalist pluralism is either a philosophy of private-*and*-public governance or only another variant of dialectical political romanticism. A reformation of large-scale administration which isn't simply directed at reducing its size and cost is unlikely to figure as a 'big idea' in any social-democratic election manifesto. But even if it does little for its popular appeal, associationalism is objectively dependent upon the development of a *supplementary* reconceptualisation of, not just the limits, but the ethical mission and routines of 'big government'.[15]

Tailpiece

In my previous book, I speculated that one of the main implications of Michel Foucault and related approaches to political and social affairs was to 'put the social back into socialism and [to leave] socialists to pick up the pieces' (Minson, 1985, p. 223). 'The social' referred to the hybrid forms and objects of liberal government. Whilst great pains were taken in that book to emphasise that the partial 'depoliticisation' of issues associated with their establishment *as* social issues ought not to be treated as a source of ideological anxiety and a subject of criticism, no attempt was made to highlight the reconstructive implications of this point from a socialist point of view. It has become quite common to note that the collapse of the communist party countries as the only actual 'alternative' to capitalism and the success stories of capitalist economies which have evolved clever national economic and industrial policies offer socialists an unexpected chance to reoccupy the middle ground of politics. The apostles of untrammelled *laissez-faire* are now the unworldly ideologists. The question is, however, what form of organised intellectual response to this opportunity to be the party of 'moderation' is open to socialists?

One option which suggests itself on the basis of this essay and its forerunners is to think again about the traditional socialist commitment to 'socialising' political and economic life. What would it amount to were it to be detached from its past association with the romantic-historicist dream of a classless society 'free' of ideological differences and the need for political institutions? With the doctrine of the withering away of the state behind them, socialists are free to think of placing their traditional commitments to the value of social cooperation and the goal of overcoming social disharmony at the service of partial and provisional depoliticisations of debilitating social conflicts. The promise to (one day) solve the conflicts between labour and capital, abolish war, eliminate crime, etc. gives way to a more modest promise to govern these conflicts which is pragmatic, yes, but pragmatic on the basis of good pluralist principles. It is a promise to find a way around these problems, to take the political heat out of them by policies aiming at institutionalising negotiation and bargaining between conflicting parties. It is a promise to secure across-the-board commitments from powerful stakeholders, not to social equality, but rather to the progressive and sustained alleviation of crippling social distress to the minimum standards prerequisite to normal social functioning.[16] What I am suggesting is that socialism needs to be rethought in such a way that its centre of gravity deliberately approximates to an ideology which believes not in abolishing ideological difference, but side-stepping it as occasions demand.

The social in socialism, then, stands for a commitment to fostering the virtues and curbing (or minimising) the baleful effects of both cooperation and competition, public and private government.

Elements of the 'associational' outgrowth of the socialist tradition would surely figure as a component. Equally, and to repeat, so would administrative apparatuses of social solidarity. And, finally, so would a certain sympathy for contemporary 'practices of the self'. Whilst not incompatible with making us more clubbable and with sentiments of social solidarity, these practices, which envelop us from the cradle to the grave, also make us capable and desirous of giving shape to our lives and managing them to a degree independently of any self-constituting or administrative ties to 'associations'.[17]

Notes

Chapter 1

1. For this information on Matisse I am indebted to the exhibition of French illustrated books mounted by the Australian National Gallery in 1991, entitled *Monet to Matisse* and in particular to the accompanying catalogue (Dixon and Leahy, 1991).

2. As a first approximation, one might speak of this intellectual 'event' as involving a shift in the centre of gravity of the ethical domain away from its idealised forms and towards its practical and calculative dimensions, making it a series of footnotes less to Plato and Aristotle than to St Augustine and the Stoa. See Bouwsma (1975). Clearly, the implication of this change of emphasis is to enlarge the traditional philosophically dominated canon of 'considerable' ethical literature. However, even the most celebrated moral philosophical texts have their 'uses' over and above that of conducting us towards the truth (or the right questions). See, for instance, Foucault's (1979) analysis of Descartes' *Meditations* as a manual of spiritual exercises.

3. Not universally, of course: like any intellectual event the historicisation of ethics creates its own precursors, notably in historical sociology and philologically oriented cultural history. But can one imagine Erasmus, for instance, figuring on a history of ethics curriculum as presently (i.e. philosophically) constituted?

4. References may be made to dimensions of existence, social meaning and mechanisms of determination (psychical, corporeal, discursive) which may or may not be reducible either to social-structural imperatives or to the resistant resources of human subjects. See Chapter 6 below.

5. Schmitt traces this Romantic resistance to causal and normative regularities to philosophical-theological doctrines of occasionalism, divine intervention in the world, here seen as a suspension of causal relations.

6. 'Joy lovely divine spark, . . . >Your magic reunites >What convention sternly separates >All men shall be brothers >There where your wings gently tarry'. From F. Schiller, 'Ode to Joy' (transl. W. Mann, modified).

7. For drawing my attention to this potentially interesting psychological concomitant of political romanticism I would like to thank Homi Bhabha (personal conversation).

8. In this respect the essays run contrary to an implicit assumption often made within the critical legal studies movement that law can be made

transparent to a critical philosophy and social theory that 'knows' its procedures, terminology and habits of mind to be ideology. On the contrary, here, the technical as well as some of the humbler ethical constituents of the law are invoked in order to create difficulties for critical philosophy and social theory.

Chapter 2

1. One should also scotch the myth that by comparison with utilitarian thought Kant's ethical rationalism is less susceptible of worldly cultural deployments. To Henry Strakosch's arguments on the utilisation of Kant's ethics in the formation of the Austrian civil code (discussed in Minson, 1985) can be added Cresson's (1897, p. 99) demonstration of the 'official' status of Kantism in late-nineteenth century France where, for example, it formed the basis of numerous manuals of child pedagogy.
2. 'Perspectivism' and 'play' are central to Enlightenment figures such as Diderot and Sterne. On the sentimentalist turn in Protestantism see Campbell (1988).
3. Significantly, Kant (1803, 1971) anticipates Schiller's point that a truly moral education must transcend 'mechanical' training or 'discipline'. 'Experimental' schools resting on principles should take precedence over 'normal' ones (*ibid.*, pp. 125–27). Duty will never be internalised by the child if its tenets are presented as external, punitively sanctioned compulsions (*ibid.*, pp. 186–77).
4. For further argument binding a Kantian view of moral obligation to the sense of guilt-as-opposed-to-shame see Lamb (1983). Undoubtedly, Kant himself uses the language of shame in connection with breaches of the moral law (Rawls, 1972, pp. 256f). Moreover, he does not talk much about moral guilt. But does this really detract from my point that for an altruistic ethics shaming as moral practice is problematic?
5. See Adkins' (1960, p. 253) view that neither in the 'archaic' era of Greek ethics nor in those associated with the city-states does 'the Greek moral scene provide . . . even the raw material from which a categorical imperative could be fabricated'.
6. The virtue of *sophrosyne* came, as North (1966) points out, to be extended to men. However, it thereby took on a different meaning, appropriate to the aim of moderating the actions of a warrior class. For men *sophrosyne* entailed the cultivation and display of 'intense passion under perfect control'. In the late European Renaissance this became the 'baroque' virtue *par excellence* (Highet, 1949, pp. 289–90).
7. For an introductory survey see Kennedy (1980); and for a more thorough and better argued, synoptic view, Vickers (1988). For all his faults, Walter Ong, S. J. (e.g. his 1971) remains an invaluable source of insights regarding the rhetorical tradition.

8. See St Augustine (1961, pp. 23, 36–9, 44, 59) for depreciations of rhetoric from the standpoint of a reformed Christian soul.
9. Pippin Burnett recounts the generic fantasy of the art: the traditional anecdote of Archilocus' composing vitriolic poems to an enemy, poems of such power that the man was driven to kill himself and his family.
10. Discourse as a way of fighting is a theme in Lyotard's (1985) linguistically-oriented take on rhetoric.
11. See Mandeville's polemics against the Society for the Reformation of Manners for their failure to acknowledge the benefits of the new commercial society (e.g Horne, 1978, ch. 1).
12. Coleman (1982) explores the dismal impact on relationships in progressive political organisations of the establishment of intimacy as the privileged standard of face-to-face relationships and the consequent suspicion which this casts on all formalities in social relationships. Compare Smith's (1989) discussion of a similar tendency in Australian official educationist thinking.
13. For example, even after the invention of the handkerchief, blowing one's nose with one's fingers is not at first prohibited outright but rather hedged round with conditions. Use only two fingers, tread the snot into the ground, avoid such behaviour in the company of superiors (Elias, 1939, 1978, pp. 143–52).
14. See, for example, Williams' (1985, pp. 192–94) account of the dependence of 'the institution of blame' on assumptions (e.g. indifference to the purely voluntary character of action) which are unacceptable or untheorisable in Kantian-humanist terms.
15. Mackeon (1942, pp. 1–3) offers an unsurpassed reminder of the complexities involved in defining the shifting subject-matter of a history of rhetoric.
16. Contrary to the common assumption that rhetoric's fall from grace was mainly brought about by the romantic revolution (e.g. Marrou, 1984, p. 199), a return to 'true' rhetoric was a component of romantic programmes from the beginning. See e.g. Schlegel's famous *Fragment No. 116* (1798, 1971, pp. 175–76) and Schiller (*op. cit.*, pp. 199–203) who places rhetoric (and manners) under the rubric of 'aesthetic semblance' (*Schein*), or 'pleasing outward form'. Romanticisations of rhetoric may transmogrify the rhetorical tradition, but outright rejection, admittedly a common phenomenon, is only one option for a romantic-aesthetic personality.
17. Compare the anthropologist Bateson's (1958, pp. 2, 118) definition of a cultural *ethos* as 'the expression of a culturally standardised system of organisation of the instincts and emotions of individuals'. Intellectualist and emotivist views of the ethical sphere concur in their neglect of the 'canny' constituents of ethical competence, e.g. being a good judge of character.

Chapter 3

1. Feminine subjectivity is frequently invested with a potential for active self-determination located in the body. For a thoughtful example, see Gatens (1988).

2. To repeat, organisational situations no less than direct action may provide 'occasions' for subverting the system. See for example Pringle's (1988, p. 265) contention that 'It is not only . . . "feminists" who have been involved in processes of resistance'. Any assertion of power is accompanied by some element of resistance, however small. The question then becomes, under what circumstances do individual resistances snowball and become part of a larger strategy?' The *power/resistance* couple here lends all 'uncooperative' conduct or demands for change a general 'political' intelligibility.

3. Echoing Schiller's romantic disdain for the 'tabularising intelligence', Stanley and Wise (1987, p. 54) pour scorn on attempts to map the statistical incidence of sexual harassment, insisting that 'neither legal nor any other formalised grievance procedures are the answer'.

4. 'The motive of role reform is individual discomfort in the existing version of the sex-role. When comfort is achieved there is nothing to carry either the politics or the analysis forward . . . Sex-role theory cannot grasp change as history, as transformation generated in the interplay of social practice and social structure . . . as a dialectic arising within gender relations themselves' (Connell 1987, p. 53).

5. As famous Victorian reformer Caroline Norton (1854, p. 38) put it: 'Masculine superiority is incontestable and with the superiority should come protection'. This is not to be refused because some hotheads talk of 'women's equality' . . . 'Women have one right (perhaps only that one) . . . to the protection of man'.

6. Farley's (1978) visionary strategy harks back to the missed opportunity of an earlier historical 'moment'. When early-twentieth-century feminists were seeking in vain to get unions to take the problem of sexual exploitation at work seriously, 'there was . . . only one voice which, had it been heeded, might have redirected history . . . ' (Farley, *ibid.*, p. 44): the voice of Emma Goldman!

7. See Chapter 6 below for instances of management policies which *provide* for many of the 'informal' responses to sexual harassment called for in the critical literature.

8. In regarding its emergence as a sixteenth- and seventeenth-century development, Foucault may be underestimating its true age (Lander, 1980, Jaeger, 1985, Guénée, 1985); but so what? The best account in English of Foucault's concept of governmentality and its uses is given by Gordon (1991).

9. For instance, from a long list of countries and policy arenas, one could cite as examples the seventeenth-century Prussian cameralist

police regulations aimed at promoting trade and enterprise, skilled immigrants, and limiting state interference in religious affairs (Small, 1909); the eighteenth-century Prussian origins of the revolt against rote-learning and attempts to transfer some of the responsibility for school discipline to the interiority of the child's conscience (Melton, 1988, p. xix); or the nineteenth-century Bismarckian social insurance initiatives.

10. In regard to the privacy of family life, Donzelot (1977) remains unsurpassed on this point (Minson, 1985, ch. 9). But for a thoughtful and very different kind of historical account of 'women's sphere' in the nineteenth century which supplements Donzelot rather well, see Karen Hansen's (1987) adaptation of Hannah Arendt's concept of 'the social' as a device for registering the hybrid character of the regions of informal existence and interactions inhabited by North American mothers and housewives.

11. Even arguments which contest the need for feminists to choose between the politics of equality and the politics of difference tend to rely on idealisations drawn from the lexicon of political philosophy (e.g. Scott, 1988).

12. All anti-sexist policies have to begin somewhere (Graycar and Morgan, 1990, p. 385). Stanley and Wise are themselves no less 'arbitrary' in their refusal to call the 'same' behaviour exhibited by women towards men sexual harassment (Stanley and Wise 1987, pp. 65–66).

13. Jaeger (1985, chs 6, 12) also demonstrates that the poetry of 'courtly love' plays only a minor role in the construction of that 'courtly' ethos and society. It was written from the standpoint of the courtly administrator-bishops as a 'sweetener' in order to urge the courtly ethos on an erstwhile warrior (and lay) nobility. The knights depicted in it were 'knights of old', mythical figures who combined elements of the new courtly ethos with traditional warrior-characteristics.

14. I thank Denise Riley for making this point in conversation.

Chapter 4

1. This progress is all the more remarkable for the fact that during the eight years since the enactment of the Civil Rights Act (1964) there had been 'no legislative history to guide the Congressional language' (*Barnes v Castle* 1977, 561 F2d, 987). The 1972 amendment merely confirmed that sex discrimination fell under the legislation. According to the chronology presented in *Tomkins v Public Service Electricity and Gas Company* (1977, 568 F2d 1044), in the legislative hearings preceding the 1964 Act, sex discrimination was not discussed. It was added on to discrimination on the basis of race, colour, religion and national origin later in the piece, during a limited House of Representatives debate (*Tomkins*, 1047). Sexual harassment was not

an issue at this stage. Thus (as MacKinnon underlines) its unlawful status was established entirely through judicial decisions.

2. See, however, the judgement in the California Supreme court case, *Sail'er Inn v Kirby* (1971, 485 p2d 529) for an early, unambiguously anti-paternalistic interpretation of sex-discrimination law.

3. For instance, see *Henson v City of Dundee* (1982, 682 F2d 897 (11th Cir.)) and *Bundy v Jackson* (1981, 641 Fed R 2d 934), discussed below. On the influence of US legal precedents and opinions, including the views of MacKinnon, in Australia, see *O'Callaghan v Loder* (no. 1 1984, EOC 90–030) or *Hill v Water Resources Commission* (1985, EOC 92–127, NSW).

4. Few would defend the proposition that everything can be encompassed in *theories*. However, 'anti-theoreticist' attitudes sometimes rest on a belief in other foundational bases for knowledge (history, experience, political struggle, sexual identity, etc.).

5. See, for example, MacKinnon's caustic assessment of the progress made by women as a result of legal reforms in her contribution to MacKinnon *et al.* (1984).

6. See, for example, the (now defunct) British feminist journal *m/f*, which made the problems of general theories of women's oppression the starting-point for both sociologically (or historically) oriented and psychoanalytically oriented contributions. A selection of articles published in the journal recently has been published (Adams and Cowie, 1990). For parallel feminist approaches see Tyler (1990); Riley (1988); and Butler (1989).

7. See Chapter 6, below, on the specifically political romantic qualities of these suspicious attitudes.

8. Title VII of the Act stipulates, notably, that: 'It shall be an unlawful employment practice for an employer . . . to fail to refuse to hire or to discharge or otherwise to discriminate against any individual with respect to his compensation, terms, conditions or privileges of employment because of such individual's . . . sex'. Title XII, pertaining to educational institutions, makes substantially the same stipulations. When, henceforth, I refer to 'Title VII discrimination', pertinence to sexual harassment in educational institutions can normally be assumed.

9. It is not necessary to prove that only gender *and no other factors whatsoever* entered into the decision-context of the alleged discrimination; hence its widespread characterisation as a 'gender-plus' criterion. See Baxter (1985).

10. In *Gilbert v General Electric* (1976, 429 U.S. 125) it was held that to exclude pregnancy from an employee's insurance plan was not discrimination based on sex, (a) since though unique it is not universal to women; and (b) in the absence of reasonable comparabilities women's disabilities (biologically) differ from men's.

11. On the contradictions arising from MacKinnon's reliance on a crude

opposition between law and (women's) experience, see Bartlett (1987, p. 1563).

12. Out of 131 cases surveyed up to March 1982, 71 involved termination of employment, 26 resignations, 19 reduced hours and 7 loss of promotion. Only in 7 cases was some direct harm to job-status not alleged (Attansio, 1982, p. 24, n. 152).

13. Notably, in *Meritor Savings Bank v Vinson* (1986, 106 S. Ct. 2399), the Supreme Court took a relatively cautious view of the vicarious liability of employers for the actions of employees.

14. Justice Wright's opinion in *Bundy v Jackson*, for instance, draws on the language of nineteenth-century moral-administrative and legal regulation of lower-class pornography in urban centres when it refers to the 'hostile environment' which may be brought into being by unlawful sexual harassment as 'illegally poisoned' (see reprint of the opinion in Bureau of National Affairs, 1981, p. 58). On legal and administrative categorisations of pornography, see Hunter, Saunders and Williamson (1992).

15. The functional concept of 'role' refers to institutionalised paradigms of action, duties and expectations associated with a status or social position, duly sanctioned or rewarded.

16. On MacKinnon's sweeping generalisations, see Brown (1990) and Bartlett (1987).

17. Indicatively, the only company policy on sexual harassment discussed is one which is so unspecific that it could only be seen as intended to enable the employer to avoid liability for the actions of employees (MacKinnon, 1979, p. 62).

Chapter 5

1. Not being a legal specialist, I have sought as far as possible to limit any assertions concerning the law to its ethical-cultural, social and political dimensions. However, to the extent that the essay bears on ethical constituents of discrimination law and attendant practice which are built into its functioning it is not always possible to leap over the legal technicalities.

2. Originally called the Human Rights Commission, the name was changed by amending legislation in 1986.

3. The first landmark instance of a Federal Court rehearing, which on the whole gave a ringing endorsement to the HREOC's findings, was *Aldridge v Booth* (1987, g.22).

4. It would be unfortunate if this label gave the impression that legal professionals who respect common-law liberties are bound to look askance at anti-discrimination law. See, for example, Lord Scarman's endorsement, cited in *Hall and Ors v A. and A. Sheiban Pty Ltd and Ors* (1989, EOC 92–250, 77, 417).

5. Sources of these objections are supplied below, i.e. at the points at which they are taken up.

6. The application of s.28 is restricted to women under the provisions of s.9 (10) of the SDA.

7. This 'exclusion' of men has not so far generated a single hard case in Australia. For an instructive (unsuccessful) complaint of sexual harassment by a man against a female superior before the New Zealand Equal Opportunities Tribunal, see *Crockett v Canterbury Clerical Workers Union and Ors* (1984, EOC, 92–025).

8. I was unable to obtain statistics from the HREOC on the proportions of male to female complaints of sexual harassment. However, informal interviews with HREOC staff in Brisbane yielded the estimation that the overwhelming majority of complaints by males (at most 15–20 per cent of the total) concerned *boys* new to the world of work and were initiated by their mothers! To that extent, complaints by men are not only the exception, they also prove the rule.

9. For *possible* implications for industrial democracy of policies addressing sexual harassment see Chapter 6 below.

10. In this famous English case, predating that country's sex discrimination legislation, a woman racehorse trainer successfully brought an action against the Jockey Club that refused to issue her with a licence. The stewards' liberty to act 'capriciously' in this manner (i.e. simply in accordance with their 'private' likes and dislikes) was denied on the grounds of a statutory and common-law right not to be unjustly excluded on the grounds of sex from engaging in a trade or profession (*Nagle v Feilden*, 1966, QB, 633).

11. For arguments that male domination works through notions of manners, see Sachs and Wilson (1978), Rich (1976, p. 57) and MacKinnon (1979, p. 172–3); and for a more historically nuanced version, Curtin (1985).

12. I am grateful to Regina Graycar of the University of New South Wales for confirming this point in conversation.

13. In which case, should we exclude the possibility of creating 'a new tort of sexual harassment' in order to supplement, and compensate for the current inadequacies of both tort law and anti-discrimination law (Schoenheider, 1986)?

14. The confidential nature of conciliation necessitated my relying on anonymous anecdotal evidence garnered from informal interviews conducted during the period 1988–89. Thanks to those conciliators who gave me the benefit of their experience.

15. For this information I am indebted to a former Deputy Commissioner at the Victorian Equal Opportunity Board, Dr Ian Siggins.

16. In this landmark race-discrimination case Justice Spender upheld a nightclub owner's claim (brought under the auspices of the Administrative Decisions (Judicial Review) Act) that a compulsory conference convened for the purposes of conciliation in a complaint brought in

under the Race Relations Act ensued in a denial of natural justice. The presiding official allegedly betrayed bias by positively intervening in the debate between the parties as to whether the entry ban imposed on the complainants contravened the Act (bringing in her daughter's experience of being banned from the nightclub). Justice Spender conceded that the respondent's personal rights were not directly affected by any decision at the conference (which only 'decided' that conciliation would have no effect, making no determination as to whether any unlawful discrimination had occurred). Nevertheless this decision exposed the respondent to further legal proceedings. Denial of natural justice by virtue of the conciliator's bias constituted a denial of the respondent's right not to be sued prior to a properly conducted conciliation attempt.

17. For this and other information I am indebted to Julian Riekert who in January 1989 was an Assistant Commissioner to the Victorian Equal Opportunity Board.

18. The Law Reform Commission Committee in this discussion paper recommended legal aid be sought from a State body independent of the EOC.

19. For example, the evidential value of 'similar facts' (e.g. evidence that the respondent had sexually harassed other women); questions of 'unconscious' intention; the burden of proof issue; and the merits of a 'reasonable woman' standard in regard to questions of intention and the distressful effects of sexual harassment.

20. See Morgan, 1988, citing in particular Justice Einfeld's controversial opinion in *Hall, Oliver and Reid v Sheiban* (1989, EOC 92–250).

21. Justice Einfeld's notorious judgement was overturned on appeal to the High Court, *Hall v Sheiban* (1990) EOC 92–319.

22. I am indebted on this point, as for much else in this chapter, to discussions with Bill Lane of the Law Faculty at Queensland University of Technology.

23. The notoriously vague formulae for the civil standard of proof were established in *Briginshaw v Briginshaw* (1938, 60 CLR 336); *Helton v Allen* (1940, 63 CLR 691); and *Rejfek v McElroy* (1965, 112 CLR 517).

24. For this information I am indebted once again to Ian Siggins, ex-Assistant Commissioner with the Victorian Equal Opportunity Board.

25. Rubinstein (1983, p. 8) sees constructive dismissal as one of the most clear-cut potential grounds on which sexual harassment may find support in English law. See *Wigan Borough Council v Davies* (1979, IRLR, 127).

Chapter 6

1. For accounts of Australian feminists' experiences of involvement in

bureaucratic settings and/or EEO programmes, see, for example, the recent essays by Chris Ronalds and Lyndall Ryan in Watson (ed., 1990); Summers (1986); Sawer (1990); Franzway *et al.* (1989); and Yeatman (1989).

2. On the interest of this concept for current feminist theory (in lieu of 'the state'), see Allen (1990).

3. For example, to qualify as a complaint in good faith it must only be made to appointed personnel with the required 'legal duty' and genuine interest. Conciliation must take place in a sufficiently private room, etc. (PSB, 1986, pp. 11, 23–24, 43–45).

4. For a sinister, 'social control' explanation of the fact that some non-unionised companies have a good record in implementing Affirmative Action policies, see Game (1984, p. 256).

5. The chances of the FPSB's documents' being comprehensively implemented within the Federal Public Service suffered a blow when in 1987, at the Hawke Labour Government's initiative, the FPSB was replaced by a skeleton organisation, the Public Service Commission. This body lacks the financial resources, powers and personnel needed for coordinated EEO reform measures. For information on the PSC I am indebted to Carol Hunt (interview, January 1989).

6. Cf. the Alliance's (1981, p. 87) complaint about feminists' needing to 'compete with management consulting firms for the opportunities to train and sensitise people'.

7. For an historical introduction to the art of casuistry, see Jonsen and Toulmin (1988) and for a balanced assessment, Arras (1991). Miller's (1990) characterisation of Sawer's (1990) text as a feminist ethical 'guidebook' through 'the bureaucratic jungle' could be read as a further example of the art.

8. For an argument commending both 'communitarian' action and more involvement in governmental initiatives as equally valid components of feminist politics, see Messinger (1985).

9. Professionalisation of the secretarial role is meant to proceed via the institution of training schemes, qualifying examinations and other means of augmenting the secretarial career-path, such as lodging 'comparable worth' wage claims.

10. ' . . . even the old typewriter can be seen as a phallic object "given" to women by men . . . With it they serve men more effectively' (Pringle, 1988, p. 175).

11. Feminist theories of the sexed subject hold no monopoly on the view of men as vaunting their independence of and superiority to the feminine whilst remaining deeply dependent on it. See, for instance, Marcus' (1989) analysis of constructions of women as healers in military propaganda enlisting their support as nurses during World War One. The analysis hinges on the echoes of theories of masculine aggression in the ancient myth of Antaeus. The son of Earth's union with Poseidon, God of Earthquakes, Antaeus was protected from harm in his martial

actions only for as long as he was able to touch the maternal life-force – the Earth and the trees (origins of 'touching wood').

12. The paradigm case of 'occasionalism' in radical politics is in the 'entrist' practice of Trotskyist organisations. Game and Pringle come closest to this posture when, after voicing scepticism about the effectiveness of a formal complaints procedure, they opine: 'Nevertheless it does give women a space to speak about sexual domination and opens up the possibility of making broader connections' (Game and Pringle, 1986, p. 290). From another perspective, any 'politicising' effects of a complaints procedure would be seen as a *bonus*.

13. See especially Hennis (1989) and *inter alia* the essays by Mommsen, Hennis, Gordon and Whimster in Lash and Whimster (eds, 1978).

14. The contrast between bureaucratic rationality and a culture of patronage must not be overdrawn. See Harding (1981) on early modern 'bureaucracies' which operated in accordance with an ethos delimiting the bounds of permissible patronage.

15. For a contrasting discussion of Oestreich, enlisting his reconstruction of neostoicism in the service of a feminist romantic-historicist argument on sexual difference in the modern era, see Outram (1989, especially pp. 67–72). But see also her illuminating contrast between the dour and disciplinary deployment of neostoicism in the seventeenth century and its self-dramatising utility for the histrionic French revolutionary élite.

16. Tacitus's works were seventeenth-century 'bestsellers'. On the pedagogical-casuistical uses of Tacitus in the ancient world see Earl (1967, ch. 4), from whom I have borrowed the idea of obedience as a skill (*ibid.*, p. 92).

17. Meaghan Morris comments on the currency of such representations in contemporary workplaces, where they 'can be far more paralysing in practice than demands for girlish display. It's a history of the distribution of myths of women as constitutionally *heavy* – the stolid earthbound beast, the killjoy, the moral overseer, the puritanical cleaner of speech, the guardian of social custom' (Morris, 1987, p. 176).

18. The power of 'homosociability' doubtless varies but should not be underestimated; neither should the dangers of mentors' becoming empire-builders.

19. On 'personal' qualifications expected of modern Australian public service administrators and executives see Meredyth (1991).

20. Fouling the ladies' toilet, abusive phone calls, threats to poison Ms Hill's 'pet' fish, etc.

21. Coeli Meyer *et al.*'s (1981, p. 121) sample memo unwittingly illustrates the absurd consequences of assuming that one can write as one speaks.

22. 'Psychoanalysis' in this 'lay' context can include everything from Freud, Lacan and Irigaray to the stock-in-trade of popular feminist characterisations such as 'boys' games', 'male bonding', etc.

23. For an example of this intellectual-political programme see Burgin *et al.*, eds (1986).

24. See Adams (1989) on the costs of attempting to evade the 'phallic' field of representations within which, according to psychoanalytic thought, female identities are predominantly constructed.

Chapter 7

1. See the contributions discussed in 'The participatory imperative' below.

2. A representative sample of these arguments is collected in Held (1989). For related comments see, again, 'The participatory imperative'.

3. Larmore's pluralism stems on his own acknowledgement from a vintage that includes Tom Paine, Max Weber and Isaiah Berlin. To *some* extent it *is* a matter of putting old wine in new bottles; and necessarily so if the old labels have come to constitute an impediment to people's appreciating its flavour.

4. Another reason for Wolff's view of the amorality of early-modern religious tolerance – romantic indifference to the conditions for stable social existence – will be taken up shortly.

5. One reason for the confusion during the Renaissance humanist era concerning what is to count as stoic (Bouwsma, 1975) is probably the alternately worldly and unworldly character of stoicism *vis-à-vis* engagements in public affairs (Foucault, 1984b, pp. 101–17).

6. On the part played by 'constructive' scepticism in early-modern arguments for social peace, see also Rabb (1973) and Tuck (1988). On the Luther–Erasmus quarrel, see Popkin (1979, pp. 1–8).

7. See Macedo's (1990, p. 255–56) citation of Voltaire's endorsement of commerce as transcending religious differences.

8. For a more recent argument along the same lines (which makes no reference to Koselleck) see Ryan (1989).

9. 'In the eyes of the hypocritical proponent of Enlightenment', comments Koselleck scornfully, 'power is identical with the abuse of power' (Koselleck, 1988, p. 119).

10. President Hafez-al-Asad's *Pax Syriana* in Lebanon, perhaps?

11. See comments by Victor Gourevitch in the Foreword to Koselleck (1988, p. ix).

12. There is of course a different usage of the concept of negotiation which is also prevalent in the post-structuralist theoretical idiom. There, negotiation refers to *a process of struggle* between oppressors and oppressed. The stable, unitary subjective identities said to be prerequisite to the reproduction of oppressive structures such as 'patriarchy' are never entirely accepted by those 'subjected' to them. Negotiation in this theoretical context refers to discursive forms of resistance, a kind of war of representations (definitions, images) in

which 'structural' limits to the autonomy of subordinate subjects are reconstructed, modified, subverted, and so on.

13. Confronted by the need to decide 'between Christ or Barabbas', says Schmitt, the liberal ' . . . answers with a motion to adjourn the meeting or set up an investigative committee' (Schmitt, cited in Ellen Kennedy's 'Introduction' to Schmitt 1988, p. xvi).

14. I am especially indebted to Mark Cousins for first introducing me to the possibilities of reorienting certain problems in political theory around the category of negotiation.

15. The force of Schmitt's polemic lies in his taking his liberal opponents at their idealistic word: 'Openness and discussion are the two principles on which constitutional thought and parliamentarism depend in a thoroughly logical and comprehensive fashion' (Schmitt, *ibid.*, pp. 48–49). Discussion he identifies with: 'an exchange of opinion that is governed by the purpose of persuading one's opponent through argument of the truth or justice of something, or allowing oneself to be [so] persuaded . . . To discussion belong shared convictions as premises, the willingness to be persuaded, independence of party ties, freedom from selfish interests' (Schmitt, 1926, 1988, p. 5). It was on this basis of his insistence on analysing liberalism at the level of its most fundamental principles that Schmitt replied to Richard Thoma's refutation of his (Schmitt's) critique of liberal Parliamentarism.

Thoma's response to Schmitt's attack took the form of broadening the criteria for what should count as liberal discussion roughly along the lines suggested in this essay: 'If one wants to examine the foundations of an institution in intellectual history one cannot confine onself to the study of a single ideology that has been used to justify it . . . one then quickly recognises that there are other and more important intellectual justifications for an elected representative assembly than Guizot's illusions . . . ' (Thoma, Appendix to Schmitt, *ibid.*, p. 79). Thoma invokes forms of discussion such as parliamentary Committees, corporatist negotiations and provisions for exchanges with technical specialists.

Schmitt retorts that 'discussion here has a particular meaning and does not simply mean negotiation' (Schmitt, *ibid.*, pp. 4–5). In the first part of his 'principled' definition of liberal discussion (cited above), however, its rhetorical component ('the purpose of persuading . . . ') is subsumed under epistemological and moral principles ('truth or justice'). In the second, this is not the case. Why should the capacity to be persuaded by opponents and to set aside party-ties and other interests in acceding to a joint-compromise decision entail being persuaded of the *truth* of that opponent's views?

16. I am grateful to Barry Hindess for pointing out the existence of this Congressional rule.

17. For example, Marshall's failure to take account of its relation to the formation of nation-states and colonial developments (e.g. Turner,

1986); his assimilation of common law civil liberties to social rights fought for by working-class organisations (e.g. Giddens, 1982); the impacts of war and the experiences of non-British nation states and forms of political rule (Mann, 1987); the critical implications of the diverse subjective identities asserted in the social movements for the 'universal' ideal of citizen-equality (e.g. Macintyre, 1985).

18. The following thoughts on the governmental anchorage of 'industrial citizenship' owe much to Ian Hunter.

19. The sole (and inadequate) basis for disclaiming that Marshall's concept of citizenship is governed by a teleology advanced by Turner (and Held, 1989, p. 193, too) is Marshall's awareness that the path to citizenship is neither smooth nor linear.

20. Another source of inequality associated with equal opportunity in education which is equally irreducible to capitalism pertains to the 'unlevel playing-field' on which educational competition is conducted. Is it feasible to entertain hopes that *any* remotely practicable raft of equal opportunity policies can overcome the problems of the inherent 'lumpiness' of certain cultural resources such as quality teachers; proximity of amenities such as opera houses; and the 'cultural capital' derived from family background (Fishkin, 1987; Gross, 1987)?

21. *Vide* Rousseau's dictum that 'keeping citizens apart has become the first maxim of modern politics' (cited in Ignatieff, 1984, p. 105).

22. Raz (1988, pp. 156–57) outlines a concept of autonomy which sets the threshold of 'adequate options' (*the* problem for the ideal of autonomy) available to a social actor at a level which *is* compatible with a genuine pluralism of values and life-orders. Usefully, he distinguishes between autonomy and self-realisation; the latter being an instance of the former.

23. The fact that the patient would, in Dr Bourne's judgement, have ended up as 'a mental wreck' had he not carried out the operation was reckoned a sufficient reason to assume that the abortion was lawful. Here, a danger to the pregnant girl's mental health was deemed equivalent to the risk to her 'life', this being the only grounds (according to the 1861 *Offences Against the Person* Act) under which an abortion might be legally performed.

24. Skegg (1984, pp. 4–19) argues that, technically, the offence of 'child destruction' (created in the Infant Life (Preservation) Act, 1929) is not prohibited in the United Kingdom's (1967) Abortion Act.

Chapter 8

1. Social-democrats no less than socialists are wont to overstate the case for active participation. See, for example, comments below on Marquand (1988).

2. Kantian conceptions of democratic citizenship also receive an intermittent critical serve.
3. As in the case of post-structuralist conceptions of negotiation.
4. For arguments on the evolving expansion of citizenship rights, see, for instance, Turner (1986) or Mathews (1988). For more radical romantic/republican arguments, see Barber (1984). On rebuilding civil society *via* the social movements see all of the above but also Keane (1988) and Held (1987). For a polyarchical/associationist autonomisation-of-civil-society argument see Hirst (1989 a, 1989 b) and my critical commentary below. Not all these arguments for extending democracy (Mathews, Hirst in particular) view participation as its highest form. To repeat, the target of criticism is only the romantic-republican stripe in this literature.
5. These limits include lack of expertise or public-minded interest in the issues; the energy to sustain involvements; lack of the confidence and capacity to speak in public; lack of opportunity to participate; the problems posed by size of population and powerful vested interests.
6. Landry *et al.* (1985) outline some of the more eccentric practical effects of this vision on radical organisations and businesses.
7. Hyperproblematisation of hierarchy is not endemic to the socialist tradition. See notably Marx's (1875, 1974, pp. 346–47) and Walzer's (1983, *passim*) insistence that (in)equality is always relative to institutionalised *measures* and differentially distributed needs and opportunities.
8. See *inter alia* Nancy Rosenblum's (1987) recent attempt to reconcile liberal-democratic philosophy and romanticism.
9. Further comment on Held's principle of autonomy can be found in Chapter 7.
10. Colin Mercer of Griffith University emphasised this point in discussion.
11. On the legal and bureaucratic-governmental conditions of civil liberties, see Chapter 7.
12. For Offe, exclusion of self-involvement in direct action is the route by which formal liberal-democratic equality turns into substantive inequality.
13. Would Lefort's animus against 'political science' would be assuaged by reminding him of political scientist Robert Dahl's (1985, 1989) arguments in favour of supplementing representative democracy?
14. I am grateful to Barry Hindess for suggesting the exemplary value of Dahl for this stage of my argument.
15. At some points, Hirst's associationalist model of a democratic polity would have to be exposed to Hindess's scepticism about the ideal of a 'self-governing community of citizens'.
16. Compare Almond and Verba's (1983) psychologistic approach to 'subjective political competences'.
17. Oscar Wilde's quip that socialism could not work because it would take

up too many evenings cannot be answered by proposing to make the institution of a greater availability of daytime for political or democratic activity a touchstone of democracy. Anyone occasionally incapable of 'finding the time' for important tasks will appreciate that the relation between time and possession of the energy and disposition for political involvement is in part psychically determined. See Hirschman's (1982, pp. 96–102) illuminating social-psychological account of the problems of 'time-overrun' in citizens' public involvements.

18. A 'developmental state', argues Marquand (1988, p. 102–107), is capable of transforming itself in accordance with publicly accepted national-economic goals.

19. See Hadley and Hatch (1981) on the resort to the participatory theme in a series of 1960s enquiries into local government.

20. This does not mean that lack of interest or involvement is never a problem. When the numbers of the voting public, the membership of a party branch, etc. fall below a certain threshold, their voice *may* cease to matter.

21. In some instances, these demands may well be driven by less edifying considerations (e.g. radical entrist strategies, conservative desires to preserve trade union block votes).

22. To illustrate the fact that this assumption of an opposition in principle between democracy and hierarchical organisation is by no means the exclusive preserve of 'radical' thinkers), consider the echoes of a thousand Enlightenment-rationalist critiques of autocratic hierarchy in the 1940s liberal administrative science scholar Mary Parker Follett's view that *managerial* authority can only be legitimated (i.e. distinguished from personal domination) on condition that 'One *person* should not give orders to another *person* but both should agree to take their orders from . . . *the order integral to a situation.* When that is found, the employee can issue it to the employer as well as the employer to the employee' (cited in Selznick, 1969, p. 24, my emphasis).

23. See Weber's anti-redemptionist views on the prospects for Germany's political and governmental development: 'The point that offends the democrats who are hostile to Parliament is . . . the largely voluntaristic character of the partisan pursuit of politics . . . The political enterprise is *an enterprise of interested persons*' (Weber, 1968, II, p. 1457, emphasis in the original).

24. For instance, in the debate preceding the establishment of the NHS, Aneurin Bevin rejected Herbert Morrison's proposal to establish a dispersed local authority-based service which could serve as 'a school of political and democratic education' as prejudicial to an efficient and evenly distributed standard of provision (Klein 1983, p. 18). Is it appropriate to characterise Bevan's position as an expression of 'the values of paternalistic rationalism' (Klein, *ibid.*, p. 19)? Too much democracy may be bad for the nation's health. The goals of promoting

higher levels of public support for renewing the NHS and 'willingness to pay' for it, by making it as efficient a service as possible, are in no way secondary to securing more active involvement by the public in running it. On efficiency as a socialist objective, see Corrigan *et al.* (1988).

25. For accounts of these theories and programmes see Williams (1982, esp. Part Two) and Hayward (1961).

26. Durkheim (1950, 1983) also, of course, placed great hopes on promoting public-spirited conduct in and through professional and civic associations. See Chapter 9.

Chapter 9

1. See Hirst (1986, 1989, and 1991a). Hirst has recently represented his recent contribution to political theory as a synthesis of associationalism, Dahl's polyarchical conception of pluralist democracy, the political edges of the 'flexible specialisation' literature in economics and a range of juristic theories especially, those of Carl Schmitt and H. L. Hart (Hirst and Jones, 1989, p. 23).

2. See the 'Introduction' and the essay, 'Socialism, pluralism and law' in Hirst (1986), for an advocacy of pluralism which addresses criticisms of pluralism by the Marxist left and the anti-liberal right.

3. For Cole's minimalist vision of the functions performed by 'the National Commune' see Cole (1920, 1980, p. 136). See also Hirst's (1988, p. 88) criticism of Laski's comparable conception of central government as merely 'the association of associations', no different in status from other associations.

4. 'Federalism', argues Laski (Hirst, 1989a, p. 189), 'applies not less to the government of the cotton industry *or of the civil service* than it does to the government of Kansas'.

5. See O'Hagan's (1984) unusual attempt to salvage a non-dialectical and non-utopian meaning out of Tönnies' distinction between *Gesellschaft* and *Gemeinschaft*.

6. Is it necessarily the fate of intelligent 'modern' men and women always to be distanced from such *sittliche* cultural worlds, as Gellner (1974, pp. 191–95) argues? Far from being a structural correlative of 'modernity', ironic distantiation is a product of a romantic person-forming procedure which is neither universally distributed nor unquestionable.

7. The familial realm is regularly the target of policies programmatically aimed at fostering its role as *inter alia* a source of identity and belongingness, a foyer of private aspirations and ambitions, a locus of consumption, a health and welfare agency, and a source of financial and material support. The community-fostering objective is not qualitatively different from the others.

8. Note, too, the interdependence of commerce, consumption and local

culture in such policies. For a detailed illustration of this sort of policy-oriented operationalisation of 'community' as a locus of 'identity', see Mercer (1991a, 1991b).

9. The 'cosmopolitan' set may of course include members of that very ethnic group.

10. Consequently, these developments do not signify a 'post-modern' trend towards more fluid relationships and forms of subjectivity (Hirst, 1989c).

11. See Mathews and Weiss (1991, pp. 21–22), however, for evidence that the successful deployment of flexible specialisation in the Italian textile industry is *not* built upon the exploitation of low-wage, non-unionised labour.

12. See Perrott's (1982) challenge to the presumption (which until recently seemed immutably established in English law since *Salomon*'s case), that corporate personality and limited liability are necessarily inseparable. On all matters concerning company law, I have benefited from the inventiveness and expertise of Robert McQueen.

13. The argument at this point owes much to a private conversation with Paul Hirst.

14. For comparable conceptions of the aims of a liberal welfare state emanating from early-twentieth-century England, see Freeden (1978).

15. Hirst's recent characterisation of associationalism as 'an axial principle of social organisation' (Hirst, 1992, forthcoming) alongside the market and state-collectivist welfare principles, rather than as a blueprint for a type of society, would license the eclectic attitude towards associationalist and centrist governance on which my argument concludes.

16. The associationalist will, correctly, insist that a prerequisite of this 'social' normality is both a reduction of social distress and an autonomisation of associations of the distressed, to levels at which they have reason to believe that they have a genuine stake in the social order (Hirst, 1992, pp. 2–3).

17. I am grateful to Ian Hunter for putting this point in discussion.

Table of Cases

For reports on Australia and New Zealand EEO cases, see Commonwealth Clearing House (CCH) Industrial Law Editors, *Equal Opportunity Law and Practice*, Canberra.

Bibliography

A.C.O.A., Queensland Women's Sub-Committee (1983) *Sexual Harassment in the Workplace*, Administrative and Clerical Officers Association Publication (Australia).

ACTU-TDC, European Mission (1987) *Australia Reconstructed*, A.G.P.S.

ADAMS, P. (1989) 'Of female bondage' in Brennan, T. (ed.) *Between Feminism and Psychoanalysis*, London: Routledge.

ADAMS, P. and COWIE, E. (eds) (1990) *The Woman in Question*, Cambridge, Mass.: MIT Press.

ADKINS, A. W. H. (1960) *Merit and Responsibility: A Study in Greek Values*, Oxford: Clarendon Press.

ALLEN, J. (1990) 'Does feminism need a theory of the State?' in Watson, S. (ed.) *Playing the State: Australian Feminist Interventions*, Sydney: Allen and Unwin.

ALLIANCE AGAINST SEXUAL COERCION (1981, 2nd edn), *Fighting Sexual Harassment: an Advocacy Handbook*, Boston, Mass.: Alyson Publications.

ALMOND, G. and VERBA, S. (1963) *The Civic Culture*, Princeton, N.J.: Princeton University Press.

ALTMAN, D. (1980) *Rehearsals for Change: Politics and Culture in Australia*, Melbourne: Fontana/Collins.

ARENDT, H. (1963) *On Revolution*, Harmondsworth: Penguin.

ARRAS, J. (1991) 'Getting down to cases: the revival of casuistry in bioethics', *Journal of Medicine and Philosophy*, XVI, pp. 29–51.

ATKINS, S. and HOGGETT, B. (1984) *Women and the Law*, Oxford: Basil Blackwell.

ATTANSIO, J. (1982) 'Equal justice under chaos: the developing law of sexual harassment', 51, *University of Cincinnatti Law Review*, 1, 1.

AUERBACH, E. (1953) *Mimesis*, Princeton, NJ.: Princeton University Press.

AUGUSTINE, SAINT (397/8,1961) *Confessions*, transl. Pine-Coffin, R. Harmondsworth: Penguin.

BAKER, J. (1979) *An Introduction to English Legal History*, London: Butterworths.

BARBELET, J. (1988) *Citizenship: Rights, Struggle, and Class Inequality*, Milton Keynes: Open University Press.

BARBER, B. (1984) *Strong Democracy: Participatory Politics for a New Age*, Berkeley: University of California Press.

BARTLETT, K. (1987) 'MacKinnon's feminism: power on whose terms?', 75, *California Law Review*, pp. 1559–1570.

BATESON, G. (1958) *Naven* (2nd edn), Stanford: Stanford University Press.

BAXTER, R. H. Jnr (1985, revised edn), *Sexual Harassment in the Work*

Place: a Guide to the Law, New York: Executive Enterprises Publications Co.

BELLAMY, E. (1888, 1920) *Looking Backwards, 2000–1887*, Sydney, Judd Publishing Co.

BLUMENBURG, H. (1983) *The Legitimacy of the Modern Age*, transl. Wallace, R., Cambridge, Mass.: MIT Press.

BOBBIO, N. (1987) *The Future of Democracy: A Defence of the Rules of the Game*, Minneapolis: Minnesota University Press.

BOURDIEU, P. (1965) 'The sentiment of honour in Kabyle society' in Peristiani, J. G. (ed.) *Honour and Shame: the Values of Mediterranean Society*, London: Weidenfeld & Nicolson.

BOURDIEU, P. (1977) *Outline of a Theory of Practice*, Cambridge: Cambridge University Press.

BOUWSMA, W. J. (1975) 'The two faces of Renaissance humanism' in Oberman H. and Brady T. (eds) *Itinerarium Italicum: the Profile of the Italian Renaissance in the Mirror of its European Transformations*, Netherlands: Leiden, E. J. Brill.

BROWN, B. (1980) 'Private faces in public places', *I and C*, 7, pp. 3–16.

BROWN, B. (1986) 'I read the *Metaphysic of Morals* and the Categorical Imperative and it doesn't help me a bit', *Oxford Literary Review*, VIII, 1/2.

BROWN, P. (1967) *Augustine of Hippo*, London: Faber.

BROWN, P. (1988) *The Body and Society: Men, Women and Sexual Renunciation in Early Christianity*, New York: Columbia University Press.

BROWN, W. (1990) 'Consciousness-razing', *The Nation*, 8 January, pp. 61–64.

BRYSON F. R. (1935) *The Point of Honour in Sixteenth Century Italy: an Aspect of the Life of the Gentleman*, Chicago: University of Chicago Libraries.

BULMER, M. (1985) 'The development of sociology and empirical social research in Britain' in Bulmer, M. (ed.) *Essays on the History of British Sociological Research*, Cambridge: Cambridge University Press.

BULARZIK, M. (1978) 'Sexual harassment at the workplace: historical notes', *Radical America*, July/August, XII, 4, pp. 25–43.

BURCHELL, G. (1991) 'Peculiar interests: civil society and governing "the system of natural liberty"' in Burchell, G., Gordon, C. and Miller, P. (eds) *The Foucault Effect: Studies in Governmentality*, London: Harvester.

BUREAU OF NATIONAL AFFAIRS (1981) *Sexual Harassment and Labour Relations*, Washington, DC: BNA Books.

BURGIN, V., DONALD, J. and KAPLAN, C. (eds) (1986) *Formations of Fantasy*, London: Methuen.

BURNS, A. and GRIEVE, N. (1986) *Australian Women: New Feminist Perspectives*, Melbourne: Oxford University Press.

BURNYEAT, M. (1981) 'Aristotle on learning to be good' in Rorty, A. (ed.) *Essays on Aristotle's Ethics*, Berkeley: University of California Press.

BURROWS, N. (1986). 'International law and human rights: the case of women's rights' in Campbell, T. (ed.) *Human Rights: From Rhetoric to Reality*, Oxford: Blackwell.

BURTON, C. (1986) 'Equal Employment Opportunity Programmes: issues in implementation' in Grieve, N. and Burns, A. (eds) *Australian Women: New Feminist Perspectives*, Melbourne: Oxford University Press.

BUTLER, J. (1989) *Gender Trouble, Feminism, and the Subversion of Identity*, London: Routledge.

CAMPBELL, C. (1987) *The Romantic Ethic and the Spirit of Modern Consumerism*, Oxford: Basil Blackwell.

CASTIGLIONE, B. (1528, 1967) *The Book of the Courtier*, transl. Bull, G., Harmondsworth: Penguin.

CAVE, T. (1979) *The Cornucopian Text*, Oxford: Oxford University Press.

CHIPMAN, L. (1984) 'The zealots: Australia's thought-police', *Quadrant*, XXVIII, 5, pp. 16—28.

CHIPMAN, L. (1985) 'To hell with equality', *Quadrant*, XXIX, 1–2, pp. 44–51.

COELI MEYER, M., OESTRICH, J., COLLINS, F. and BERCHTOLD, I. (1981) *Sexual Harassment*, Princeton, N.J.: Petrocelli Books.

COHN, E. J. (1968) *Manual of German Law*, 2 vols, London: Dobbs Terry.

COLE, G. D. H. (1920, 1980) *Guild Socialism Revisited*, New Brunswick: Transaction Books.

COLEMAN, M. (1982) *Continuous Excursions: Politics and Personal Life*, London: Pluto Press.

CONNELL, R. W. (1987) *Gender and Power*, Sydney: Allen and Unwin.

CONSTANT, B. (1988) *Political Writings*, Fontana, B. (ed.) Cambridge: Cambridge University Press.

COORAY, L. (1985) *Human Rights in Australia*, Sydney: ACFR Community Education Project.

COORAY, L. (1989) 'An assault on our free speech', *The Australian*, 30 March.

COPJEC, J. (1989) 'Cutting up' in Brennan, T. (ed.) *Between Feminism and Psychoanalysis*, London: Routledge.

COPJEC, J. (1990) '*m/f*, or nor reconciled' in Adams, P. and Cowie, E. (eds) *The Woman in Question*, Cambridge: MIT Press.

CORRIGAN, P., JONES, T., LLOYD, J. and YOUNG, J. (1988) *Socialism, Merit and Efficiency*, London: Fabian Society.

CRESSON, A. *(1897) La Morale de Kant: Étude Critique*, Paris: Alcan.

CURTIN, M. (1985) 'A question of manners: status and gender in etiquette and courtesy books', *Journal of Modern History*, 57, pp. 395–423.

CURTIUS, E. (1953) *European Literature and the Latin Middle Ages*, London: Routledge and Kegan Paul.

DAHL, R. (1956) *A Preface to Democratic Theory*, Chicago: University of Chicago Press.

DAHL, R. (1985) *A Preface to Economic Democracy*, New Haven: Yale University Press.

DAHL, R. (1989) *Democracy and Its Critics*, New Haven: Yale University Press.
DAVID, R. and BRIERLEY, J. (1985) (3rd edn) *Major Legal Systems in the World Today*, London: Stevens.
DAY, A. N. (1599, 4th edn 1967) *The English Secretorie, or Methods of writing Epistles or Letters with, A Declaration of such Tropes, Figures and Schemes as either usually or for Ornament's Sake are therein required*, Gainsville, Fla.: Scholars Facsimiles & Reprints.
DEFERT, D. (1991) '"Popular Life" and Insurance Technology', in Burchell *et al.* (eds) *The Foucault Effect: Studies in Governmentality*, London: Harvester.
DE PISAN, C. (1405, 1983) *The Book of the City of Ladies*, Harmondsworth: Penguin.
DÉTIENNE, M. and VERNANT, J-P. *et al.* (1986) *The Cuisine of Sacrifice Among the Greeks*, Chicago: Chicago University Press.
DI PALMA, G. (1990) *To Craft Democracies: an Essay on Democratic Transitions*, Berkeley, L.A.: University of California Press.
DIXON, C. and LEAHY, C. (1991) *Monet to Matisse: French Illustrated Books*, Canberra, A.C.T.: Australian National Gallery.
DIXON, P. (1971) *Rhetoric,* London: Methuen.
DONZELOT, J. (1977) *The Policing of Families*, New York: Pantheon.
DONZELOT, J. (1979) 'The poverty of political culture', *I and C*, No. 5, pp. 73–86.
DONZELOT, J. (1983) *L'Invention du Social: Essai sur le Déclin des Passions Politiques*, Paris: Fayard.
DURKHEIM, E. (1950, 1983) *Professional Ethics and Civic Morals*, transl. Brookfield, C., Westport, Conn.: Greenwood Press.
DZIECH, B. W. and WEINER, L. (1984) *The Lecherous Professor: Sexual Harassment on Campus*, Boston: Beacon Press.
EARL, D. (1967) *The Moral and Political Tradition of Rome*, Ithaca, N.Y.: Cornell University Press.
ECKSTEIN, H. (1966) *Division and Cohesion in Democracy*, Princeton, N.J.: Princeton University Press.
EDWARDS, S. (1985) *Female Sexuality and the Law: a Study of Constructs of Female Sexuality as they Inform Statute and Legal Procedure*, London: Croom Helm.
EISENSTEIN, H. (1985) 'The gender of bureaucracy: reflections on feminism and the state' in Goodnow, B. and Pateman, C. (eds) *Women, Social Science and Public Policy*, Sydney: Allen and Unwin.
EISENSTEIN, H. (1990) 'Femocrats, official feminism and the uses of power' in Watson (ed.) *Playing the State: Australian Feminist Interventions*, Sydney: Allen and Unwin.
ELIAS, N. (1939, 1978) *The Civilising Process, Volume One: The History of Manners* transl. Jephcott, E, Oxford: Basil Blackwell.
ELIAS, N. (1939, 1982) *The Civilising Process, Volume 2: Power and Civility*, transl. Jephcott, E., Oxford: Basil Blackwell.

ELIAS, N. (1969, 1983) *The Court Society*, transl. Jephcott, E., Oxford: Basil Blackwell.

ELLIS, E. (1988) *Sex Discrimination Law*, London: Gower.

FARLEY, L. (1978) *Sexual Shakedown: the Sexual Harassment of Women in the Working World*, N.Y.: McGraw-Hill.

FEDERAL PUBLIC SERVICE BOARD (1987) *Eliminating Sexual Harassment: Guidelines for Sexual Harassment Contact Officers*, Canberra: Australian Government Publishing Service.

FERGUSON, A. (1767, 1966) *An Essay on the History of Civil Society*, Edinburgh: Edinburgh University Press.

FISH, S. (1989) 'Commentary: the young and the restless' in Aram Veeser, H. (ed.) *The New Historicism*, London: Routledge and Kegan Paul.

FISHKIN, J. (1987) 'Liberty Versus Equal Opportunity', in Frankel Paul, E. *et al.* (eds) *Equal Opportunity*, Oxford: Blackwell.

FOUCAULT, M. (1975) *Discipline and Punish: Birth of the Prison*, transl. Sheridan Smith, A., London: Allen Lane.

FOUCAULT, M. (1978) *History of Sexuality vol. 1: The Will to Knowledge*, transl. Hurley, R., Harmondsworth: Penguin.

FOUCAULT, M. (1979) 'On governmentality', *I and C*, No. 6, pp. 5–23.

FOUCAULT, M. (1981) '*Omnes et singulatim*: towards a criticism of "political reason"' in McMurrin, S. (ed.) *The Tanner Lectures on Human Values, Vol. 2*, Cambridge: Cambridge University Press.

FOUCAULT, M. (1984a) *L'Usage des Plaisirs*, Paris: Gallimard.

FOUCAULT, M. (1984b) *Le Souci de Soi*, Paris: Gallimard.

FOUCAULT, M. (1987) 'The ethic of the care of the self as a practice of freedom', *Philosophy and Social Criticism*, 2–3, pp. 121–31.

FOUCAULT, M. (1991) 'Questions of method' in Burchell, G., Gordon, C. and Miller, P. (eds) *The Foucault Effect: Studies in Governmentality*, London: Harvester.

FOUCAULT, M. (1979) 'My body, this paper, this fire', *Oxford Literary Review*, IV, 1.

FRANZWAY, S., COURT, D. and CONNELL, R. W. (1989) *Staking a Claim: Feminism, Bureaucracy and the State*, Sydney: Allen and Unwin.

FREEDEN, M. (1978) *The New Liberalism: An Ideology of Social Reform*, Oxford: Clarendon Press.

FREEMAN, M. D. (ed.) (1984) *The State, the Law and the Family*, London: Tavistock.

FRENCH, P. (1979) 'The corporation as a moral person', *American Philosophical Quarterly* XVI, 3, pp. 207–215.

FRIEDLANDER, J. (1985) 'Sexual harassment – who should really pay?', *The Australian*, 4 July.

GAME, A. (1984) 'Affirmative action: liberal rationality or challenge to patriarchy?, *Legal Services Bulletin*, IX, 6, December, pp. 253–57.

GAME, A. and PRINGLE, R. (1986) 'Beyond *Gender at Work*: secretaries' in Grieve, N. and Burns, A. (eds) *Australian Women: New Feminine Perspectives*, Melbourne: Oxford University Press.

GATENS, M. (1988) 'Towards a feminist philosophy of the body' in Caine, B., Grosz, E. and de Lepervanche, M. (eds) *Crossing Boundaries: Feminisms and the Critique of Knowledges*, Sydney: Allen and Unwin.

GELLNER, E. (1974) *Legitimation of Belief*, Cambridge: Cambridge University Press.

GELLNER, E. (1983) *Nations and Nationalism*, Oxford: Blackwell.

GOODIN, R. (1986) 'Laundering preferences', in Elster, J. and Hylland, A. (eds) *Foundation of Social Choice Theory*, Cambridge: Cambridge University Press.

GOODIN, R. and DRYZEK, J. (1987) 'Risk-sharing and social justice: the motivational foundations of the post-war welfare state' in Goodin, R. and LeGrand, J. (eds) (1987) *Not Only the Poor*, London: Allen and Unwin.

GOODSELL, C. T. (1985) *The Case for Bureaucracy: A Public Administration Polemic*, 2nd edn, Chatham, N.J.: Chatham House Publishers.

GORDON, C. (1986) 'Government rationality: an introduction' in Burchell, G., Gordon, C. and Miller, P. (eds) *The Foucault Effect: Studies in Governmentality*, London: Harvester.

GRAY, H. (1968) 'Renaissance humanism: the pursuit of eloquence' in Kristeller, P. and Wiener, P. (eds) *Renaissance Essays*, New York: Harper & Row.

GRAYCAR, R. and MORGAN, J. (1990) *The Hidden Gender of Law*, Sydney: The Federation Press.

GREENBLATT, S. (1980) *Renaissance Self-Fashioning from More to Shakespeare*, Chicago: University of Chicago Press.

GREGORY, R. (1981) 'The great conciliation fraud', *New Statesman*, 3 July, p. 6.

GROSS, B. R., (1987) 'Real equality of opportunity' in Frankel Paul, E. *et al.* (eds) *Equal Opportunity*, Oxford: Blackwell.

GROSZ, E. A. (1988) 'The in(ter)vention of feminist knowledges' in Caine, B., Grosz, E. A. and de Lepervanche, M. (eds) *Crossing Boundaries: Feminisms and the Critique of Knowledges*, Sydney: Allen and Unwin.

GUÉNÉE, B. (1985) *States and Rulers in Later Medieval Europe*, transl. Vale, J., Oxford: Basil Blackwell.

GUTEK, B. (1985), *Sex and the Workplace: the Impact of Sexual Behaviour and Harassment on Women, Men and Organisations*, San Francisco: Jossy-Bass Publishers.

HABERMAS, J. (1970) *Towards a Rational Society: Student Protest, Science, and Politics*, Boston: Beacon Press.

HADJIFOTIOU, N. (1983) *Women and Harassment at Work*, London: Pluto.

HADLEY, R. AND HATCH, S. (1981) *Social Welfare and the Failure of the State: Centralised Social Services and Participatory Alternatives*, London: Allen and Unwin.

HANSEN, K. (1987) 'Feminist conceptions of public and private: a critical analysis', *Berkeley Journal of Sociology*, 32, pp. 105–28.

HARDING, R. (1981) 'Corruption and the moral boundaries of patronage in the Renaissance' in Orgel, S. and Lytle, G. (eds) *Patronage in the Renaissance*, Princeton, N.J.: Princeton University Press.

HARTLEY, T. and GRIFFITH, J. (1981) *Administrative Law*, London: Weidenfeld and Nicolson.

HAYWARD, J. E. S. (1961) 'The official social philosophy of the French Third Republic: Leon Bourgeois and Solidarism', *International Review of Social History*, 6, pp. 19–48.

HEATH, S. (1986) 'Joan Rivière and the masquerade' in Burgin, V., Donald, J. and Kaplan, C. (eds) *Formations of Fantasy*, London: Methuen.

HEGEL, G. W. F. (1821, 1952) *The Philosophy of Right*, transl. Knox, R., London: Oxford University Press.

HEINEMAN, R., BLUHM, W., PETERSON, S., and KEARNEY, E. (1990) *The World of the Policy Analyst: Rationality, Values and Politics*, Chatham, N.J.: Chatham House Publishers.

HELD, D. (1987) *Models of Democracy*, Cambridge: Polity.

HELD, D. (1989) *Political Theory and the Modern State*, Cambridge: Polity.

HELD, D. and POLLITT, C. (1986) (eds) *New Forms of Democracy*, London: Sage.

HENNIS, W. (1988) *Max Weber, Essays in Reconstruction* transl. Tribe, K., London: Allen and Unwin.

HIGHET, G. (1949) *The Classical Tradition: Greek and Roman Influences on Western Literature*, London: Oxford University Press.

HINDESS, B. (1983) *Parliamentary Democracy and Socialist Politics*, London: Routledge and Kegan Paul.

HINDESS, B. (1987) 'Citizenship and the market', in his *Arguments on Social Policy*, London: Tavistock.

HINDESS, B. (1990) 'Sources of disillusion in Labour and social-democratic politics', Unpublished paper, given at V. Gordon Childe Centenary Conference, Brisbane: University of Queensland, September.

HINDESS, B. (1991a), 'Taking socialism seriously', *Economy and Society*, XX, 4, pp. 363–79.

HINDESS, B. (1991b) 'The imaginary presuppositions of democracy',*Economy and Society*, 1991, XX, 2, pp. 173–95.

HIRSCHMAN, A. (1977) *The Passions and the Interests: Political Arguments for Capitalism before Its Triumph*, Princeton University Press.

HIRSCHMAN, A. (1982) *Shifting Involvements: Private Interest and Public Action*, Oxford: Blackwell.

HIRST, P. Q. (1986) *Law, Socialism and Democracy*, London: Allen and Unwin.

HIRST, P. Q. (ed.) (1989a, *The Pluralist Theory of the State: Selected writings of G. D. H. Cole, J. N. Figgis and H. J. Laski*, London: Routledge.

HIRST, P. Q. (1989b) *After Thatcher*, London: Collins.

HIRST, P. Q. (1989c) 'After Henry', *New Statesman and Society*, 21 July, p. 18.

HIRST, P. Q. (1990a) 'Democracy: socialism's best answer to the right', in Hindess, B. (ed.) *Reactions to the Right*, London: Routledge.

HIRST, P. Q. (1990b) 'From statism to pluralism' in Pimlott, B., Wright, A. and Flomer, T. (eds) *The Alternative*, London: W. H. Allen.

HIRST, P. Q. (1991a) *Democracy and its Limits*, Cambridge: Polity Press.

HIRST, P. Q. (1991b), 'Associationalist democracy in a pluralist state' in Hirst, P., *Democracy and its Limits*, Cambridge: Polity Press.

HIRST, P. Q. (1992, forthcoming) 'Associational democracy' in Held, D. (ed.) *Prospects for Democracy: North, South, East, West*, Cambridge: Polity Press.

HIRST, P. and WOOLLEY, P. (1982) *Social Relations and Human Attributes*, London: Tavistock.

HIRST, P. Q. and JONES, P. (1987) 'The critical resources of established jurisprudence', in Fitzpatrick, P. and Hunt, A. (eds) *Critical Legal Studies*, Oxford: Basil Blackwell.

HIRST, P. Q. and ZEITLIN, J. (1988) (eds) *Reversing Industrial Decline?*, Oxford: Berg.

HITCHING, G. (1983) *Rethinking Socialism*, London: Methuen.

HODGES, J. and HUSSAIN, A. (1979) 'Review article: Jacques Donzelot *La Police des Familles*', I and C, 5, pp. 87–123.

HOHFELD, W. (1909) 'The nature of stockholders' individual liability for corporate debts', IX 4 *Columbia Law Review*, 287.

HOLCOMBE, L. (1983) *Wives and Property*, London: Martin Robertson.

HORNE, T. (1978) *The Social Thought of Bernard Mandeville*, New York: Columbia University Press.

HUMAN RIGHTS AND EQUAL OPPORTUNITY COMMISSION. 'Guidelines for handling complaints under Commonwealth legislation' (unpublished).

HUME, D. (1963) *Essays Moral Political and Literary*, Oxford: Oxford University Press.

HUNTER, I., SAUNDERS, D. and WILLIAMSON, D. (1992) *On Pornography: Literature, Sexuality and Obscenity Law*, London: Macmillan.

HUNTER, I. (1988) *Culture and Government: The Emergence of Literary Education*, London: Macmillan.

HUNTER, I. (1992, forthcoming) 'The pastoral bureaucracy: towards a less principled understanding of state schooling', in Meredyth, D. and Tyler, D. (eds) *Child and Citizen*, Institute for Cultural Policy Studies, Griffith University.

IGNATIEFF, M. (1984) *The Needs of Strangers*, New York: Viking.

JAEGER, C. S. (1985) *The Origins of Courtliness: Civilising Trends and the Formation of Courtly Ideals*, Philadelphia: University of Pennsylvania Press.

JEFFREYS, S. (1985) *The Spinster and her Enemies: Feminism and Sexuality 1880–1930*, New York: Pandora.

JESSOP, B. (1980) 'Parliamentary democracy: the limits of Hindess', *Politics and Power*, 2, pp. 259–62.

JOHNSTON, D. (1986) *The Rhetoric of Leviathan: Thomas Hobbes and the Politics of Cultural Transformation*, Princeton University Press.

JONSEN, A. and TOULMIN, S. (1988) *The Abuse of Casuistry: a History of Moral Reasoning*, Berkeley, Ca.: University of California Press.

KANT, I. (1781, 1933) *The Critique of Pure Reason*, London: Macmillan.

KANT, I. (1784, 1970) 'Idea for a universal history with a cosmopolitan purpose' in Reiss, H. (ed.) *Kant's Political Writings*, Cambridge: Cambridge University Press.

KANT, I. (1785,1948) *Groundwork of the Metaphysics of Morals (The Moral Law)*, transl. Paton, H. J., London: Hutchinson University Library.

KANT, I. (1788, 1956) *Critique of Practical Reason*, transl. Beck, L., New York: Bobbs-Merrill Co.

KANT, I. (1797,1964) *The Metaphysics of Morals, Part 2: The Doctrine of Virtue*, transl. Gregor, M., New York: Harper Torchbooks.

KANT, I. (1803, 1971) 'Lecture Notes on Pedagogy' in Buchner, F. B. (ed.) *The Educational Theory of Immanuel Kant*, New York: AMS Press.

KANT, I. (1875–80, 1963) *Lectures on Ethics*, transl. Infield, L., New York: Harper Torchbooks.

KÄSTNER, K.-H. (1981) 'From the social question to the social state', *Economy and Society*, X, 1. pp. 7–26.

KEANE, J. (1988) *Democracy and Civil Society*, London: Verso.

KENNEDY, E. (1988) 'Introduction, Carl Schmitt's *Parlamentarismus* in its historical context', in Schmitt, C., *The Crisis of Parliamentary Democracy*, London: Cambridge, MIT Press.

KENNEDY, G. (1963) *The Art of Persuasion in Greece*, Princeton: Princeton University, Press.

KENNEDY, G. (1980) *Classical Rhetoric and its Christian and Secular Tradition from Ancient to Modern Times*, London: Croom Helm.

KLEIN, R. (1983) *The Politics of the National Health Service*, London: Longmans.

KOSMAN, L. A. (1980) 'Being properly affected: virtues and feelings in Aristotle's ethics' in A. Rorty (1980) (ed.) *Essays on Aristotle's Ethics*, Berkeley: University of California Press.

KOSELLECK, R. (1985) *Futures Past*, transl. Tribe, K. T., Cambridge, Mass.: MIT.

KOSELLECK, R. (1988) *Critique and Crisis: Enlightenment and the Pathogenesis of Modern Society*, Oxford: Berg.

LA BAUME, P. (ed.) (1980) *Beyond their Sex: Women in the European Past*, New York: New York University Press.

LACLAU, E. and MOUFFE, C. (1985) *Hegemony and Socialist Strategy*, London: Verso.

LAMB, R. (1983) 'Guilt, shame and morality', *Philosophy and Phenomenological Research*, XLIII, 3, pp. 329–46.

LAND, H. and ROSE, H. (1985) 'Compulsory altruism for some or an altruistic society for all?' in Bean, P., Ferris, J. and Whynes, D. (eds) *In Defence of Welfare*, London: Tavistock .

LANDER, J. R. (1980) *Government and Community: England, 1450-1509*, Cambridge, Mass.: Harvard University Press.

LANDRY, C., MORLEY, D., SOUTHWOOD, R., WRIGHT, I. (1985) *What a Way to Run a Railraod: an Analysis of Radical Failure*, London: Comedia.

LANHAM, R. (1976) *The Motives of Eloquence*, New Haven: Yale University Press.

LARMORE, C. (1987) *Patterns of Moral Complexity*, Cambridge: Cambridge University Press.

LASCH, C. (1985) 'Historical sociology and the myth of maturity: Norbert Elias' very simple formula', *Theory and Society*, XIV, 5, pp. 705-20.

LASH, S. and WHIMSTER, S. eds. (1987) *Max Weber, Rationality and Modernity*, London: Allen and Unwin.

LAW REFORM COMMISSION (VICTORIA) (1990). *Equal Opportunity Act Review: Second Discussion Paper* (Melbourne: Law Reform Commission of Victoria, 7th Floor, 160 Queen Street, Victoria, 3000).

LE DOEUFF, M. (1980) *L'Imaginaire Feministe*, Paris: Payot.

LE GALL, J. (1974) *French Company Law*, London: Oyez Publishing.

LEFORT, C. (1988), *Democracy and Political Theory*, Cambridge: Polity Press.

LEITES, E. (ed.) (1989) *Conscience and Casuistry in Early Modern Europe*, Cambridge: Cambridge University Press.

LEVIN, M. (1984) 'A rejoinder to Kate Caro', *Quadrant*, XXVIII, 1-2, pp. 61-62.

LIPJHART, A. (1980) *Democracy in Plural Societies: a Comparative Exploration*, New Haven: Yale University Press.

LITTLETON, C. (1987) 'Reconstructing sexual equality', 75 *California Law Review*, 1279.

LLOYD, G. (1984) *The Man of Reason: "Male" and "Female" in Western Philosophy*, Minneapolis: University of Minnesota Press.

LOCKE, J. (1667, 1956) *The Second Treatise of Government* and *A Letter Concerning Toleration* (edited J. W. Gough), Oxford: Basil Blackwell.

LOGIE, J. (1989) 'Affirmative action in the law of tort: the case of the duty to warn', XL, 1, *Cambridge Law Journal*, 115.

LORAUX, N. (1986) *The Invention of Athens: the Funeral Oration in the Classical City*, Cambridge, Mass.: Harvard University Press.

LUCAS, J. (1976) *Democracy and Participation*, Harmondsworth: Penguin.

LÜHMANN, N. (1989) *Political Theory in Welfare States*, New York: de Greytes.

LYNCH, L. (1984) 'Bureaucratic feminisms: bossism and beige suits', *Refractory Girl*, 27 (May), pp. 38-44.

LYONS, D. (1973) *In the Interests of the Governed*, Oxford: Clarendon Press.

LYOTARD, J. (1985) *Just Gaming*, transl. Godzich, W. Manchester: Manchester University Press.

LYTLE, G. and ORGEL, S. (eds) (1981) *Patronage in the Renaissance*,

Princeton, N.J.: Princeton University Press.

MACEDO, S. (1990) *Liberal Virtue: Citizenship, Virtue and Community in Liberal Constitutionalism*, Oxford: Clarendon.

MACGREGOR, S. (1988) *The Poll Tax and the Enterprise Culture: the Implications of Recent Local Government Legislation for Democracy and the Welfare State*, Manchester, Centre for Local Economic Strategies.

MACINTYRE, A. (1981) *After Virtue: a Study in Moral Theory* (1st edn), London: Duckworth.

MACKEON, R. (1942) 'Rhetoric in the Middle Ages', *Speculum*, XVII, pp. 1–32.

MACKINNON, C. (1979) *Sexual Harassment of Working Women*, New Haven: Yale University Press.

MACKINNON, C. (1987) 'Sexual harassment: its first decade in court' in *Feminism Unmodified: Discourses on Life and the Law*, Cambridge, Mass.: Harvard University Press.

MACKINNON, C. (1987a) *Feminism Unmodified: Discourses on Life and the Law*, Cambridge, Mass.: Harvard University Press.

MACKINNON, C., DUBOIS, C., DUNLAP, M., GILLIGAN, C. and MENKEL-MEADOW, C. (1984), 'Feminist discourse, moral values and the law: a conversation', 34, *Buffalo Law Review*, 4, 11–87.

MANDEVILLE, B. (1732, 1971) *An Enquiry into the Origins of Honour and the Usefulness of Christianity in War* (2nd edn), London: Frank Cass.

MANN, M. (1987) 'Ruling class strategies and citizenship', *Sociology*, XXI, 3, pp. 339–354.

MARCUS, J. (1989) 'The asylums of Antaeus: women, war and madness – is there a feminist fetishism?' in Aram Veser, H. (ed.) *The New Historicism*, London: Routledge and Kegan Paul.

MARQUAND, D. (1988) *The Unprincipled Society: New Demands and Old Politics*, London: Fontana.

MARROU, H. I. (1984) 'Education and Rhetoric' in M. I. Finley (ed.), *The Legacy* of Greece, Oxford: Oxford University Press, 185–201.

MARSHALL, T. H. (1949, 1977) 'Citizenship and Social Class' in his *Class, Citizenship and Social Development*, Chicago: Chicago University Press.

MARTIN, J. and MURPHY, S. (1988) 'The rise of sex in the workplace', *The Age*, 10 September, p. 7.

MARX, K. (1875, 1974) 'Critique of the Gotha Programme', in *The First International and After, Political Writings*, Volume Three, Fernbach, D. (ed.) Harmondsworth: Penguin.

MATHEWS, J. (1988) *A Culture of Power: Rethinking Labour Goals for the 1990s*, Sydney: Pluto Press.

MATHEWS, J. and WEISS, L. (1991) '*A tale of two industries: textiles in Italy and Austria'*, *Industrial Relations Working Papers*, School of Industrial Relations and Organisational Behaviour, University of New South Wales.

MATISSE, H., (1947) *Jazz*, Paris: Tériade.

MCQUEEN, R. (1992) 'Why company law is important to realist criminology' in Lowman, J. and MacLean, B. (eds) *Realist Criminology: Crime and Policing in the 1990s*, Toronto: University Press of Toronto Press.

MEADOWS, A. (1957) 'Personal qualifications in an executive', *Public Administration* XVI, 4, pp. 178–181.

MEINECKE, F. (1924, 1957) *Machievellism: The Doctrine of Reason of State and its Place in Modern History*, London: Routledge and Kegan Paul.

MENDUS, S. (1988) (ed.) *Justifying Toleration: Conceptual and Historical Perspectives*, Cambridge: Cambridge University Press.

MENDUS, S. (1987) 'Kant: an honest but narrow-minded bourgeois?' in Kennedy, E. and Mendus, S. (eds) *Women in Western Political Philosophy*, New York: St. Martin's Press.

MERCER, C. (1991a) *A Cultural Development Strategy – towards a Cultural Policy for Brisbane. Main Report*, Brisbane City Council.

MERCER, C. (1991b) 'Little supplements of life: cultural policy and the management of urban populations'. Unpublished paper presented to the Institute of Cultural Policy Studies Seminar, Griffith University.

MEREDYTH, D. (1991) 'Personality, participation and personnel: translations between the Academy and social administration' in Hunter, I. and Meredyth, D. (eds) *Accounting for the Humanities*, Institute for Cultural Policy Studies, Griffith University.

MESSINGER, R. (1985) in Eisenstein, H. and Jardine, A. (eds) *The Future of Difference*, New Brunswick: Rutgers University Press.

MILL, J. S. (1838, 1969) 'Bentham', *Collected Works of John Stuart Mill, Vol. X: Essays on Ethics, Religion and Society*, Robson, J. M. (ed.) London: Routledge Kegan Paul.

MILLER, D. (1988) 'Socialism and toleration' in Mendus, S. (ed.) *Justifying Toleration: Conceptual and Historical Perspectives*, Cambridge: Cambridge University Press.

MILLER, P. (1990) 'Feminist finesse', *Australian Left Review*, 123, November, p. 41.

MILLER, P. and ROSE, N. (1990) 'Governing economic life', *Economy and Society*, XIX, 1.

MINSON, J. (1985) *Genealogies of Morals: Nietzsche, Foucault, Donzelot and the Eccentricity of Ethics*, London: Macmillan.

MINSON, J. P. (1986) 'Entertaining ethics: review article on Michel Foucault (1984), *L'Usage des Plaisirs* and *Le Souci de Soi*', *m/f*, 11–12.

MINSON, J. P. (1988) 'The new romantics', *Australian Left Review*, 107.

MOORE, W. (1962) *The Conduct of the Corporation*, New York: Random House.

MORGAN, J. (1988) 'Sexual harassment: one man's view', *Legal Services Bulletin*, XIII, 4 August.

MORRIS, M. (1987) 'In any event' in Jardine, L. and Smith, P. (eds) *Men in Feminism*, New York: Methuen.

MOUFFE, C. (1988) 'The civics lesson', *New Statesman*, 7 October.

MOUFFE, C. (1989) 'Radical democracy: modern or post-modern?', in

Ross, A. (ed.) *Universal Abandon? The Politics of Post-Modernism*, Minneapolis: University of Minnesota Press.

MURRIN, M. (1969) *The Veil of Allegory*, Chicago: University of Chicago Press.

NIETZSCHE, F. (1969) *On the Genealogy of Morals and Ecce Homo*, transl. Kaufmann, W., N.Y.: Vintage.

NORTH, H. (1966) *Sophrosyne: Self-Knowledge and Self-Restraint in Greek Literature*, London: Cornell University Press.

NORTON, C. (1854) *English Law for Women in the Nineteenth Century*, London: Wertheimer.

O'HAGAN, T. (1984) *The End of Law?*, London: Blackwell.

OESTREICH, G. (1982) *Neostoicism and the State*, Cambridge: Cambridge University Press.

OFFE, C. (1985) 'Two logics of collective action' in his *Disorganised Capitalism: Contemporary Transformations of Work and Politics*, Cambridge: Polity Press.

OLSEN, F. (1983) 'The family and the market: a study of ideology and legal reform', 96 *Harvard Law Review*, 1997.

ONG, W. (1971) *Rhetoric, Romance and Technology*, London: Cornell University Press.

OUTRAM, D. (1989) *The Body and the French Revolution: Sex, Class, and Political Culture*, New Haven: Yale University Press.

PASQUINO, P. (1978) 'Theatrum politicum: the genealogy of capital – police and the state of prosperity', *I and C*, 4, pp. 41–54.

PATEMAN, C. (1970) *Participation and Democratic Theory*, Cambridge: Cambridge University Press.

PATEMAN, C. (1988) *The Sexual Contract*, Cambridge: Polity.

PERROTT, D. (1982) 'Changes in attitude to limited liability – the European experience' in T. Orhnial (ed.) *Limited Liability and the Corporation*, London: Croom Helm.

PIAGET, J. (1965) *The Moral Judgement of the Child*, New York: Free Press.

PIPPIN BURNETT, A. (1983) *Three Archaic Poets: Archilochus, Alcaeus, Sappho*, London: Duckworth.

POCOCK, J. (1985) 'Virtues, rights and manners: a model for historians of political thought' in *Virtue, Commerce and History*, Cambridge: Cambridge University Press.

POINTER, G. and WILLS, S. (1991) *The Gifthorse*, Sydney: Allen and Unwin.

POPKIN, R. (1979) *The History of Scepticism from Erasmus to Spinoza*, Berkeley: University of California Press.

PRINGLE, R. (1988) *Secretaries Talk: Sexuality, Power and Work*, Sydney: Allen and Unwin.

PRINGLE, R., and WATSON, S. (1990) 'Fathers, brothers, mates: the fraternal state in Australia' in Watson, S. (ed.) *Playing the State: Australian Feminist Interventions*, Sydney: Allen and Unwin.

Bibliography 269

PROBERT, J. and WOOTEN, D. (1984) 'Human Rights Commission: just
another toothless tiger', *Legal Services Bulletin*, IX, 5, pp. 227–30.
RABB, T. (1973) *The Struggle for Stability in Early Modern Europe*, Oxford:
Oxford University Press.
RABIL, A. Jnr., (1988) 'Desiderius Erasmus', in Rabil, A. Jnr (ed.) *Renais-
sance Humanism: Foundations, Forms and Legacy*, 3 vols, Philadelphia:
University of Pennsylvania Press.
RAMAZANOGLU, L. (1987) 'Sex and violence in academic life, or you can
keep a good woman down' in Hanmer, J. and Maynard, M. (eds) *Women,
Violence and Social Control*, London: Macmillan.
RAWLS, J. (1972) *A Theory of Justice*, Cambridge: Harvard University
Press.
RAZ, J. (1988) 'Autonomy, toleration, and the harm principle' in Mendus,
S. (ed.) *Justifying Toleration: Conceptual and Historical Perspectives*,
Cambridge: Cambridge University Press.
RICH, A. (1976) *Of Woman Born*, New York: Norton.
RICHARDS, D. (1971) *A Theory of Reasons for Action*, Oxford: Oxford
University Press.
RILEY, D. (1989) *Am I That Name?*, London: Macmillan.
RONALDS, C. (1987, 1st edn) *Affirmative Action and Sex Discrimination: a
Handbook on Legal Rights for Women*, Sydney: Pluto Press.
ROSE, N. (1987) 'Beyond the public/private division: law, power and the
family' in Fitzpatrick, P. and Hunt, A. (eds) *Critical Legal Studies*, Oxford:
Basil Blackwell.
ROSE, N. (1990) *Governing the Soul: the Shaping of the Private Self*, London:
Routledge and Kegan Paul.
ROSEN, G. (1974), *From Medical Police to Social Medicine*, New York:
Science History Publication.
ROSENBLUM, N. (1987) *Another Liberalism: Romanticism and Reconstruc-
tion in Liberal Thought*, Cambridge, Mass.
RUBENSTEIN, M. (1983) 'The law of sexual harassment at work', 12,
Industrial Law Journal 1.
RYAN, A. (1988) 'A more tolerant Hobbes?' in Mendus, S. (ed.) *Jus-
tifying Toleration: Conceptual and Historical Perspectives*, Cambridge:
Cambridge University Press.
SACHS, A. (1978) 'The myth of male protectiveness and the legal subordi-
nation of women' in C. and B. Smart (eds) (1978) *Women, Sexuality and
Social Control*, London: Routledge and Kegan Paul.
SACHS, A. and WILSON, J. (1978) *Sexism and the Law: A Study of
Male Beliefs and Legal Bias in Britain and the US*, Oxford: Martin
Robertson.
SAWER, M. (1990) *Sisters in Suits: Women and Public Policy in Australia*,
Sydney: Allen and Unwin.
SCHILLER, F. (1801, 1982) *On the Aesthetic Education of Man*, Oxford:
Clarendon Press.
SCHLEGEL, F. VON (1798, 1971) *Friedrich Schlegel's Lucinda and the*

Fragments, transl. Firchow, P., Minneapolis: University of Minnesota Press.

SCHMITT, C. (1924, 1986) *Political Romanticism*, Harvard, Mass.: MIT Press.

SCHMITT, C. (1926, 1988) *The Crisis of Parliamentary Democracy*, Cambridge, Mass.: MIT.

SCHOENHEIDER, K. (1986) 'A theory of tort liability for sexual harassment in the workplace', 34 *University of Pennsylvania Law Review* 1461.

SCHUMPETER, J. (1943) *Capitalism, Socialism and Democracy*, London: Allen and Unwin.

SCOTT, J. W. (1988) 'Deconstructing equality-versus-difference: or the uses of post-structuralist theory for feminists', *Feminist Studies*, XIV, 2, pp. 33–50.

SCUTT, J. (1985) 'In pursuit of equality: women and legal thought, 1788–1984' in Goodnow, J. and Pateman, C. (eds) *Women, Social Science, and Public Policy*, Sydney: Allen & Unwin.

SCUTT, J. (1986) 'The privatisation of justice: inequality and the palliative of conciliation, counselling and mediation', paper presented at a Conference on Alternative Dispute Resolution, Australian Institute of Criminology, 23 July.

SELZNICK, P. (1969) *Law, Society and Industrial Justice*, New York: Russell Sage Foundation.

SEX DISCRIMINATION ACT (1984) Canberra: GPS.

SILTANEN, J. and STANWORTH, M. (1984) 'The politics of private woman and public men', *Theory and Society*, 13, pp. 91–118.

SKEGG, P. (1984) *Law, Ethics and Medicine: Studies in Medical Law*, Oxford: Clarendon Press.

SMALL, A. (1909) *The Cameralists: the Pioneers of German Social Polity*, New York: Burt Franklin.

SMITH B. (1989) 'Discipline from the Classroom to the Community', Occasional Paper, Institute for Cultural Policy Studies, Griffith Universitv, Nathan, Qld, 4111, Australia.

SMITH, P. (1966) *The Anti-Courtier Trend in Sixteenth Century French Literature*, Travaux d'humanisme et Renaissance, Vol. 84, Geneva: Droz.

STANLEY, S. and WISE, L. (1987) *Georgie Porgie: Sexual Harassment in Everyday Life*, London: Pandora.

STATEN, H. (1984) *Wittgenstein and Derrida*, Oxford: Blackwell.

SUMMERS, A. (1986) 'Mandarins or missionaries: women in the Federal bureaucracy' in Grieve, N. and Burns, A., (eds) *Australian Women: New Feminist Perspectives*, Melbourne: Oxford University Press.

TEAD, O. (1945) *Democratic Administration*, New York: Association Press.

TIFFIN, S. (1984) 'Against the odds: fighting sexual harassment under Anti-Discrimination legislations', *Refractory Girl*, 27, May, pp. 7–12.

TOFFLER, A. (1981) *The Third Wave*, London: Pan.

TUCK, R. (1988) 'Scepticism and toleration in the seventeenth century', in Mendus, S. (ed.) *Justifying Toleration: Conceptual and Historical*

Perspectives, Cambridge: Cambridge University Press.

TULLY, J. (1988) 'Governing Conduct' in Leites, E. (ed.) *Conscience and Casuistry in Early Modern Europe*, Cambridge: Cambridge University Press.

TURNER, B. (1986) *Citizenship and Capitalism: the Debate over Reformism*, London: Allen and Unwin.

TYLER, D. (1990) 'Going too far: the function of "Foucault" in recent feminist writing' (unpublished typescript).

VAN HORN MELTON, J. (1988) *Absolutism and the Eighteenth Century Origins of Compulsory Schooling in Prussia and Austria*, Cambridge: Cambridge University Press.

VERKAMPF, B. J. (1977) *The Indifferent Mean: Adiaphorism in the English Reformation to 1554*, Albens, Ohio: Ohio University Press.

VERNANT, J-P. (1982) *The Origins of Greek Thought*, Ithaca, N.Y.: Cornell University Press.

VICKERS, B. (1988) *In Defence of Rhetoric*, Oxford: Clarendon.

VICTORIAN EQUAL OPPORTUNITY ACT (1984) Melbourne Government Printers.

VOGEL, U. (1987) 'Humboldt and the romantics: neither hausfrau nor citoyenne' in Kennedy, E. and Mendus, S. (eds) *Women in Western Political Philosophy*, New York: St. Martin's Press.

VON STEIN, L. (1964) *The History of the Social Movement in France 1789–1850*, transl. Mengelberg, K., Totowa, N.J.

WALZER, M. (1983) *Spheres of Justice: a Defence of Pluralism and Equality*, Oxford: Basil Blackwell.

WALZER, M. (1984) 'Liberalism and the art of separation', *Political Theory*, XII, 3, pp. 315–30.

WEBER, M. (1920, 1965) *The Protestant Ethic and the Spirit of Capitalism*, London: Unwin.

WEBER, M. (1947) 'Politics as a vocation' in Gerth, H. H. and Mills, C. W. (eds) *From Max Weber: Essays in Sociology*, London: Kegan Paul.

WEBER, M. (1968) *Economy and Society* (2 vols), Berkeley: University of California Press.

WELCH, K. (1988) 'The platonic paradox: Plato's rhetoric in contemporary rhetoric and composition studies', *Written Communication*, V, I pp. 3–21.

WETTENHALL, R. (1986) 'Review: T. L. Cooper *The Responsible Administrator: an Approach to Ethics for the Administrative Role*', *Australian Journal of Public Administration* XLV, 4, pp. 363–4.

WILENSKI, P. (1989) *Public Power and Public Administration*, Sydney: Hale and Iremonger.

WILLIAMS, B. (1985) *Ethics and the Limits of Philosophy*, London: Fontana.

WOLF, R. P. (1969) 'Beyond tolerance' in Wolf, R. P., Moore, B. and Marcuse, J., *A Critique of Pure Tolerance*, London: Cape.

WOUTERS, C. (1977) 'Informalisation and the civilising process', in Gleichman, P.R. *et al.* (eds) *Figurations: Essays for Norbert Elias*, Amsterdam: Sociologisch Tijdschrift.

WYNDHAM, S. (1985) 'The persecution of Jane Hill', *Sydney Morning Herald (Magazine Section)*, pp. 6–8.

YEATMAN, A. (1989) *Bureaucrats, Technocrats, Femocrats*, Sydney: Allen and Unwin.

YEATMAN, A. (1992) 'Minorities and the politics of difference' *Political Theory Newsletter* (Australia) IV, 1, pp. 1–11.

ZIZEK, S. (1989) *The Sublime Object of Ideology*, London: Verso.

Index

273